THE APACHE INDIANS

CHARLES MORGAN WOOD

THE
APACHE
INDIANS

BY

FRANK C. LOCKWOOD

Foreword by Dan L. Thrapp

University of Nebraska Press
Lincoln and London

First Bison Book printing: 1987
Most recent printing indicated by the first digit below:
1   2   3   4   5   6   7   8   9   10

Library of Congress Cataloging-in-Publication Data
Lockwood, Frank C. (Frank Cummins), 1864–1948.
   The Apache Indians.
   "Bison book"
   Reprint. Originally published: New York:
Macmillan, 1938.
   Includes index.
   1. Apache Indians—History. 2. Indians of
North America—Arizona—History. I. Title.
E99.A6L6 1987   979.1'00497   86-25103
ISBN 0-8032-2878-3
ISBN 0-8032-7925-6 (pbk.)

Reprinted by arrangement with Elizabeth Hampsten

Inscribed to the Memory of
CHARLES MORGAN WOOD

FOREWORD
By Dan L. Thrapp

When Frank C. Lockwood's *The Apache Indians* was published in 1938 it proved a milestone for the understanding and history of those remarkable people considered by many Americans at the time as among the most savage and warlike of the frontier saga. Other important works had included much on the Apaches, but they were concerned with different themes. Among these were *Massacres of the Mountains* by J. P. Dunn, Jr., which appeared in 1886, and scattered primary accounts, including John Gregory Bourke's *An Apache Campaign in the Sierra Madre* (1886) and his unforgettable *On the Border with Crook* (1891), as well as Britton Davis's *The Truth about Geronimo* (1929). But among secondary writers, Lockwood was perhaps the first to combine respectable research with a disciplined avoidance of literary flamboyance and extravagance. Rather, the restless Arizona intellectual turned out a study in some depth, rounded in concept and written gracefully, if with an occasional professorial touch that, however, never turned pedantic.

In another book Lockwood once wrote it was ever his aim "to tell the truth and . . . to make the truth interesting." In *The Apache Indians* he explained further his "deep desire to be accurate and just." He achieved these twin goals so well that today, half a century after its appearance, the book remains basically sound and as pleasantly readable as ever. It is not dated. Thus, its value for today's readers will be as marked as for those for the two previous generations. Of course, the intervening fifty years have seen the appearance of fresh stud-

ies, of new insights, of the published results of diligent research into almost every aspect of Apache customs and history. Yet most of Lockwood's basic understandings remain
sound. Upon rereading this, perhaps the major work of his
accomplished literary career, one develops renewed admiration for his sound analyses, for his confident selection of the
significant from the mass of materials before him, for his
capacity for synthesis, and for his sure touch in extracting the
thread of narrative for his gripping story. And from this work
even the most practiced specialist of today may draw re-
freshing, provocative insights.

The Apache Indians, rather than the product of a single mind,
was actually a collaborative effort of two uncommon men, as
Lockwood generously makes clear. Undergirding his scholarship was the tireless research of Charles Morgan Wood
(1870–1927), who originated the project.

In his preface Lockwood describes something of Wood's interesting background and the sort of man he was, leaving only
a few points to be clarified. A Dayton, Ohio, manufacturer,
Wood had spent four winters in the beneficent climate of Tucson, where he had come for reasons of health. During that
time he had become acquainted with Lockwood. They found
common interests. On field trips to areas of special concern
for one or the other, Lockwood had come to accept amiably
Wood's growing enthusiasm for Apache Indian study,
although at the time he did not intend to do anything with the
subject himself.

Wood returned east for about half of each year. His home
was in Ohio; he had a summer place at Ipswich, Mas-
sachusetts; and he also found time for Washington, D.C.,
where he diligently rummaged through War Department records and photograph collections held in the old Munitions
Building and elsewhere, following wherever opening leads
took him. That was before the day of the centralized National
Archives, which were not formally established until 1934. It

also was before easy duplication of records, and copies had to be made laboriously by the researcher himself or by hired typists. Fortunately, Wood was no more strapped for funds than he was for time, and his collection of pertinent documents grew steadily. Each winter he transported a new batch to Tucson. At the same time, he collected books relating to his subject until he possessed "one of the most complete libraries of its kind in the country," as a local newspaper put it. Mrs. Wood, an accomplished artist whose paintings were often on exhibit, came to love the desert Southwest as much as her husband. They decided to settle at Tucson permanently. Wood purchased a property near that of famed novelist Harold Bell Wright, planning to build a retirement home upon it. Then, in February 1927, he contracted pneumonia. Within a few days, at midnight on the ninth of the month, he was gone.

Mrs. Wood at first planned to remove her husband's library and papers to Dayton, but eventually they were turned over to Lockwood, who knew more about Wood's project than anyone else and had shared in some of its research—and whose literary skills offered the best hope for eventual publication. So in the early 1930s he seriously commenced work on what would become *The Apache Indians*.

Francis Cummins Lockwood was born May 22, 1864, at Mount Erie, a tiny crossroads community northeast of Fairfield in Wayne County, Illinois.[1] He was raised on the Kansas frontier, where his father, a Methodist minister, had secured a land grant for Civil War service. Young Lockwood was graduated Phi Beta Kappa from Baker University at Baldwin City in eastern Kansas in 1892. He went on to Northwestern University, Evanston, Illinois, where in 1896 he received a doctorate in philosophy with a minor in history. In the interim he had studied briefly at Garrett Biblical Institute, still a major Methodist theological school at Evanston. He preached regularly at Chicago and held a pastorate for some months at Salt Lake City, being ordained in 1897 before finally deciding that, after all, the ministry was not his calling. So he enrolled for more graduate study at the University of Chicago and in 1902 earned a master's degree in English literature at Wesleyan University of Middletown, Connecticut. He taught at several midwestern and eastern colleges, studied for a year at Oxford, moonlighted as a Chautauqua lecturer when he found his preaching skills easily convertible to platform speaking, wrote articles on a variety of subjects, did temperance work, and dabbled in politics, stumping Pennsylvania for Theodore Roosevelt during the Bull Moose campaign.

Lockwood had been married in 1901 to young Mary Pritner (they became in time the parents of two daughters). In the spring of 1916 he resigned his position at Allegheny College, Meadville, Pennsylvania, and was immediately invited to join the University of Arizona faculty at Tucson. He was given a full professorship and taught English literature at the small school (the student body was under 500 while the population of the new state was only around 230,000, Tucson having 22,000 of that number). The Lockwoods had barely settled in when America entered World War I. Frank Lockwood became a chaplain on the transport *Pastores*, making nine transAtlantic voyages. By 1919, then fifty-five years of age, he returned to Tucson, where he would live the rest of his life. He was very active in university affairs, directed its Extension Service, became dean of the College of Letters, Arts, and Sciences, and even served as interim president for a few months in 1922.

Interested in the history of Arizona almost from the moment of his first arrival, Lockwood wrote newspaper articles on pioneers, many of whom were still around and whose memories of the stirring events of the recent past he assiduously cultivated. Four of his ten historical books are collections of such biographies. Two major studies are *Pioneer Days in Arizona* (1932), and *The Apache Indians* (1938), both published by the Macmillan Company.

After the publication of *Pioneer Days,* he turned to the Indian work in earnest. He had already found his way about such
important historical collections as those at the Bancroft Library of Berkeley and the Huntington Library of San Marino,
California, the Arizona Pioneers' Historical Society of Tucson, the Southwest Museum of Los Angeles, and the Newber-
ry Library of Chicago, and he had a fair idea of the immensity
of the task he was taking on. In addition, he had the wealth of
documentation and the photograph collection assembled by
Charles Wood to wade through and digest. He had learned
how to research and what to do with his material; he was careful to avoid the trap that caught so many aspiring scholars who
wound up their careers in unending study with little in print
to show for it. Lockwood had an organized mind, his industry
was phenomenal, his output steady, and to lighten and balance his work he cultivated a finely honed sense of humor. It is
a matter of pictorial record that as he grew older he came to
resemble ever more markedly Samuel Clemens (Mark
Twain), and the quiet humor that sparks even his most serious
works also was reminiscent, to some modest degree, of the
pungent wit of that great American novelist and raconteur.
Lockwood died on January 12, 1948.

Lockwood's *The Apache Indians* appeared early in 1938. It
was universally well received. Many of those commenting on it
then either had personal, sometimes thrilling experience in
fighting hostile Apaches, or they wrote when at least the memory of southwestern Indian troubles was still vivid.

Retired Brigadier General Thomas Cruse had firsthand experience of the Apaches. As a shavetail second lieutenant, he
had won a brevet and a Medal of Honor at the action of Big
Dry Wash, and Lockwood closely followed his unpublished (at
that time) narrative, *Apache Days and After* (1941). Cruse wrote
a glowing review of *The Apache Indians* for the *Cavalry Journal:*
"I have been hoping for forty years that someone would write
a book like this. And what a book! Thank Heaven Professor

Lockwood has had the courage to tell . . . not just of the Apache's treachery and brutality toward the white man, but also of the great wrongs the white man committed toward him."

Charles B. Gatewood, Jr., son of the hero of the last Geronimo outbreak and avid collector of documentation on the Apache wars with particular reference to the career of his father, thought it "an outstanding contribution to the history of our Southwest, a book interesting to read and a reference work of permanent and unique value." He conceded in two California newspaper reviews that the work was "not without flaw. The meticulous student may find statements here and there with which he will disagree. But these . . . are nowhere of basic importance, and they do not appreciably mar the well-balanced impartiality and faithfulness of the whole." Gatewood agreed with Cruse that "tribute must be paid to Dr. Lockwood's courage" in giving a fair shake to the Indians from his desk in an Arizona where anti-Apache passions still raged fifty years after the bloodshed had ceased.

That rage against the Apaches was stressed by Harvey L. Mott in a discussion that rambled on for a column and a half in the *Arizona Republic.* He thought that readers might find "one of two things [happening]. They will absorb a generous amount of knowledge about these wildest of Arizona's primitive people, or they will become blindly, unreasonably angry." He had discovered that "most long-time residents of Arizona can't speak calmly about the Apache. Usually the name is sufficient to evoke, in what until that minute had been a quiet conversation, an explosive tirade that may last until well into the dawn. The [very] name is anathema to most pioneers."

Carl Trumbull Hayden was more charitable, and he spoke with considerably more authority. He was something of a pioneer himself. Hayden had represented Arizona at Washington in House and Senate since the state was created.

He would continue to occupy his Senate seat until in his nineties, having a longer term of service in the two houses than any other of record. He also had made the study of the history of his beloved state his lifelong avocation. In a review for the *Washington Post,* Hayden wrote, "[Until the appearance of Lockwood's book] there has never been any thoroughly unbiased and connected history of the Apaches. . . . There has been too much fiction . . . , and it is a relief to find . . . the true story interestingly and fascinatingly told." He went on to explain that "the broad human understanding of the book is what makes it most remarkable," with as much attention given to the "blundering ineptitude" of the whites as to the "cruelty of the Indians." Lockwood, he concluded, "has made a distinct and worthwhile contribution to the literature of the Southwest. It is honest, straightforward history written simple and strong."

Historical writers most familiar with the West and its Indians appreciated the book, even if some criticized it mildly, according to their personal points of view. Novelist Oliver La Farge (he won the Pulitzer Prize with his Navaho tale, *Laughing Boy,* in 1929) thought Lockwood's work "the best study we have of its central subject, the military campaigns," though in his *Saturday Review of Literature* article he found it "not a rounded study of the Apaches, but [only] a generous foeman's account of their subjugation," tending to be told "from the army's point of view and to whitewash that organization." The six-thousand Apaches who never warred, or at least not for very long, against the whites were ignored while the book concentrated on the "less than two hundred outlaws" who did, La Farge complained. Paul I. Wellman, whose *Death on the Desert* (1935) had covered in somewhat fictionalized form some of the ground Lockwood worked, was more generous. "No better history of this people ever has been written," he concluded in a long and informed review-article in the

Kansas City Times. Appreciating the difficulties Lockwood had overcome, Wellman thought he had succeeded in a remarkable manner in fashioning a connected and coherent account of a people buffeted by "decades of the cruelest kind of warfare." Don Russell, a nationally known book reviewer and himself author of significant works on western subjects, assessed Lockwood's book favorably for the *Chicago Daily News* and the *Journal of the American Military History Foundation.* In a letter to the author, he called it "certainly the best book ever written about the Apache Indians. I do not see how anyone could have done it better." In the *New York Sun*'s "Book of the Day" column Jerry Rand wrote that "a wide reading of this book is necessary if a true picture of the Indian question is desired. It is one more of the really worth-while works that American historians are giving us." The *Christian Science Monitor* said, "The book is a splendid synthesis, careful, complete, dispassionate and contains much new material from oral accounts of eyewitnesses . . . undoubtedly the best account for the general reader."

William James Ghent, a social activist and the author or coauthor of several worthy books on the West as well as numerous brief sketches of frontier figures for the *Dictionary of American Biography,* wrote a half-page, generally favorable essay on Lockwood's work for the *New York Times Book Review.* He found it "the first comprehensive study of the one-time Ishmaelites of the Southwest," useful to general reader and student alike, "and it aims to treat fairly the ever-baffling question of the rights and wrongs of the two contending races." However, Ghent attacked Lockwood's view that the Apaches were "a moral people" and the statement that their "code of morals [was] as deeply rooted and binding as that of civilized man." He went on to reflect common white perceptions of Apache "barbarism" and the white "enlightenment" of which they presumably were in desperate need.

Lockwood's remarks on this subject—notably enlightened for the time and place—were taken almost verbatim from a letter from Grenville Goodwin, a foremost field ethnologist who worked among the Western Apaches and whose first-hand knowledge of that people has never been surpassed. Goodwin's own work on the Apaches may have been inspired in part by a lecture by Lockwood he had attended years before. He wrote the author that "these people are governed by strict moral ideals in all their conduct . . . Almost everything a person did was governed by conventions . . . I think that it would be fairly safe to say that the people were probably greater adherers to their own conventions than were our own ancestors at the same time. As for morals, their observance was very much in evidence, and their moral code came up to ours in quality easily." Not content with that, Goodwin went on to splinter common white preconceptions and prejudices with his conclusion that "in general these people are honest, truthful, generous, and extremely kind. They have a very keen sense of humor, and they love fun and play. I have never yet seen an Apache lose his temper with an inanimate object, with a child who was too young to understand, or with a dumb animal—something I can't say for the Whites. . . . The above has been proved to me so many times that I can not doubt it." Whether Dr. Lockwood ever brought these persuasive views to Ghent's attention is not remembered.

The Apache Indians, of course, is not flawless history; there may be no such thing. Occasionally there is confusion. Lockwood in the beginning approvingly quotes Fray Alonso de Benavides that Apaches "pride themselves much on speaking the truth, and hold for dishonored him whom they catch in a lie." Then in subsequent contexts he goes on to write: "they were shifty," or "they turned traitors to the Spaniards," or, still later, "of course the Spaniards knew that the Apaches were not to be trusted." Errors of fact can also be found. In the book, Albert Sterling, popular chief of San Carlos Indian police, is killed twice: once in Juh's bolt of 1881, although he was truly slain, as the book records, in the Loco outbreak of 1882.

The author tends to rely not rarely upon a solitary version for his description of some operation that may be too complicated for such treatment. Reliance upon a single source may move a narrative, but it can weaken history. He depends, for example, almost entirely upon John Clum for his account of the transfer of Apaches from Ojo Caliente, New Mexico, to San Carlos, Arizona. The accuracy of Clum's version has been questioned by many, although perhaps such challenges were not fully available in Lockwood's time. He depends substantially upon Bourke for the famed Battle of the Cave and upon Cruse for the celebrated action at Big Dry Wash. He adapted his narrative of the Battle of Apache Pass from John C. Cremony, who was in that affair, but who recent scholarship shows is not the most reliable source on anything.

Such captious criticisms aside, the writer's balance and good judgment are what make *The Apache Indians* a worthy book. This is nowhere shown more clearly than in his support of the true hero of the Geronimo campaign, and the spartan manner in which he slices through fifty years of army bickering over who should get credit for the final surrender of the Apache and the ending of the southwestern Indian wars. "That distinction," he wrote crisply, "was reserved for First Lieutenant Charles B. Gatewood, though he long was denied the full meed of honor he deserved through Army jealousies and through the pettiness and vanity that marred the really great soldierly qualities of [Nelson] Miles." That was about all he had to say on the matter, and it was enough. His verdict brought a semblance of finality to a long and bitter argument.

He wraps up his story, too, with a very good summary of the Apaches' lives after their wars with the United States, taking them from exile down to the moment in which he wrote. He does this with the geniality and tolerance that colors everything else he reports of them, even though his conclusive remarks on the outlook for their future may seem a bit out of step with modern thinking on that perplexing subject.

For a long time *The Apache Indians,* out of print since its earliest years, has been a hard book to find. Its rising prices have reflected that scarcity. Thus the reissuing of this western classic in an economical edition should be widely hailed. It will make the book once again available for a new and wider readership to enjoy and learn and profit from.

NOTE

1. The best biographical treatment is John Bret Harte, "Frank C. Lockwood: Historian of the Southwest," *Arizona and the West* 9, no. 2 (Summer 1967): 109–30.

PREFACE

A BOOK on the Apache Indians was to have been the work of my friend, Charles Morgan Wood. Indeed, he gave much thought and labor to the subject and at the time of his death had made considerable progress toward the achievement of this cherished purpose. He had long been in poor health, but he had leisure and unbounded enthusiasm for the enterprise, and its pursuit enlivened and brightened the closing days of his life. We were fellow enthusiasts in the field of Southwestern history, drawn to our studies and researches more in the spirit of cultural recreation and by a desire to be of service to the state we both loved than by the ambition to be known as historians. As friends we read, planned, talked, and traveled together—each absorbed in his particular project. My comrade was suddenly taken from my side with his task unfinished.

Ten years have passed, and having completed the three books I had set my heart on writing, I turn to the theme that had always interested both of us but which was his by common consent and priority of claim—The Apache Indian. Mr. Wood's book, both in aim and execution, would have been a very different one from this that I have written. Nor has it been my intention in any manner to attempt to carry out his unfinished work. His genial temper—half serious, half whimsical—always mellow with humor and the milk of human kindness—would have invested the book with a charm all his own that I must not hope to capture. But it would be ungracious, indeed, if I did not at the very beginning offer a tribute of friendship to my comrade along the way; explain that, in a measure and through use of material he collected, I have entered into his labors; acknowledge the inspiration that came from association with him; and, so far as possible, commemorate a true and manly personality. I have thought it fitting, therefore, to dedicate this book to him, to reproduce his photograph as a frontispiece, and briefly to interpret his character.

Fate often plays havoc with a man's ambitions and plans in life, yet, in spite of obstacles and adverse circumstances, a strong man somehow in the long run carves out a semblance of his passionately cherished ideal. Charles Morgan Wood was in most respects a favored child of fortune. Descended from a fine old Virginia family in easy circumstances, enjoying the typical life of a wholesome American boy, a graduate of Yale, endowed with business energy and acumen, social-minded, widely traveled, a happy husband and fond father—his lot was indeed cast in pleasant places. Yet from boyhood he had suffered with bronchial asthma, and throughout life was continually baffled and often thwarted by ill health. Notwithstanding this ever-present handicap, however, he achieved a well-rounded, fruitful life, attaining notable success in the chief objects of his ambition. He was distinctively a man of culture, a lover of home and family, and a knight-errant of the romantic and the ideal.

It is as a lover of books, adventure, and travel that I wish to envisage Mr. Wood in this sketch; and also as an example of symmetrical manhood and genial, undaunted living. He should have been a scholar and writer; and, indeed, he did acquire much knowledge and wrote not a little with both conviction and grace. At Yale he entered the Scientific School; but he was a member of the Glee Club, wrote for the *Record*, was initiated into the Cloister, or Book and Snake Society, and upon graduation was invited to remain in the college as an instructor. During a two years' residence in Italy in search of health, he at once betook himself to study and letters. At Siena for six months he studied Italian under the distinguished teacher-priest, Dan Orlandi; and as he learned, he made use of his knowledge by translating considerable portions of Dante. He translated also a book entitled *The Early Life of Siena,* which was later published. During a residence of some years in New York, where for a time he found comparative relief from his malady, he began work at Columbia for his master's degree, specializing in the field of sociology and economics.

No sooner had Mr. Wood taken up his residence in the Southwest, whither he was finally directed by the doctors in his search for health, than he entered into the study of its fascinating and remote past. From boyhood the West and the Indians had exercised a strong spell upon his imagination and his sympathies. At Santa Fe he came into contact with eminent archaeologists and with them visited many of the prehistoric ruins of New Mexico. An entire summer was spent, in company with his wife, visiting the Navajo country and Hopi Indian pueblos. He took a deep interest in the various Indian ceremonies that they were permitted to see and also spent several weeks with the Wetherills at Kayenta. When he came to Tucson, he entered one of Dr. Byron Cummings' classes in archaeology at the University of Arizona and both afforded stimulus to his associates in this department and added solid material to his fund of information concerning the prehistoric Indians of the Southwest.

For a long time Mr. Wood had been eager to fix upon some suitable theme for the exercise of his literary gifts. In the Southwest he found contentment, and he was comparatively well. Not only did he find the climate of Tucson favorable to his health but here, also, he entered into fellowship with a circle of cultivated friends who afforded him both enjoyment and

mental stimulus. Since the Indians had always been a prime
center of his interest, here in Arizona he found his El Dorado.
Right at hand was his laboratory—spread out all around him
under the unclouded skies, on the mesas and in the canyons
and mountains that he loved to traverse and explore. So he
decided that for the future the Apache Indians should be the
center of his thought and literary endeavor. This choice may
have been prompted by Dr. Frederick W. Hodge. At any rate
he approved and confirmed it, pointing out to Mr. Wood that
a history of the Apache Indians should be written and that, by
virtue of his deep interest in the subject, his leisure, his present
location, and his ability as a writer, he was admirably fitted for
the undertaking.

With great ardor Mr. Wood now set about the work of collecting materials and familiarizing himself still further with
the Apache country. He rapidly accumulated a considerable
library on the Apaches and the Southwest. He made leisurely
visits to the Apache reservations, interviewing leaders, Indian
agents, and scouts who had survived the bloody wars of the
seventies and eighties, and taking photographs of historic figures
and scenes. He also engaged in prolonged research in the
Library of Congress and the archives of the War Department
at Washington. Many Arizona pioneers, who had themselves
taken part in the Indian hostilities of fifty and sixty years ago,
were interviewed by him. It was at this period of Mr. Wood's
activities that I came into most intimate contact with him; for
I, too, for a considerable time, had made the study of Arizona
history my chief recreation. We took field trips together,
identifying and photographing spots of tragic interest, and
interviewing pioneers who had known the Apaches and fought
with them in the early days. We had planned to meet each
other in Los Angeles, in March, 1927, for the purpose of
jointly interviewing several former residents of Arizona who

had borne a main hand in Apache affairs half a century before. Then, suddenly, while in the full enjoyment of life, and doing the best work he had ever done, Mr. Wood died of pneumonia; and his eager plans were all at an end.

I take this opportunity to thank the following people who, in various ways, have graciously helped me in preparing this book for the press. Acknowledgment is due to my daughter, Mrs. Shiras Morris, Jr., and to my colleague, Dr. A. Laurence Muir, of the English Department of the University of Arizona, for the critical reading of my manuscript and the constructive criticism offered by them; to my colleague, Mr. Rudolph H. Gjelsness, Librarian of the University of Arizona, for constant expert assistance and advice; to Dr. Frederick W. Hodge, for encouragement and scholarly suggestions; to the late Will C. Barnes for vivid accounts of Apache battles in which he himself participated; to Thomas Cruse, Brigadier General, U. S. Army, Retired, for the use of his unpublished autobiography and for numerous letters that he wrote me concerning famous battles and campaigns in the early eighties in which he, modestly as he obscures the fact, bore a heroic and conspicuous part; to Mr. William Donner, Superintendent of the White River Apache Indian Reservation, and Mr. J. B. Kitch, Superintendent of the San Carlos Reservation, for friendly assistance rendered me during extended visits to these reservations for the purpose of gathering first-hand material about the Apaches at the present time; to Dr. J. G. Brown for his generous and skillful work in photographing for me numerous historic illustrations found in old books and magazines, particularly the remarkable series of Remington drawings made half a century ago to illustrate some of the very battles and scenes that I describe in my text.

All the photographs of Apache Chiefs and warriors and of the concluding scenes in the long war with the Apaches were secured by Charles Morgan Wood from the Photograph Section of the Signal Corps, Munitions Building, Washington. In footnotes and bibliographies I have tried to give full credit for other material that I have drawn upon, whether for the printed page or for purposes of illustration.

In conclusion I wish to express to the personnel of the following institutions my sincere thanks for the courteous assistance they have rendered me: Biblioteca Nacional, Mexico City; Pioneers Historical Society, Tucson; the Los Angeles Public Library; the Bancroft Library, Berkeley; the Stanford University Library; and the Library of the University of Arizona.

FRANK C. LOCKWOOD

University of Arizona

CONTENTS

ILLUSTRATIONS

THE APACHE INDIANS

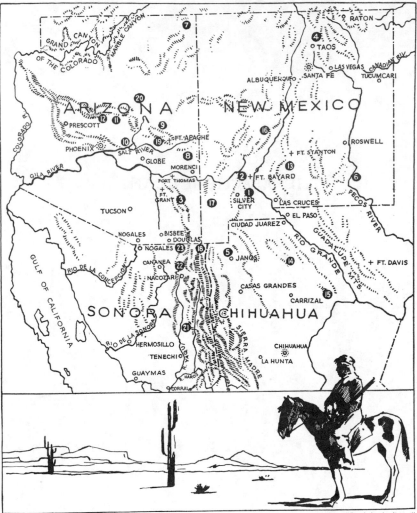

SKETCH MAP
OF THE APACHE COUNTRY

1. Santa Rita del Cobre, scene of Johnson's massacre.
2. Piños Altos, where Mangus Colorado was flogged.
3. Apache Pass, where two battles were fought.
4. The Pueblo de Taos.
5. Where Governor Carasco massacred the Mimbrenos in 1858.
6. The Bosque Redondo Reservation.
7. Canyon de Chelly, the Navajo stronghold.
8. The San Carlos Reservation.
9. The Tonto Basin, scene of Crook's campaign of 1872–73.
10. The Salt River Canyon battle.
11. Turret Butte.
12. The Camp Verde Reservation.
13. The Mescalero Reservation.
14. The Candelaria Mountains, where Victorio's double massacre occurred.
15. The Tres Castillos Mountains, where Victorio made his last stand.
16. Nana's camp in the San Andreas Mountains.
17. Horse Shoe Canyon fight.
18. Where Colonel Garcia ambushed Loco's band.
19. Hentig's fight on Cibicu Creek.
20. The Cevelon Fork battle.
21. Where the Mexicans shot Captain Crawford.
22. Country where Lieutenant Gatewood found Geronimo.
23. Canyon des Embudos where Crook was double-crossed by Geronimo.

CHAPTER I

Origin and Distribution

IT is the way of certain learned writers when they set out to tell the story of a particular country or people to go back to the beginnings of time in order to lay firm and deep foundations. Washington Irving, in his *Knickerbocker's History of New York,* burlesques this pedantic manner with extravagant humor. He devotes one entire book to the setting forth of "divers ingenious theories and philosophic speculations concerning the creation and population of the world, as connected with the history of New York." Chapter I is entitled "Description of the World"; Chapter II, "Cosmogony, or Creation of the World, with a multitude of excellent theories, by which the creation of the world is shown to be no such difficult matter as common folk would imagine"; Chapter III, "How that famous navigator, Noah, was shamefully nicknamed, and how he committed an unpardonable oversight in not having four sons; with the great trouble of philosophers caused thereby, and the discovery of America"; Chapter IV, "Showing the great difficulty philosophers have had in peopling America; and how the Aborigines came to be begotten by accident—to the great relief and satisfaction of the author"; and so on to the end of Book I.

The author of this volume has no desire to put on a wise look or to ape the manner of erudite scholars. He prefers, rather, to come to grips at once with the subject that interests him—the Apache Indians. The fact is, no scholar has been able to trace satisfactorily the exact origins of this spectacular people or to say just when they made their appearance in the Southwest as a distinct nation. Concerning one simple fact all ethnologists agree: the Apache belongs to the Athapascan family, the most widely scattered of all North American Indian linguistic families. In remote times it covered the greater part of the continent. Its various tribes inhabited the Arctic and the Pacific coasts and extended as far south as northern New Mexico and as far east as the Rio Grande.

Such are the peculiarities of the Athapascan languages that they may be definitely discriminated from the languages of all other American Indians, even though, during the long period of time that this family has been dispersing itself over the North American continent, differences in language and physical appearance have arisen in widely separated groups. The peculiarities of the languages of the Athapascan family Dr. Frederick W. Hodge describes as follows: "Phonetically they are rendered harsh and difficult for European ears because of a series of guttural sounds, many continuants, and frequent checks and aspirations. Morphologically they are marked by a sentence verb of considerable complexity, due largely to many decayed prefixes and to various changes of the root to indicate the number and character of the subject and object. Between the various languages much regular phonetic change, especially of vowels, appears and while certain words are found to be common, each language, independently of the others, has formed many nouns by composition and transformed the structure of its verbs."

The Reverend Frank Uplegger, of San Carlos, Arizona, a linguistic scholar of eminent ability, who has lived among the Apaches for fifteen years and has preached to them regularly in their own tongue, kindly prepared for me the following account of the genius and peculiarities of the Apache language:

"The chief characteristic of the Apache, as of other languages of the large Athapascan family, consists in its being a tone language in a very strict sense of this term. Of vowel sounds it has those of Spanish, but tone-coloring, modulation, quantity, pitch, bring their number up to sixty, all serving to form mental pictures, in their combination with consonants and glides of the voice from middle to a higher or lower position in the scale, which are to the non-Apache ear often as unnoticeable as a quarter note deviation of tone is to many a beginner at violin-playing.

"The consonant register comprises more than thirty sounds, omitting f, p, r, v, and x, but having a number of consonant colorings and combinations foreign to European languages. The language is not 'guttural,' but frequent in it are aspirates, explodent sounds, final breathings, breath checks or glottal stops. Rich in sound variations, it also has a copious vocabulary at its command. In fact, with its wealth of word stems or roots, there is no limit to the easy formation of new words, as new objects enter the speaker's vision. These stems are so easily joined together that values expressing action, its subject, object, indirect object relation to what preceded, mode of execution, together with indication of time, smoothly form one word where we in English hear, as units standing apart, a leading concept or statement with a relative phrase or sentence. This feature of expressing a very complex thought in a single word, together with its character as a tone language, and the facility of utterance to the native, requiring only little noticeable movement of the organs of speech, renders it difficult for European ears and tongues and has kept interested non-Apache listeners from proceeding toward a true appreciation of its logic and its music."

The Athapascan family consists of three divisions: the Northern, the Pacific, and the Southern. It is the Southern division with which we are interested. The tribes that constituted this division were dispersed over a wide area in the Southwest—including parts of southern Colorado and Utah, Arizona, New Mexico, the western portions of Kansas and Texas, and Mexico as far as the 25th degree of latitude. Among the Athapascan tribes that inhabited this region were the Navajo and the Apache. That these two peoples are closely related is shown both by their languages and their physical characteristics. Adaptability, a marked quality of the Athapascan family in general, is illustrated in both the Apache and the Navajo by virtue of the fact that they in common adopted and absorbed various rites and ceremonies from the Pueblo Indians with whom they have had long, and at times, close contacts. The vocabularies and basic characteristics of the Apache and Navajo languages are almost identical.

The inclusive name of the Athapascans who inhabited Canada is Tinnë. Both the Apaches and the Navajos belong to this branch. Originally, the Apaches and the Navajos were one people. When these two tribes separated, and for what cause, is unknown. The Navajos have always outnumbered their cousins, the Apaches. It may be that the latter were ejected by the Navajos because of their mischief-making proclivities and excessive turbulence. On the other hand, the Apaches may have withdrawn on account of their desire for a more roving and adventurous way of life. During historic times the Navajos have been more given to agriculture—particularly to pastoral pursuits—than have the Apaches. The Apaches have not adhered so closely to the culture of the Athapascans of the North as have the Navajos, nor have the Pueblo Indians left so definite a mark upon them. There seems to be little doubt that when the Apaches first appeared upon the historical horizon, in 1540, they were wholly detached from the Navajos and were neither a very numerous nor a very important people.

Patient inquiry shows that the Apaches have no definite

knowledge as to their racial origin or earliest habitat. It is rare indeed to find an Apache who is able to give any information concerning an ancestor more remote than his grandparent. The creation myth is the only widely known legend of the origin of their people, though several clans among the Western Apaches have definite stories concerning migrations of their people from the north and northeast—that is, from the regions now occupied by the Navajo and the Hopi. Though there is great vagueness with respect to the time at which this southern movement took place and the exact country from which they came, there can be little doubt that at no remote time there was a migration from somewhere in the northeast to the region they now occupy south of the Little Colorado River and north of the Southern Pacific Railroad.

Tradition attributes great cruelty to the Apaches, even before historic times. The Apache was the original "bad man" of the Southwest. The Pueblo Indian was his victim long before the coming of the white man. Not until after the Pueblo Indians came under the sway of the Spanish—and, in consequence, under their protection—did warfare against the white invaders become the order of the day. From the first, the Apaches have been the most hardy, warlike, mobile tribe known to history. They "wandered everywhere and dwelt nowhere." Marauding and murdering, they were constantly on the move—the most disconcerting and harassing of enemies. So cunning were they in ambush and so stealthy in attack that a handful of them could keep a community in terror or an army in disorder. Says Bandelier: "They stood toward the land-tilling Indians in the relation of a man-eating tiger to the East Indian communities. Nobody knew, even if there were but a single enemy in the neighborhood, where he might strike next. One Apache could keep a pueblo of several hundred souls on the alert, and hamper them in their daily work. He had nothing to attend to but his purposes of murder, rapine, and theft, which were his means of subsistence, whereas the others had their modest fields to till, and in the performance of such duties danger was lurking unseen, always likely to display itself when and where it was least expected."

The Apaches gave fixed allegiance to no supreme leader, did not acknowledge hereditary chiefs. The position of leadership, so far as it existed and so long as it lasted, was won by military prowess in time of great emergency. The Apaches, more than any other force, changed the ethnological map of the Southwest. They constituted such a threat to the Pueblo Indians as to halt their natural advance toward the east, and even drove back their eastern limits. At a later period their pressure upon the Sobaipuri Indians of the San Pedro Valley in Arizona caused this tribe to retire westward to the Santa Cruz, there to unite themselves to their Pima cousins, the Papagos, and at last to lose their tribal identity altogether. Other hostile tribes that were induced to enter into alliances with them were eventually absorbed—if not exterminated as a result of such unhappy alliance, as in the case of the Mabos. Even in the memory of living Americans, during the Civil War and just afterwards, the Apaches made large areas of the most fertile parts of Arizona uninhabitable.

From the dawn of Southwestern history there have been confusion and uncertainty with respect to the geographical distribution of the Apaches, their numbers, and the names by which widely separated tribes or divisions were designated. They are first referred to in history by Castañeda, chronicler of the Coronado Expedition. The Spaniards first met them in eastern Arizona, near the Gila River. A very different division of the Apaches was encountered by Coronado and his army early in 1541 in northeastern New Mexico. Castañeda calls these Indians "Querechos." More than a generation later, Oñate comes across a tribe of them and calls them the "Apiches" or "Apaches"; and Benavides, in *The Memorial*, classifies them Gila Apaches, Navajo Apaches, and Apaches Vaqueros. This same confusion persists down to modern and even present times. The Spaniards gave the generic name Apache to the Tontos, Chiricahuas, Gileños, Membreños, Taracones, Mescaleros, Llaneros, Lipanes, and Navajos. The specific names are Spanish words descriptive of some animal, or product of the soil, or geographic feature, or peculiarity that marked a particular group.

BIBLIOGRAPHY

BANDELIER, A. F. *Final Report on Investigations in the Southwest.* Papers of the Archaeological Institute of America, American Series III, 1890.

BOURKE, J. G. "Apache Mythology." In *Journal of American Folklore*, Vol. III, p. 209.

BOURKE, J. G. *Medicine Men of the Apache.* Bureau of Ethnology Report.

BOURKE, J. G. *On the Border with Crook.* New York, Scribner, 1895.

CURTIS, E. S. *North American Indian*, Vol. I. 1907.

GODDARD, P. E. *Indians of the Southwest.* American Museum of Natural History Handbook, Series No. 2. New York, 1921.

GODDARD, P. E. *Various Apache Texts* (including Creation Myths, etc.). American Museum of Natural History, Anthropological Papers, Vol. VII and Vol. XXIV, Parts 1–4.

HODGE, F. W. "The Early Navajo and Apache." In *American Anthropologist*, old series, July, 1895. Washington.

HODGE, F. W. *Handbook of the American Indian*, Vol. I, p. 63.

HRDLICKA, ALES. *Notes on the San Carlos Apaches*, September, 1905, p. 480.

Pacific Railroad Reports, Explorations, and Surveys, Vol. III. Washington, 1856. Whipple, etc., on Apaches.

CHAPTER II

The Apaches in Spanish Times

THE first mention made of the Apaches is by Castañeda in his report, *The Journey of Coronado*. The Spaniards encountered them near Chichilticalli, the famous "red house," believed by Bandelier to have been in the neighborhood of modern Fort Thomas, Arizona. Castañeda says this house must "have been destroyed by the people of the district, who are the most barbarous people that have yet been seen. They live by hunting."

The next reference to the Apaches occurs in 1541 and is found in Castañeda's *Report*. Coronado's army, after spending some time at Pecos in northeastern New Mexico, set out to find Quivira. The Spaniards had marched ten days beyond the Pecos River in a northeasterly direction when they "came to some settlements of people who lived like Arabs and who are called Querechos in that region. . . . These people follow the cows, hunting them and tanning the skins to take to the settlements in the winter to sell, since they go there to pass the winter, each company going to those which are nearest. . . . That they were intelligent is evident from the fact that although they conversed by means of signs they made themselves understood so well there is no need of an interpreter. . . . These people are called Querechos. . . . They have better figures than the Pueblo Indians, are better warriors, and are more feared." [1]

[1] Castañeda. *The Journey of Coronado*. Chicago, Laidlaw.

8

Castañeda states further that these Indians dried the flesh of the buffalo, powdered it, and made a kind of soup of it. They ate raw flesh, also. They skinned the buffalo with remarkable quickness and skill with a piece of flint as large as a man's finger, which they tied to a stick and used as a knife. They gave this flint instrument an edge with their own teeth. The Spaniards saw a village consisting of two hundred tents, made of buffalo skins, tanned white, so that they looked like army tents. The whole living of these people came from the buffaloes. From the skins they clothed themselves and made shoes; and they wove rope from the long shaggy hair. Their dogs were of good size and were trained to serve as beasts of burden. Whenever a band moved, pack saddles were placed on the dogs and fastened with leather thongs. From thirty to fifty pounds was placed on each dog; and the tent poles, covered with the tent which served as a net into which various camp articles could be thrown, were tied onto the pack saddle at the sides, so that they would drag behind. If the loads got disarranged, the dogs would howl, in this way calling someone to come and fix them right. In 1583, mention is made by Espejo's party of the Querecho Indians, a mountain tribe hostile toward the tillers of the soil who lived at Acoma.

One more reference to the Apaches as first known to the white man must suffice. Oñate came in contact with them in 1569, during his travels in New Mexico; and it is in accounts of his expedition, published in 1599, that we have for the first time the word Apache (enemy) applied to this people. In one document, *Obediencia San Juan Baptista*, the spelling of the name is "Apaches"; while in another, *Carta Escripta*, the word appears as "Apiches": "*es infinita gente los Apiches de que tambien hemos visto algunos.*"

In *The Memorial* of Fray Alonso Benavides, a missionary Franciscan priest in New Mexico, printed at Madrid in 1630, we get a rather comprehensive account of the Apaches as they existed at the time. This report was compiled for the King of Spain. Benavides refers to all the outlying native tribes in New Mexico as Apaches, and he classifies them as Gila Apaches, Navajo Apaches, and Apaches Vaqueros. Even then they were a terror to other native tribes, but as yet they had given the Spaniards little trouble. At one time Benavides speaks of them as "the huge Apache nation," and in another place alludes to them as the largest tribe of the world. The fact is, Benavides greatly exaggerates the Indian population of New Mexico in his day. He does this through ignorance rather than with the desire to deceive; but of course it was impossible for him either to count or to make a just estimate of roving tribes, forever on the move.

The important fact is that the Pueblo villages on the Rio Grande were surrounded by the Apache nation. Says Benavides: "It is a people very fiery and bellicose, and very crafty in war. Even in the method of speaking, they show a difference from the rest of the nations. For these speak rather softly and deliberately, and the Apaches seem to break their heads with the words. They do not dwell in settlements, nor in houses, but in tents and huts, for as much as they move from mountain range to mountain range, seeking game, which is their sustenance. However, each hut of a principal or individual has its recognized land on which they plant corn and other seeds. They go clad in skins of deer, very well tanned and adorned in their fashion, and the women gallantly and honestly clad. They have no more idolatry than that of the Sun, and even that is not general to all of them, and they scoff much at other nations that have idols.

"They have as many wives as they can support; and upon her whom they take in adultery they irremissibly execute their law, which is to cut off her ears and nose; and they repudiate her. They are very obedient to their elders and superiors and hold them in great respect. They teach and chastise their children differently from other nations, who have no chastisement whatever. They pride themselves much on speaking the truth, and hold for dishonored him whom they catch in a lie. The tongue varies somewhat, as they are a great nation, though each can understand the other. They occupy a vast expanse of country. . . . It is a nation so bellicose, all of it, that it has been the crucible for the courage of the Spaniards."

The Apaches, as well as the other tribes of New Mexico, grew more warlike during the next two decades, and killed several of the Spaniards. For this they were hung or sold into slavery. The Apaches of northern New Mexico became more and more dangerous as time went on. In a raid on a Zuñi town, about 1672, and other pueblos farther east, they killed several friars. There was open war between the Pueblo Indians and the Apaches at this time. Affairs continued to grow worse, and about 1676, the Apaches destroyed churches and towns and killed a good many Spaniards. The Spanish settlements were without suitable defense, each frontier station having only five men poorly armed and almost no horses.

In August, 1684, vigorous retaliatory action was taken—a combined force of Spanish and Indians making an attack on an Apache *rancheria* with the avowed purpose of killing all the men and taking captive the women and children. Near Zuñi, in the autumn of 1692, a herd of Spanish cattle was stampeded and driven off by the Apaches. They kept up a continual attack upon the forces of Vargas during his return march after the conquest of the Pueblos, and succeeded in wounding a soldier and capturing a number of horses. A friar, P. Casanes, was led into an ambush by the Apaches, in March, 1696, and was beaten to death with clubs and stones.

Toward the close of the 17th century, Sonora and Nueva Viscaya suffered greatly from Apache incursions. The commanding officer responsible for the protection of this region lived at San Juan. There was a garrison at Frontéras and one at Janos to the eastward, also; and they cooperated with each other in efforts to hold the enemy in check. In cases of great need reenforcements were drawn from distant points. The savages were continually raiding the exposed towns and missions. They would make a whirlwind dash upon a community, drive off the livestock, and swiftly retreat into their northern strongholds. The soldiers would pursue, often tardily, and rarely with signal success. Sometimes the stolen stock would be recovered, two or three warriors killed, and a few women and children captured; but never were they able to achieve a decisive victory.

In 1693 Don Domingo Jironza, a brave and capable officer, was placed in command of a "flying company" organized for the defense of Sonora against the savages. He immediately made two spirited attacks upon the enemy, and in 1694 conducted four energetic campaigns against the Apaches and other hostile tribes. A band of Apaches had stolen thousands of horses in northern Sonora. These marauders Jironza pursued, killing thirteen of them and capturing seven. Later in the same year, with the aid of Pima warriors, he gained a smashing victory over six hundred of the invaders, killing large numbers of them. In cooperation with Captain Fuente of the presidio at Janos, and with the aid of the Pimas, he invaded the territory of the Apaches, but with only meager results. Young ensign Juan Mateo Manje was associated with his uncle, Commander Jironza, in these Apache wars and was later assigned as military escort to the Jesuit padres on their dangerous journeys into new territory. In his *Lux de Tierra Incognita*, Manje makes frequent allusion to Apache raids into Sonora for the purpose of stealing horses and ravaging the Spanish settlements. He comments, too, on the great difficulty of winning any of the Apaches to the church; and consoles himself with the thought that, hard as it may be to instill the Faith into the hearts of these people, when once the impression is made it will be as if stamped on bronze.

A joint campaign of considerable importance was waged against the Apaches and their allies in September, 1689, by the three commanders, Jironza, Teran, and Fuente. Many Indians were slain. General Teran died during this campaign. The following March the persistent foe again swept down on a village and drove off two hundred horses. Pursuit was prompt; one of the horses was recovered and eighteen of the Indians were killed; but scarcely had the soldiers returned to their presidio before the enemy attacked and murdered a party from Arispe, consisting of Captain Cristóbal León, his son, two other Spaniards, and six Indian servants. Jironza followed the Indians with his "flying company" and killed three of them; while from Janos came Fuente to join in the punitive expedition. The punishment was severe; the Apaches were forced back to the Gila River, and thirty-two of their warriors were slain.

Repeated vicious attacks were made by the Apaches on the Pima villages of northern Sonora. They were after the corn and livestock that the Christian Indians had accumulated. In a raid on Cocospera in February, 1698, Father Contreras was wounded and barely escaped with his life, and two Pima women were killed. The savages descended three hundred strong, robbed the town, burned the Church and the house of the Father, and killed the women mentioned above. The native men were nearly all away at the time on a trading trip to the northward. The few Pima men that were left in the town followed the enemy, but were ambushed and slain.

A month later, flushed with their victory at Cocospera, the Apaches fell upon the Ranchería Santa Cruz (where Fairbank, Arizona, is now located). The chief of the village and two or three of his followers suffered immediate death. Padre Eusebio

Francisco Kino, the brave and devout pioneer Jesuit missionary
to the Upper Pimas, had erected an adobe house here, and
had brought cattle and horses for the beginnings of a mission.
The house was built with embrasures and was surrounded by
a corral. After the death of the chief the surviving inhabitants
were driven into this house, three more of the people having
been killed as the fight progressed. The Apaches now climbed
onto the roof and began burning the building. With an arquebus
they had taken in battle they killed another man, slaughtered
a number of horses and cattle, set fire to the corral and buildings,
and took whatever they could lay hands on. Thinking they
had won a complete victory, they began feasting on the animals
they had killed and the maize and beans they had stolen.

But a terrible vengeance now descended upon them. Three
miles down the San Pedro River at Quiburi, where also Kino
had started a mission, dwelt Captain Coro, a warm friend of
Father Kino's and the most redoubtable fighter in the Pima
nation. When word was brought to him of the destruction and
slaughter of Santa Cruz, he at once went to the relief of his
kinsmen. At the time there happened to be at his village a
large number of Pimas from San Xavier, who had come over
to trade. These visiting Pimas joined him in his expedition.
Capotcari was the name of the Apache leader. He was a bold,
capable wight and, withal, an insolent one. In the parley that
took place after Coro arrived on the scene Capotcari made fun
of Coro and his band, calling them women, and declaring that
the Spaniards, with whom they were allied, were poltroons. He
said he had killed many Pimas and Spaniards, and dared Coro,
instead of fighting a general battle, to match ten Pimas against
ten of his party and fight it out in this way. Nothing daunted,
Coro accepted his proposal and picked ten brave Pimas to meet
Capotcari's ten. Capotcari, as daring as he was abusive and
boastful, led his band in person. The Apaches were very effec-

RUINS OF COCOSPERA

AQUEDUCT AND CHURCH OF SANTA RITA, CHIHUAHUA

Reproduced from John R. Bartlett's "Personal Narrative"

JANOS, CHIHUAHUA

Reproduced from John R. Bartlett's "Personal Narrative"

tive in offensive warfare, with spears and bows and arrows, but they were not so good at warding off the missiles of their foes. The Pimas were good both in defensive and in offensive battle. Very soon nine of the Apaches were either killed or out of the fighting; so Capotcari was left to bear the brunt of the fight. He was so skillful that he could catch with his hand the arrows that were launched at him. But when the antagonist who had engaged him saw this, he rushed upon him, threw him to the ground, and pounded him to death with a stone.

It was a great victory, indeed, for the Pimas. Perhaps never before had the Apaches suffered a defeat so impressive. The routed enemy sought to escape by fleeing to the woods and mountains, but were mercilessly pursued and scores of them killed. Captain Coro sent word of the victory to Kino, and the Padre, with Manje and Escalante, Spanish military representatives, came to view the scene of battle and to count the dead. They actually counted fifty-four dead bodies; and it was known that many who had been wounded by poisoned arrows died on the retreat after the engagement ended. Kino states that three hundred of the enemy were killed in this fight and that an equal number presented themselves at the nearest presidios seeking peace.

We have little information concerning Apache depredations between 1700 and 1724. No doubt the settlements continued to suffer as in the past. But in the autumn of 1724 matters grew worse. The Apaches had become so aggressive that it looked as if white civilization in northern Mexico would be wiped out. To add to the woes of the exposed settlements, the Government at this time issued orders to the commanding military officer that he was to make no more aggressive campaigns against the Apaches, but was to conduct a purely defensive warfare, waiting until an attack was made and then pursuing and punishing the foe. To the settlers and missionaries this policy seemed very weak and dangerous, for it was well known that attacks by the Apaches were always aimed at undefended points. The Father Visitor, Miguel Almanza, strongly remonstrated against the new policy, but we do not know what the outcome was.

The Lipan Apaches of Texas, a very troublesome tribe, were crafty enough, when hard-pressed by their wild foes, the Comanches, to seek peace with the Spanish and a settled mission life. Neither the padres nor the soldiers put much faith in their sincerity. The Fathers were willing to experiment, however, and a mission was founded for the Apaches on the Guadalupe River. This action was approved as early as 1750 but was not carried out until 1756, and then the mission was located, not on the Guadalupe, but on the San Saba River. The Apaches were now friendly enough, but when elaborate preparations had been made for missionary supervision, they were shifty and, for one reason or another, declined to settle permanently at the mission. Their real object was to secure the Spanish as their allies against the Comanches and other enemies. As a result of what had already been done, the animosity of the Comanches was now directed against the Spanish. The Apaches warned the Spaniards that the Comanches, now their common foe, were about to strike a blow; but it was too late. Under friendly guise, a Comanche chief with a thousand warriors gained entrance to the Apache mission. They made a thorough job of it—plundering and burning the buildings and killing nearly all the Spaniards. Two padres were killed, and a party sent from the presidio to reenforce the mission was led into ambush. The wily Apaches suffered little, for only a few of them were present at the time of the attack.

This disaster brought such blame upon the padres that they offered to abandon the mission, but their suggestion was set aside. Instead, a punitive expedition made up of five hundred Spanish soldiers and a considerable number of Apaches marched northward against the common enemy. A surprise attack was made on a *rancheria* and more than five hundred of the Comanches were killed; but when the Spaniards advanced against the towns in the region of San Teodoro, the enemy, not waiting to be attacked, came out against them six thousand strong and put them to flight. After this, for several years, it was all the Spaniards could do to hold their ground against the bold assaults of the Comanches; so no aggressive steps were taken. Peace having been finally effected with the Comanches through the friendly overtures of Padre Calaborra, there was talk of moving the Spanish presidio and mission to the north, but this idea did not meet with the approval of the Apaches. Indeed, they turned traitors to the Spaniards, and in crafty raids against the Comanches left articles behind that seemed to give evidence of Spanish perfidy, and they finally attacked the Spanish posts and then retreated. Of course, the northern tribes now became as hostile as ever toward the Spanish. Yet the Apaches were still able to convince them that they wanted missions; so, in 1761, Missions San Lorenze and Candelaria were established, and four hundred Apaches came together at these places. Conditions seemed so propitious that steps were taken to begin work again at Saba; but nothing came of all these efforts; the enterprise was finally given up; and, in 1767, the missions were abandoned.

At this point it may be well to clarify and summarize the Apache situation as it confronted the Spanish Government during the period between 1700 and 1772. By 1700 the Spanish had pushed their settlements almost to the present northern borderline of Mexico. It was a vast region; the scattered population was to be found in mining camps and missions and on ranches, not far removed from the presidios that had been established for their protection. "Flying squadrons" too, as we have seen, were kept in the field in times of special danger or emergency. However, this frontier military organization was marked by great corruption and incompetence, and, in view of the fact that these northern provinces, especially Sonora, were continually pouring wealth into the royal treasury, the Spanish Government itself was to blame for the failure to provide a strong and coordinated frontier program and administration.

Nowhere is there a better statement in brief space of the weakness and defects of the Government in its dealing with the Apache problem than Dr. C. E. Chapman's summary of a memorial addressed to the King by Pedro de Labaquera, who had long served in Mexico as Lieutenant Captain-General:

"The Apaches, when attacked, habitually retired to the mountains which were inaccessible to the presidial troops. This was due not merely to the fact that the latter were cavalrymen, but to the nature of the soldiers themselves. Most of them were mulattoes of very low character, without ambition, and unconquerably unwilling to travel on foot, as was necessary in a mountain attack. Moreover, their weapons carried so short a distance that the Apaches were wont to get just out of range and make open jest of the Spaniards. Furthermore, some presidial captains were more interested in making a personal profit out of their troops, arising from the fact that part of the latter's wages was paid in effects, than they were in subjecting the enemy, nor did the various captains work in harmony when on campaigns. Continuance of the Apaches in Apachería was in the highest degree prejudicial. Not only were they a hindrance to conquests toward the Colorado and in the direct route between Sonora and New Mexico, but also they endangered regions already held by Spain, leading subjected Indians, either from fear or from natural inclination, to abandon missions and villages, and whether in alliance with the Apaches or by themselves, to commit the same kind of atrocities as the

Apaches did. Labaquera recommended that two hundred mountain fusileers of Spanish blood be recruited in Spain, equipped among other things with guns of long range, and despatched to New Spain for service against the Apaches. These men, under a disinterested leader, would quickly subject the Apaches, and might then be given lands in the region." [2]

It is necessary to stress the fact that most of the presidio captains were given to greed and tyranny. Not all of them, but most of them, were addicted to graft. They practiced their greed at the expense of the soldiers under their command. Instead of paying the men in the specie provided by the royal government they took the cash and paid off the soldiers in goods purchased from stocks owned or controlled by them. The prices they charged were excessive. As a natural result of the unjust advantage thus taken by the captains, the troops were often ill-disposed toward their commanders and indifferent in the discharge of duty. Both Viceroy Francisco de Croix and Visitador José de Gálvez state bluntly that "the Sonora presidios served chiefly to enrich captains and their backers." [3] The Marques de Rubi and Bucareli point out their shameful delinquencies with equal force.

After all, the failure to control the Apaches was the fault of the Spanish Government. It was their duty to see the fact that the adequate protection of the northern frontier absolutely demanded a coordinated and steadfast program; and it was obligatory upon them to devise and enforce such a program. The problem of controlling the Apaches along the far-flung northern frontier was a single problem—not one to be coped with separately by this province or that, spasmodically. The line of attack was along an exposed border, twelve or fifteen hundred miles in extent. The blows fell thickest and heaviest

[2] Chapman, C E. *The Founding of Spanish California*, pp. 65–66. New York, Macmillan, 1916.
[3] *Ibid.*, p. 141.

on Nueva Viscaya (Chihuahua) and Sonora; but any point on the frontier was subject to attack at any time, and so shrewd were the Apaches that it was their habit when resistance and offensive tactics became very strong in a particular province to turn with lightning speed to some front that had been left weakened or unprotected. Indeed, some of their most successful raids were directed against the presidios themselves at times when the troops were in the field on some ambitious campaign into their territory.

How criminally lacking in cooperation were the various provinces, presidios, and commanders, may be illustrated by the conduct of a captain of the presidio at Janos. About 1770 he entered into a sham armistice with enemy Apaches, by the terms of which they were allowed to go through the pass that his presidio was responsible for guarding. They were thus enabled to enter Nueva Viscaya and make contact with their friends, the Tarahumara Indians (supposedly a pacified tribe) who were stealing horses and mules from the presidio at Chihuahua and trading or selling them to the Apaches whenever they made their appearance. In 1771 a band of Apaches from the Gila profited by this infamous arrangement, slipping by the presidio of Janos and attacking *locales* not far from Chihuahua. It proved to be a very destructive raid. Two Spanish settlers were killed near Chihuahua, two wood choppers in the mountains suffered a like fate, in another place a cowboy was slain, and sixteen others on a large ranch. The Indians also took several captives, and drove off a large herd of animals. Upon investigation it was found that seventeen hundred of the Tarahumara Indians were in collusion with the invaders. They had a regular rendezvous with the Apache raiders, in the Sierra de Rosario, where there was good pasture for their stolen animals.

But at last great statesmen and great soldiers set seriously to work to rectify the long-existing evils. During the years 1765–1768 the famous Marques de Rubi devoted himself to the task of studying and reforming the whole military organization along the border. His proposals were submitted to his superiors, and in 1772, by a royal decree, his plans were put into effect. Some presidios were dropped, and others, for strategic purposes, were relocated. The result was a line of fifteen presidios, stretching from Matagordo Bay to Altar, Sonora, in the extreme West.

Each fort was assigned a captain, a lieutenant, a chaplain, an *alferez*, a sergeant, two corporals, and forty men. Ten Indian scouts were attached to each presidio, also. The presidios were spaced about a hundred miles apart so that exposed points all along the line could be protected. More effective military discipline was enforced; and, all in all, opposition to the Apaches became stiffer and more efficient than ever before.

To the distinguished soldier General Don Hugo Oconor was assigned the task of carrying out the reorganization. For a period of five years he was engaged in the very difficult task of remaking the military system along the border. At the same time that he was selecting new sites, and shifting the location of various forts, he carried on wide and devastating campaigns against the daring, shrewd, and ever-hostile foe. The Apaches repeatedly suffered severe punishment, and at times sought terms of peace. However, only at brief intervals was there cessation of active warfare; and, usually, the Apaches got the better of the fighting. In Sonora, most of the time, the conditions were very distressing.

The Apaches carried on their raids under the very shadow of the presidios—at Tubac, killing a soldier and driving off a hundred horses, and likewise at Terrenate, killing the horse-guard and getting away with two hundred and fifty-seven animals. In December, 1772, they murdered an Indian and a Spanish settler at another settlement and escaped with one hundred head of cattle. An expedition against the Apaches had been planned for January, 1773, but the governor of Sonora, disheartened by these bold raids, wrote to his superiors that no more inopportune time for an aggressive campaign into the Apache territory could be chosen, as the residents of Sonora were finding it impossible to protect their own homes. A year later the enemy made another attack on Tubac. This time they killed a sergeant and stampeded one hundred head of cattle. Most outrageous of all, in a third descent upon the presidio of Tubac a little later, they stole one hundred and thirty horses—the best mounts to be had in northern Sonora— that Captain Anza had collected for his famous overland expedition to the Pacific coast. May 7, 1774, a great number of Apaches made a savage assault on Frontéras and drove off three hundred horses from that garrison. In July Tubac was again robbed of thirty horses. As if the impudence and daring of the Apaches knew no limit, in September they got away with thirty-six animals that were used in carrying the mail from Sonora to the Viceroy. And all this time, individual settlers—miners, wood choppers, and ranchmen in lonely places—were being robbed and murdered.

But, in the summer of 1775, Oconor made plans for concerted action along the whole front from Sonora to Texas. Orders to mobilize were issued to governors and captains of presidios in Coahuila, Chihuahua, New Mexico, and Sonora. More than two thousand men, including settlers and Opata Indian allies, were mustered for active service. Every presidio on the border supplied its quota, and Oconor brought into action under his immediate command three hundred soldiers from the various flying squadrons. It was his purpose to strike the Indians hip and thigh, front and rear, in camp and on the move. Buffeted from this direction and that, whether they stood or retreated, they were to be found, repulsed, and beaten. Fifteen defeats of devastating proportions were administered to the Apaches during this campaign. The Spaniards killed, in all, one hundred and four of the enemy and recaptured nearly two thousand animals.

Again, in 1776, Oconor massed his forces for concerted attacks. The results were somewhat disappointing to the Spanish, but in five battles twenty-seven Indians were killed and eighteen captured. It was very plain that Oconor's repeated blows were beginning to tell. From Zuñi, October 12, 1776, Fray Francisco Garcés wrote to the General stating that all the Western Apaches were returning to their old haunts in the north with their families and horses and were very much inclined toward peace with the Spaniards. Now came the climax of their woes. As they were attempting to escape toward the northeast, they encountered large numbers of their hereditary enemies, the Comanches. Caught, thus, between the upper and the nether millstone, they perished by hundreds.

Favorable as the situation, in general, had been for the Spanish, hostilities still continued on the Sonora border. At eight o'clock one morning in November, 1776, Magdalena was attacked by forty Apache and Seri Indians and almost completely destroyed. At the time there were only four ablebodied Pima men in the village. When the attack began, the priest and the women and children were engaged in the regular religious exercises of the day. At once they all took refuge in the home of the missionary. The leader of the attacking party placed a ladder against the wall of the house and, climbing it, set fire to the grass that formed the covering of the roof.

The savages next began to rob and desecrate the church. They carried off the vestments and the altar utensils and tore up the missal and threw it away. Meantime, some of the band had driven the cattle into the mountains. The house by this time was in flames and the people—men, women, and children —on the point of suffocation. With heavy stones the enemy managed to batter down one of the doors. But this proved their undoing; for the three brave Pima warriors within were able to discharge their arrows through the opening, and so, for a time, drove off the foe. As all were now momentarily expecting to die in the flames, the priest prepared to administer absolution. Salvation came from a different quarter, however. The fourth Pima brave, soon after the attack began, had slipped away to San Ignacio where there was a detachment of soldiers; and, barely in the nick of time, the soldiers arrived and drove off the murderers, not, however, before they had mortally wounded one woman and carried another one and two children into captivity.

Oconor's health gave way under the strain of his long and unremitting duties on the border, and at the beginning of 1777 he was relieved. Don Teodoro de Croix now took over responsibility for the control of the Apaches. Frequent and deadly raids still continued in New Mexico and Chihuahua, and bleeding Sonora had never been given time even to bandage her wounds; but Croix's immediate and most urgent task was the suppression of the apparently irrepressible Gila Apaches. On October 12, 1777, a band of these Indians attacked Janos. But they met a hot reception, and were not only repulsed, but were pursued so energetically that they found it convenient to ask for a peace parley. Stern and bitter, indeed, were the conditions offered them. However, the time had come when they must either come to terms or perish. They were between the devil and the deep sea—that is, the merciless Comanches and the unremitting concerted action of the Spanish.

It was left to Croix to determine upon a course of action. He was a humane man, but a shrewd one, too. He saw that to deal with a widely scattered people, every member of which was a

FRONTÉRAS, SONORA

Reproduced from John R. Bartlett's "Personal Narrative"

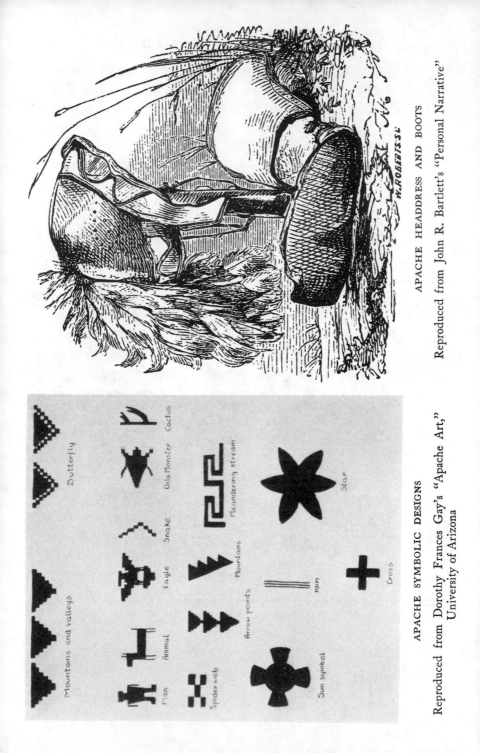

APACHE HEADDRESS AND BOOTS

Reproduced from John R. Bartlett's "Personal Narrative"

APACHE SYMBOLIC DESIGNS

Reproduced from Dorothy Frances Gay's "Apache Art," University of Arizona

Butterfly

Gila Monster

Cactus

Snake

Meandering stream

Star

Mountains and valleys

Eagle

Mountains

Man

Animal

Arrow points

rain

Cross

Spider web

Sun symbol

law unto himself, was all but impossible. No binding treaty could be made with the nation as a whole. He could not suppose that these savages would ever give up robbery and butchery, trained to it as they had been from infancy. They could not change their nature overnight; it was impossible that the thought of good faith to the Spaniards could find permanent lodgment in the brain of an Apache. It was too much to expect that they would give up roaming the plains, abandon the hunt, and settle down to the life of Christians. Nor did he believe that they would return their white captives, or the horses they had stolen, or that they would give hostages. In short, he felt confident that their present overture was simply a makeshift. What they were trying to do was to gain time, and escape immediate destruction at the hands of the Comanches.

A renewed application for peace on the part of the Apaches in the region of Janos brought matters to a head. Croix offered peace on the following terms: they were to come together at Janos, and at other places with their families and live in regularly organized pueblos; were to obey the captain of the presidio, or such justices as Croix should designate; were to select one of their own leading men as governor; were to give up a roving life, and not leave the pueblo without permission; were to set about the building of their houses and the cultivation of the patch of ground that would be allotted to each head of a family; and were also to help cultivate the mission fields (for it was required that they should be under the instruction of the padres). It was further stipulated that, for one year, rations should be issued each week by families; but that at the end of the year they were to support themselves from their own herds and from the crops that they were to raise. They were to be provided with necessary tools, were to be supplied with horses to tend their herds, and were not to be required to return animals previously stolen.

But, as Croix had feared, this attempt at a peaceful solution was in vain. Depredation went on as usual. A party of twenty-five Spaniards was set upon and a soldier badly wounded. Raids were made on San Elezario and El Paso. Early in the year 1778 the very Indians who had sought peace at Janos killed a settler near the fort. In August, only a short distance from Chihuahua, one hundred and thirty-three horses and mules were stolen. When Croix sent Captain Gil to punish the marauders and to make exchange of prisoners, the Indians refused to come down from their mountain retreats to talk with him. Other military expeditions sent out to punish these recalcitrants all failed.

Just about this time the able and experienced explorer and Apache fighter, Don Juan Bautista de Anza, was entering upon his duties as governor of New Mexico. For the next two years Croix and Anza worked hand in hand for the complete conquest of the Apaches. Croix was convinced once for all that the Spanish must adopt an aggressive policy and pursue it relentlessly. He determined that from this time on the war should be carried into the heart of the Indians' own territory, and that a constant stream of detachments should be poured in from all of the frontier states, so that the Indians might have no rest. It was his plan to have expeditions concenter upon the Apaches from Santa Fe, Zuñi, El Paso, Chihuahua, and Sonora and encircle them with a ring of iron. To Anza was assigned the task of breaking a direct road from the Pueblos on the Rio Grande into central Sonora as a line of communication. He was also required, if possible, to enter into an alliance with the Comanches.

Croix carried on one well-coordinated campaign that reached to the remote strongholds of the enemy, but the result was not highly successful. He had intended to follow this campaign up with a similar one the following season, but emergencies arose that prevented him from doing this. Likewise, Anza, because of a crisis in New Mexico, was forced to give his immediate attention to the suppression of the destructive Comanches in the north and to vital negotiations with the Pueblo Indians of northeastern Arizona. So it was not until November, 1780, that he was able to undertake the all-important road-breaking expedition through the Apache country into Sonora. Even when he was free to make this long and perilous march, the result was disappointing. He merely skirted the eastern edge of the Apache wilds; and so failed to penetrate to their strongholds on the Gila—the main purpose of the expedition.

Croix's ambitious plans were carried out to some extent by his successor, Felipe de Neve; and Anza, also, between 1783 and 1787, made solid gains against the Apaches. Neve launched a great drive during April and May, 1786, for the purpose of dislodging the enemy from their mountain *rancherías* near the frontier and forcing them back into more remote fastnesses. As a result sixty-eight Apaches were killed and eleven captured; two Spanish captives were delivered and one hundred and sixty-eight animals recovered. Nor were the spoils of war inconsiderable—in the form of buffalo robes and deer skins. Perhaps most important of all was the shock that must have come to the savages when they found themselves confronted by the Spanish in remote *sierras* where white men had never before been seen. Indeed, they were so alarmed and depressed that they sought an alliance with the Navajos.

The Navajos, however, were unstable allies. They were bound by a treaty of peace entered into with the former governor of New Mexico; and Anza forced them to stand by this former agreement. Anza's skill in effecting an alliance with the Comanches, and then in mustering Comanches, Navajos, and Spanish unitedly in active operations against the Apaches, is deserving of great praise. However, when he resigned as Governor, the good work he had done came to naught. In 1796 the Navajos again established friendly relations with the Apaches, and again the Spanish were at war with both tribes.

Coincident with the increased rigors of war that had been visited upon the Apaches by Oconor, Croix, and Neve, was the Spanish policy of encouraging friendly Indians to make settlements near the presidios and missions along the border; and this policy was made to include well-disposed bodies of Apaches, as well as Opatas and Pimas. So, occasionally, groups of Apaches did thus settle down peaceably. Eventually treaties were entered into with such communities, and these agreements in some instances were mutually observed. The Indians found it to their advantage to keep these treaties, for the Government expended from eighteen to thirty thousand pesos a year in cash for their support. Of course the Spanish knew that the Apaches were not to be trusted, even in this seemingly friendly relation. They were aware that the spirit of hostility was not fully allayed. That such attempts at peace were very uncertain and dangerous is illustrated by an incident at Arispe when Apaches came there to make a peace treaty in 1795. Says Bancroft: "Being lodged in the barracks they rose in the night, killed the sentry, and fled to the mountains, killing all they found on the way." [4]

Nevertheless, from 1790 to 1810, there was a nearer approximation to peace than at any previous time. It is true that recalcitrant bands, operating independently, continued to make raids now and then and that the soldiers had to be forever on the alert to meet these attacks and to pursue and chastise the troublemakers; but, as compared with earlier conditions and with those that were, unhappily, to follow, there was a state of peace between the red man and the white. For the first time in generations there was an opportunity for constructive de-

---

[4] Bancroft, H. H. *North Mexican States and Texas*, Vol. I, p. 681.

velopment along the border, and it was during these years of respite that mines were opened and successfully operated, churches built and beautified, and ranches prosperously conducted.

BIBLIOGRAPHY

BANCROFT, H. H. *North American States and Texas.* San Francisco.

BENAVIDES, FRAY ALONSO DE, *The Memorial of,* tr. by Mrs. Emma Burbank Ayer.

BOLTON, HERBERT E. *Kino's Historical Memoirs of Primaria Alta.* Cleveland, Arthur H. Clark, 1919.

CASTAÑEDA, DE NAGERA, PEDRO. *The Journey of Coronado,* tr. by George Parker Winship. Chicago, Laidlaw.

CHAPMAN, C. E. *The Founding of Spanish California.* New York, Macmillan, 1916.

COUES, ELLIOTT. *The Expeditions of Zebulon Montgomery Pike.* New York, F. P. Harper, 1895.

LOCKWOOD, FRANK C. *With Padre Kino on the Trail.* University of Arizona Bulletin, Tucson.

MANJE, JUAN MATEO. *Lux de Tierra Incognita.*

THOMAS, ALFRED B. *Forgotten Frontiers.* Norman, University of Oklahoma Press, 1932.

CHAPTER III

The Apaches in Mexican Times

NOVEMBER 6, 1813, a Congress that had been called together by José Maria Morelos y Pavon declared the Independence of Mexico from Spain; but it was not until February 19, 1823, that the patriots were able to make good their freedom. During these ten years there was trouble and confusion throughout Mexico. Nothing could have been more pleasing to the amiable Apache. It was his gentle task to compound trouble and make "confusion worse confounded."

During this turbulent transition period from Spanish Royal Dominion to Mexican Independence, the frontier military defenses were sadly weakened. The garrisons were neglected and the whole military organization was disintegrating. There were continual changes of military as well as civil officers, and the result was hopeless confusion and inefficiency. Some of the presidios were depleted in numbers; the soldiers were unpaid and most of them had lost all hope of receiving the back pay due them. This neglect was chiefly chargeable, of course, to lack of funds; though it was not so much lack of money as misappropriation of the money supplied for military purposes that did the mischief. The shell of the presidio system was kept intact, however, and as an offiset to the diminishing number of troops, local guards were enlisted. But these men were not supplied with firearms and were little skilled in the use of bow and arrow. The Indians were quick to see the crumbling of all effective military resistance and their attacks grew bolder and more frequent.

Sonora suffered severely from Apache raids in 1813. Troops under Captain Narvona made retaliatory campaigns and claimed to have meted out severe punishment, but results were anything but convincing. The fact is, the Mexicans were in such mortal fear of their tormentors and so desirous of getting rid of them that they showed undue eagerness to make terms with them. Nothing could have been more injurious to the ultimate peace and welfare of the country than this spirit of abject weakness on the part of both military and civil officers; for, in proportion as the astute foe saw that he was dreaded, he grew bolder and more insolent. For example, in 1817, a famous chief, Chiquito, was taken captive. The governor of the province treated him with great deference; and when other chiefs came seeking terms of peace, he freed Chiquito. Thereupon, Chiquito and the other chiefs repaid this courtesy by murdering the guard and running away with some good Spanish weapons.

The Apache strategy was incomparably effective. When a raid was to be made, a few warriors would be left behind to guard the camp and the women and children, while a large force, consisting sometimes of several hundred, would approach within striking distance of the community they intended to raid. They would then divide up into bands, having first agreed upon a place where they would all come together again upon the completion of their devilish work. By scattering out thus in small parties, they were able to keep the whole region distracted, the soldiers and settlers not knowing where to attack or whom to pursue, the various bands meanwhile picking up booty and driving off animals everywhere. When the stock was once on the run, the Indians would break up into still smaller parties, so that if some were followed so hotly that they had to abandon their herds, others would be sure to get away with the stock. In case the Spanish attacked in force, a swift-riding rear guard would be left to hold off the enemy or to mislead them in their pursuit. Sometimes a number of the bands would reunite, make a stubborn stand, and hold off the pursuers until their comrades had a safe lead with their stampeded cattle. After the raid, all the bands and detachments would meet at the preappointed rendezvous, divide the booty, and hold high carnival, feasting, dancing, and rejoicing. Mexican women and children were often captured and adopted into the tribe. The boys as they grew up were trained in the arts of Apache warfare.

It was a rare thing for the Apaches to engage in open battle, though they did sometimes risk it; and it must be said that on such occasions they were able to give as good an account of themselves as did either American or Mexican troops, and they always won the respect, if not the approval, of their foes. Captain Zebulon Pike reports the conversation of a brave New Mexican officer, Malgares, who escorted him from Santa Fe to Chihuahua. He had had many encounters with the Apaches and was well able to discuss their methods of warfare. On one occasion when he was on a march with a hundred and forty men, he was attacked by a band of Apaches, both horse and foot, and a battle of four hours ensued. Whenever the dragoons would make a general charge, the Apache cavalry would retire behind the infantry, while the infantry would send a shower of arrows against the Spaniards, and then retreat. Malgares declared that "it was not to be thought of that the Spanish cavalry could break the Apache infantry."

Gálvez had initiated a policy warmly approved by both settlers and soldiers, of sending out reconnoitering parties once a month and of habitual readiness for instant attack, but in

Mexican times both of these vital precautions had been abandoned. Discipline in the presidios, too, had almost ceased to exist. Then, too, long before the American war with Mexico, the Apaches had been able to arm themselves with modern weapons purchased from American traders and taken from victims slain in battle. Indeed, they were better marksmen with firearms than were the Mexicans. Taking into account all the points of superiority on the part of the Apache warriors, it is easy to understand the pitiful state of suffering, terror, and desolation that hung like a nightmare over the Mexican population of the northern frontier.

In Chihuahua in 1831 there was a renewed and violent Apache outbreak. The immediate cause was the failure on the part of the Mexicans to provide the Indians with the accustomed allowances and rations. Prompt efforts were made to repress and punish the savages and troops were sent out against them. But, as usual, the military demonstrations were weak, and when the shrewd troublemakers, in 1832, again offered to come to terms, the overture was acceded to with unseemly haste and timidity. The malefactors were able to dictate, practically, the terms of surrender. Then, almost at once, they continued their raids, and with such vigor and daring that the capital of the province was in danger of being captured and destroyed.

The renewed hostilities soon extended into Sonora. The Apaches along the Gila River and in the mountains to the southward took advantage of the revolt among the Yaquis, Opatas, and Seris to descend upon Sonora. The northern part of the province was laid waste and almost depopulated. Mines, missions, and *ranchos* were abandoned. The raids extended as far south as Hermosillo and Arispe. At least one hundred *ranchos* and towns were deserted by the Mexicans, and it was not until Arispe was threatened that the general populace and the sluggish government at last rallied in an effort to check and drive out the invaders. Special rewards were offered for volunteers; the border provinces formed an alliance; and in 1834 some encouraging victories were won and a famous Apache chief was caught and executed. But this spasm of valor soon spent itself, so far as the military was concerned, and the *Commandante* now made the usual futile attempt to make terms with the savages. The civilians, however, repudiated such a proposal. The Governor declared that the military might again make peace treaties if they saw fit; but that as for the citizens, they proposed to carry on a war of extermination against every Apache in arms. This was all in the spirit of noble and righteous indignation. The legislature approved the Governor's stand, and voted to carry on the campaign to the bitter end. The war went on, therefore, for a year longer to the advantage of the aroused citizens. But, alas, in the summer of 1836, the fever of rage and determination again died out, peace terms were again agreed upon, and the savages had a welcome breathing spell before renewing their ravages all along the line, for it never entered into the minds of the Apaches to keep a truce longer than was "necessary for the disposal of their plunder. As soon as more mules were needed for service or for traffic— more cattle for beef—more scalps for the war-dance—they would invariably return to their deeds of ravage and murder." [1]

The blame for this ever-continuing orgy of murder and destruction must, of course, be laid at the door of the Mexican Government, both local and central. Foresight, and determined cooperation on the part of the exposed provinces and the central government, might at any time have proved successful in holding the savages in check, if not in their complete suppression; but the ruling powers never actively bestirred themselves until some supreme emergency arose; and, always, as soon as the urgent danger was abated, they relapsed into neglect and

[1] Gregg, Josiah. *Commerce of the Prairies.*

inactivity. Not only was the central government weak and careless as to the havoc wrought on its frontiers; the frontier provinces themselves failed to cooperate in a sensible and honorable way. One province would shamelessly secure peace by some bargain with the enemy, and immediately the wily beneficiaries would transfer their operations to another province. Says Josiah Gregg in *Commerce of the Prairies:* "Such is the imbecility of the local governments that the savages, in order to dispose of their stolen property without even a shadow of molestation, frequently enter into partial treaties of peace with a department, while they continue to wage a war of extermination against the neighboring states. This arrangement supplies them with an ever-ready market for the disposal of their booty and the purchase of munitions wherewith to prosecute their work of destruction."

Such a truce was made at Janos, in Chihuahua, in 1842. John C. Cremony, in *Life among the Apaches,* shows the concrete effects of such dealings in a quotation from General Carasco, Military Governor of Sonora, with whom Cremony conversed at Frontéras in 1850.

"There is a small town named Janos, in Chihuahua, near the eastern boundary of Sonora, where the Apaches have for several years been received and provided with rations by the Government of that State, although the same Indians were at the time in open war with the Mexicans of Sonora. Not being able to comprehend the virtue of a policy which feeds Indians in one State that they might prey upon and destroy the citizens of another, I concluded that my duty was to destroy the enemy wherever I could find him. Acting upon this decision, I waited until the allotted time for the Apaches to visit Janos to obtain their regular quarterly rations, and, by forced marches at night, succeeded in reaching the place just as the carnival was at its height. We killed a hundred and thirty and took about ninety prisoners, principally women and children. Col. Medina, commanding the State of Chihuahua, was so enraged at my action that he made formal complaint to the Supreme Government, which, however, after some unnecessary delay approved of my course."

Indeed, according to Josiah Gregg, still deeper iniquities may be laid at the door of Mexican civil authorities of the forties. He says that he himself saw a large party of traders leave Santa Fe in 1840, provided with implements of war and abundant supplies of whisky to be traded to the Apaches for mules and other plunder that they had stolen from the settlers in the southern provinces. "This traffic was not only tolerated but openly encouraged by the civil authorities, as the highest public functionaries were interested in its success—the governor himself not excepted."

Perhaps no border province suffered more bitterly from Apache depredations than Chihuahua. The whole country became almost depopulated; the people took refuge in the towns and cities. The savages became so daring that they would appear in bands of only three or four on the very outskirts of the City of Chihuahua in open day, kill the herders and field laborers, and drive off herds of horses and mules unmolested. To be sure, detachment of soldiers might later give pursuit; but they were careful not to begin the chase too soon or approach the enemy too close. As a final and desperate resort, the various states began to offer bounties for the scalps of Apaches, both male and female, young and old. The price paid for a scalp was large—one hundred dollars for the scalp of a male and fifty dollars for that of a woman—so both settled Indians and foreigners took up the gainful occupation. One enterprising fellow named James Kirker organized a company of two hundred, made up of Americans, Shawnee Indians, and Mexicans, to go out after scalps. Kirker was a Scotchman—a trapper who had been captured by the Apaches at one time, and then had risen to a place of leadership among them. When the Apaches entrusted him with some booty that he was to sell for them, he ran away and entered upon the more agreeable employment of scalping his former associates. Kirker was very enterprising, and he brought in so many heads that the government refused to pay the full amount promised. The grisly business had tended to check the raids, but when it was abandoned the Apache onslaught was more fierce than before. It must be said to the credit of the Mexican Republic that the scalp-hunting project was only in operation a few weeks and that it never had the official approval of the central government. It was, however, strongly endorsed by many of the leading citizens of Chihuahua.

Threat of American invasion from the north in 1843 brought about almost instant organized resistance on the part of the Mexican people, such as generations of bloody Apache incursions had never been able to accomplish—the prompt strengthening of frontier defenses, the enlistment of new regiments, and the calling to arms of thousands of volunteers. These attempts proved to be as futile against the Americans as former attempts against the Apaches—and for a time as bloody. The presence of two armies in northern Mexico did, it is true, for a time relieve the citizens from the marauding expeditions of their ancient foe. However, by 1848, renewed irruptions on the part of the Apaches became so fierce that the central government felt obliged to initiate some effective policy of resistance. In July, 1848, a law was passed providing for the establishment of eighteen military colonies along the northern border. It was hoped that these settlements would both take the place of the old presidio system and at the same time encourage the growth of civilian communities on the frontier. No great enthusiasm was shown for this project and little came of it, for funds were lacking to put it into successful execution. And so three more years passed with only slight beginnings in the work of frontier settlement and defense. At about the same time the central government also named a committee of congressmen from the region most afflicted by Apache hostilities, and requested that they make recommendations looking toward a more effective joint policy for the protection of the frontier. No concrete benefits seem to have resulted from the deliberations of this committee.

As for Chihuahua and Durango, there was no time for deliberation. They were being robbed, murdered, and tortured once more by their fiendish foes from the north. The country was devastated and all but depopulated. So, again, in desperation, they turned to the policy of scalp hunting. American hunters got two hundred dollars for every scalp brought in. A live warrior brought two hundred and fifty dollars. To say nothing about the wisdom and humanity of this practice, it failed to work out successfully. Men who would hire themselves out to decapitate Indians and bring in their heads were not the sort of men it was a pleasure to do business with. Though they were sometimes paid in advance and provided with arms, they were too often inactive just at the time their services were most needed; and, besides, it was safer and easier to take the scalp of a tame Indian (or a Mexican, even) than it was to capture or scalp a wild warrior—and what officer was wise enough to know in every case just what sort of scalp it was that was turned in? There was something to be said on the other side, too; for the hunters were not always sure of their pay.

During the closing months of the war between Mexico and the United States, Sonora suffered almost as much from Apache raids as did Chihuahua. So distressing was the situation by 1848 that the presidio of Tubac had to be abandoned. The depopulation of Sonora went on apace. In addition to the hundreds of citizens who were killed or driven off, Sonora lost heavily as a result of the gold rush to California. She lost many of her strongest and ablest citizens in this way. Great caravans left Hermosillo for the California gold fields in 1849 and 1850, aggregating five or six thousand people.

A good illustration of the feeble and dilatory manner in which the scheme for military colonies along the border worked out may be found in Sonora, which had been granted five military colonies. The designated locations were Tucson, Altar, Frontéras, Santa Cruz, Bavispe. Frontéras was the only one of these five settlements to be fully established by 1850. Some beginnings had been made at Santa Cruz—how pitifully inadequate we may learn from the reports of travelers such as Benjamin Hayes and John R. Bartlett, who visited and described Santa Cruz during the years 1849, 1850, and 1851. Nothing had been done at Bavispe, Altar, and Tucson. The total armed force in these towns amounted to only three hundred and thirteen men. The state was instructed to enlist and equip four companies of mounted troops at federal expense with fifty men and four officers in each company. All told, there were in 1850 only about five hundred armed men and a majority of this number were simply colonists supplied with arms. The Apaches of the Gila, with grim jocularity, viewed Sonora "as their *rancho* and depot of supplies."

In 1851 the enemy penetrated even as far south as Mazatlan and devastated it. That year in Sonora they killed two hundred citizens and stole two thousand head of stock, to say nothing of a wealth of other plunder with which they enriched themselves. Little damage was inflicted upon them by the troops. In 1853 one hundred and seventy settlers were killed. There was a slight revival of effort on the part of the people to protect themselves, but it was too weak and unorganized to be of much use, and—as always—temporary. The Apache death toll in 1860 was fifty, and in 1863 the invaders almost reached the ancient and important city of Ures in the central part of Sonora. So alarming and desperate had the situation now grown that the Government offered one hundred dollars for every Apache scalp turned in. As usual, money was a potent incentive, and so great was the stimulus of this cash offer that two hundred Apaches were killed or captured. But the energy and vindictiveness of the savages only grew more terrible, and as their bloodthirstiness increased, the price of a scalp went up to three hundred dollars. Indian heads were rarely brought in, but the slaughter of whites by Indians went on steadily up to 1872. After the Mexican War and the Gadsden Purchase, the Mexicans claimed that their woes were due, not only to the slackness of the United States in controlling their Apache wards, but also to the work of criminal Americans. Diaz in his day strengthened the border defenses; Arizona gradually became well populated; and at last comparative safety came to the distressed border people after their centuries of suffering.

BIBLIOGRAPHY

BANCROFT, H. H. *A History of Arizona and New Mexico*. San Francisco, 1889.

BANCROFT, H. H. *North Mexican States and Texas*. San Francisco.

BARTLETT, JOHN R. *Personal Narrative*, Vol. I. New York, Appleton, 1854.

CREMONY, JOHN C. *Life among the Apaches*. San Francisco, 1868.

GREGG, JOSIAH. *Commerce of the Prairies*. New York, Langley, 1845.

HAYES, BENJAMIN. *Diary of a Journey Overland from Socorro to Warner's Ranch*. Unpublished manuscript. Berkeley, Bancroft Library, 1849.

CHAPTER IV

The Primitive Apache

THE earliest Americans who came in contact with the Apache
were able to study him in his original condition. As yet he was
untouched by the ways of civilized man. He was strictly the
creature of his environment; and, for her part, Nature had
turned him out a perfect physical specimen. In appearance he
was attractive rather than repulsive. The head, well formed
and somewhat broad, was set firmly on a short, muscular neck.
He had high cheekbones, well-formed nose, black eyes that
blazed with fire and energy, strong jaws, and firm-closed lips—
not thin, yet not too full. The hair, black, thick, and very coarse,
was allowed to fall to the shoulders, but in front was trimmed
straight across at the level of the eyebrows. Apache men had
sparse beards. Such scattered hairs as did grow on their faces
were plucked out one at a time with tweezers made of bent
strips of tin.

The lean, supple, sinewy body of the Apache was capable
of extraordinary activity and endurance. The legs and arms
of an Apache brave, neither round in contour nor scrawny and
thin, were shapely enough, and lacked nothing in agility and
dexterity. The back was well developed and sturdy, the
chest both broad and very deep, the waist slender. Rarely did
the Apache attain a height of more than six feet, and just as
seldom did he fall below five feet. Dr. John B. White in
1873 actually measured one hundred Arizona Apache men and

41

one hundred women. The average results he reported as follows: "The men measured without any selection five feet, six and one-half inches and the women about five feet. The tallest man measured, standing in his bare feet, six feet and the tallest woman five feet, two inches, though there are doubtless many women among them who may exceed this height.

"The shortest man measured five feet and three-fourths of an inch, and the shortest woman four feet and seven and three-fourths of an inch."

All writers who describe the Apaches as they were when they became known to Americans emphasize their superior mental qualities. They showed instinct and sagacity akin to that of animals. They were endowed with great acuteness of perception; marked ingenuity in overcoming the asperities of climate, soil, and topography; shrewdness in forecasting the actions of their enemies and in coordinating their plans, though operating in widely scattered bands over a vast region of country. They were witty, possessed of a quick sense of humor, cheerful, companionable, and little disposed to heed the annoyances and uncertainties of life. They were ever on the alert, however, and were excitable. Unusual sounds or happenings would arouse them at once to tremendous activity.

It is a mistake to suppose that the Apaches were not a moral people. The fact is, their code of morals was as deep-rooted and binding as that of civilized men. To be sure, they were guided in their conduct by principles very different from those professed by the white man. Their highest conception of a virtuous man was that he engage in war and excel as a thief; of a woman that she toil hard and faithfully. All other people they looked upon as their enemies. Their occupation was murder and robbery. The man who could kill without being killed, and could steal without being caught, was the most honored and admired individual among them. These ideals were held before the child from his infancy; and the whole ambition of the growing boy was to be—a brave warrior, yes—most of all a successful raider and killer. Daring and gallant action, in itself, meant little to him. Indeed, it seemed very foolish. But to outwit and destroy his foe by craft was meritorious in the highest degree; and the evidence of such cunning and hardihood was the bringing home of the bacon. The suitor who throve best in the eyes of the maid he desired to marry was the one richest in stolen horses and cattle and best able to deck her out with spoils snatched from his murdered foe. And it was to the standard of such a leader that the ambitious young braves eagerly pressed. It is true that the very highest admiration was reserved for the very ablest warriors and chieftains, who, because of their preeminence in action and diplomacy, were equal to the task of protecting and leading the whole tribe in times of supreme emergency. To the qualities of raider, such a chief added those of intellect, strategy, and indomitable resolution. Cochise and Victorio were such leaders, and Mangas Coloradas in diplomacy and intellect, though not in military powers.

Pity was a feeling unknown to the Apache; cruelty an ingrained quality. It must be admitted that he was never able to conceive of pains more cruel than those he had suffered from his Christian enemies. The only difference between them and him was that the Apache openly confessed and practiced his creed of cruelty and rapacity, whereas the white man hypocritically professed mercy and honesty and at the same time surpassed the Apache in deeds of dishonor and blood.

So much with respect to the Apache in his attitude toward the rest of mankind. The story is a very different one if we study his conduct as it affected his own people. From birth to death he was held irrevocably to well-defined attitudes and duties toward his family and his clan or group, and disloyalty to the standards erected by his people brought pains and penalties upon him quite as severe as those that rule civilized society. Indeed, viewed from this standpoint, he was as moral a man as is the typical white man. In fact, he adhered more strictly to his social code than the white man does to his. For one thing, the Apache held it a high virtue to speak the truth. Again, he did not steal from his own tribesmen; nor would he fail to pay his debts. He was openhanded—would share what he had with his fellows. Parents fondly loved their children, and they supported other dependent members of their families. Also, at whatever the cost to their own safety and comfort, they demanded just satisfaction for injuries to their kith and kin. The labor and expense involved in marriage and burial ceremonies were shared by relatives; and in many other ways habitual regard was given to ties and obligations universally recognized among them. And, to an extraordinary degree, their women were loyal to their marriage vows and patient in the discharge of the heavy menial tasks laid upon them.

The primitive Apache man went unclothed save for breechclout, mocassins, and, on raids or in battle, a close-fitting helmet of hide decorated with feathers. Originally the breechclout was made of dressed deerskin, but at a later date, a strip of muslin about six feet long was used for this purpose. This band was passed between the legs and around the loins and so adjusted that the ends fell to the knee, both in front and behind. The moccasins were of buckskin and were peculiarly fitted to protect the feet and legs from venomous reptiles and thorny desert plants. They reached halfway up the thigh, and had tough soles extended and curved up at the toe, terminating in a sort of button the size of a half-dollar. The tops were often pushed down below the knees and the folds were used as pockets for such small articles as the Apache might desire to carry on his person. After the coming of the Americans, an

Apache warrior nearly always wore a band of flannel or cotton cloth tightly bound about his head to hold his hair in place. The women wore skirts of deerskin extending from the waist to the knees, with a fringe of thongs and, possibly, ornamented with bits of bright metal or glass. The moccasins worn by the women were of a different kind from those used by the warriors—not of such great length nor so durable. They came only a little above the ankle, though they had the usual button-like projection at the toe.

The Apache dwelling place was a circular or oval shack, called a wickiup. It was built by the women from saplings and brush. The long, slender poles were thrust into the ground about two feet apart, bent inward until they met, and then bound together at the top, a little hole being left to let the smoke out. Brush or branches were now woven into the frame-work, and in some instances the whole was covered with bark, or even with deerskins. After the structure had been com-pleted, a place was scooped out in the floor, from eighteen inches to two feet deep, to serve as bedroom. The dirt was packed around the base of the wickiup and was useful both in giving solidity to the shack and in affording protection against driving storms. In cold weather a very small fire was made in the center, and around this the family huddled. When an Apache moved from one place to another, and after a member of the family had died, the wickiup was burned. These huts were from ten to twelve feet by about eight or nine feet in dimensions. The doorway was low, and sometimes there ex-tended from it on each side a little windbreak made of poles and brush. The Apache never erected his wickiup at a distance from others; ordinarily four or five of these shelters were built in proximity to each other.

The food of the Apache was exceedingly varied. Of course he ate abundantly of flesh. He liked mule meat best of all, and next to that horse flesh. The fact is, almost any sort of animal suited his taste—from deer and buffalo to gopher and lizard. He did not eat bear meat or pork or the flesh of the turkey. He would not eat fish, nor devour any other creature that lived in the water. Yet he hunted the turkey, as well as the hawk and the eagle, for their feathers, and the mink, the beaver, and the muskrat for their skins. At times, of course, so arid and destitute was the country, that he was compelled to subsist for the most part on roots, berries, and nuts, and the seeds of grasses. Acorns, mescal, and mesquite beans were staple articles of food. The pulpy head of the mescal meant almost as much to the Apache as bread does to us. Available nearly everywhere on the desert, it was gathered by the women and roasted in pits. It could be stored and carried about. The mesquite bean and the acorn were pounded into meal and made into cakes. The fruit of the giant cactus, and the pitahaya were much in favor; and, indeed, in times of necessity the fruit of various other species of cactus was acceptable, as well as that of the yucca. Travelers likened the taste of these fruits, when cured, to the fig, the date, and the banana. After being ground or pounded to a powder on a large flat stone, the grass seeds were made into a paste with water, and were shaped into cakes.

The Apaches were a sociable people. After the chief meal of the day, which was usually eaten in the evening, they would sit or lie about their camp talking endlessly about the happenings of the day or exchanging tales of past deeds in raids and battles. On many occasions they met for feasting, or dancing; and there were innumerable ceremonial dances. Before and after battle the braves indulged in characteristic war dances while the women looked on. There were social dances in which the young men and young women were the chief participants, the older people looking on, commenting and conversing—

APACHE WICKIUP

SAN CARLOS TWINED AND WEAVE BURDEN BASKETS

Reproduced from Helen H. Roberts' "Basketry of the San Carlos Apache"
Courtesy, American Museum of Natural History

SAN CARLOS PITCHED WATER JARS

Reproduced from Helen H. Roberts' "Basketry of the San Carlos Apache"
Courtesy of American Museum of Natural History

enjoying themselves as much apparently as did the young people. They all swam well, and in summer swimming was a favorite sport. Every Apache was a gambler, man, woman, and child; and there was nothing they would not stake, from their horse to their shirt (or what, in the Apache mind, took the place of the shirt). There were ball games of various kinds —the most popular and famous, that played with hoop and pole, from which women were excluded. The women raced and played games akin to our modern shinny. There were guessing games, too, and wrestling matches, and games of skill in the shooting of arrows and the tossing of rocks at a hole.

After children were big enough to run about, parents made little effort to control them and rarely scolded or punished them. Small boys ran races, tussled together, threw stones at each other, or practiced with bow and arrow. The little girls were more given to play than were the boys. They made mimic houses with sticks and stones, shaped dolls from bits of rag or buckskin, or from bunches of flexible plants, tied around at the top. Their miniature houses were built in imitation of their own homes and their dolls were placed in them, very much as little white children do; and, when mud could be had, they molded it into the forms of dolls, horses, men and women, even mounting their men and women upon animals.

The Apaches seem to have had little desire to create things of beauty. This is not strange in view of their nomadic and marauding propensities. In the designing and shaping of devil-dance masks, medicine shirts, and violins, they did display some decorative and pictorial skill; but their most notable achievement in art is to be seen in their basketry. This work was of two kinds—burden baskets and water jugs. Originally, in both kinds, beauty was subordinated to function; though in course of time Apache women attained considerable skill in the shaping and decorating of these very useful and durable domestic ar-

ticles. Two techniques were employed: the twined and the
coiled. Specimens of their work are preserved in various
museums. The finest examples of craftsmanship and beauty
are to be seen in their coiled work. It is difficult to determine
to what extent the art of basketry was original and distinctive
among the Apaches and to what degree it was a cultural bor-
rowing. Very likely the development of the art among them
was influenced by the work in the same kind of the Pueblo,
Pima, and California Indians. A certain intermediate, very
ornate, and florid type may have been derived from the Yumas.
Probably influences from the sources just named were introduced by individuals held as captives among the Apaches who,
by some chance, had come in contact with California, Yuma, or
Pima Indians.

Both socially and economically the family was the basic unit
in the integration of the Apache nation. Each family was
bound together by rights and duties that were formal and well
defined. Families camped together. The home of the mother
was the family center. She was the head. If there were married
daughters, their husbands came to dwell in the maternal camp;
though it was forbidden them to look upon the face of their
mother-in-law or to hold converse with her. Once for all, an
individual was bound to his family. Robert Frost writes in
one of his most perfect poems:

> *Home is the place where, when you have to go there,*
> *They have to take you in.*

Most assuredly this was true in the Apache economy. The
family was supremely interested in each of its members, was
responsible for his education, had much to say with·respect to
his choice when he married, partook of his disgrace and shared
in his glory, braved defilement and the possibility of "ghost
sickness" in preparing him for burial after his death, and in

case he suffered a violent and undeserved death, was under solemn obligation to avenge him.

When an Apache girl reached puberty there was a simple family celebration of the event. It might last a day or two, though it was in no way formal or ceremonial. As an indication that she had arrived at womanhood, she was told to run toward the east whence the sun arises. A month or two later, however, she was given a grand coming-out party. This was as much a society event as a formal ball given in honor of a Washington débutante by her proud mother. It lasted four days, and relatives and friends from far and near were invited to attend. The festival, considered as a whole, was as beautiful in design and symbolic significance as the most involved and elaborate pattern woven upon a richly artistic Navajo rug.

The expense was borne by the parents, though other relatives often assisted, as the cost was not inconsiderable. Sometimes a father would begin saving up and making preparations many months ahead, and not infrequently closely related families would give a joint party for two or more girls. When the appointed day arrived, people from a distance would begin to make their camps near the silvan spot selected for the exercises. Here on a smooth space, properly laid out and marked off, a tepee had been set up in which the girl was to spend the next four days and nights in strenuous vigils and ceremonial dances. The host engaged a medicine man to take charge of the religious rites and made abundant provision for the feeding and feasting of the crowd. After gifts and food had been carried to the lodge of the maiden, she would make her appearance in her finest array. Bright ornaments were displayed to the best advantage on the fringe of her buckskin skirt and along the sides of her moccasins. With her attendants she entered the tepee. Outside there were social dances, and within, the girl would alternately kneel for long hours in statuesque supplication and dance her stately measures. The second day, morning and afternoon, there was dancing by the crowd; and at night the girl resumed her vigils and her exhausting dancing. The second or third night, disguised in the skins of various savage animals, the devil dancers would come and dance around a central fire. At first the warriors and the old women would seem alarmed at the appearance of these wild beasts, but, when they found that they were unable to drive them away, they would join with them in the dance, and the young girl would dance with them also. The climax came on the fourth night. All that night the dancing of the girl, as well as the social dancing outside, continued. At sunrise the final ritualistic exercises were completed by the medicine man. Then the tepee was demolished, and the girl ran swiftly toward the east. Dr. M. E. Opler writes: "It is a sun ceremony—a prayer that the force which causes all plant life to thrive, may also grant this young Apache girl health and vigor." [1]

For an Apache girl, the mother's wickiup was the hub of the universe. Mother and daughter were almost constantly together. They toiled side by side in domestic work, accompanied each other on expeditions to gather food; and, after the maiden had made her début, she went with her mother to dances and other social affairs where she met the young men. In the social dance she chose her own partner. Cupid was no less adept with Apache than with Greek bow and arrow; in spite of the severity of the social code by which they were hedged about, young people found ways to make known their mutual love. It is true that the families both of young men and young women exerted a powerful influence over them in their choice of a life partner. Yet in most cases

---

[1] For a full and scholarly account of this festival, read Dr. M. E. Opler's *An Analysis of Mescalero and Chiricahua Apache Social Organization*. In Mrs. White Mountain Smith's *Indian Tribes in the Southwest*, there is a fragmentary but attractive description. I have drawn upon these accounts, as well as upon oral descriptions given me by the Reverend Frank Uplegger and others who live in the Apache reservations.

they chose for themselves. After an Apache youth had made his choice, he must secure the consent of his own family to the union. Next it was necessary to make known to the girl's parents his desire to marry their daughter. His father or his brother would probably discharge this office for him. Now came the actual proposal. This formality consisted in the offering of presents to her and her family. As his wealth consisted chiefly of horses, in the night he would take one, or two, or more animals, and tie them near the girl's wickiup. The number of horses he brought indicated to the family the measure of his riches and the degree of his ardor for the girl. The offer of only one horse would be thought a "one-horse affair." If the girl took care of the animals—led them to water and fed them—the youth knew that his suit was successful; but if they were left uncared for, it was all too plain that he was rejected. The maiden was allowed four days to come to a decision. It was not good form to care for the animals the first day; but on the other hand, if she allowed them to suffer without forage or drink more than two days, she would be thought vain and proud. If the horses remained on the picket, neglected and starving at the end of the fourth day, there was nothing for the lover to do but to take them back.

After a suitor had been accepted, there followed a wedding feast that extended over three days. During this time the engaged couple were not allowed to speak to each other; but on the third night they would suddenly disappear—eluding, supposedly, the vigilance of the older people—and escape to the temporary wickiup provided by the groom in some hidden place in the woods not far away. After an absence of a week or more, they would return to the parental camp as suddenly as they had departed, unheralded and unnoticed. They would now erect their wickiup near that of the girl's mother, but facing in an opposite direction. "Avoidance" was the term applied to the very definitely fixed formality that forbade a son-in-law to see his mother-in-law or to talk with her. In order to observe the strict amenities, the son-in-law, even though his own wickiup faced in an opposite direction from that of his wife's mother, had to acquire a good deal of skill in quick dodging and sudden skipping. A man was not limited to one wife. If he was able to do so, he might at any time marry one or more additional wives, though he would be limited in his choice to sisters or unmarried cousins of his first wife. In case of the death of his first wife, he would be expected to remain in mourning for one year and then to espouse a sister or a cousin of his former wife.

When once married, a man said good-by forever to his own family. They no longer had any claim upon him. His whole obligation after that was to the family of his mother-in-law. As long as he lived he must support and protect the domestic circle into which he had married. He must bring to them the spoils of the chase and must be their avenger in case they suffered unjust injury. When he returned from the hunt, loaded with game, it was carried by the daughter to her mother's wickiup; was there dressed and cooked, along with other food; and then their share was brought by the wife to be eaten with her husband and children in their wickiup. Divorces were few. No matter how dissatisfied a husband might become, or how hard his lot, he dare not seek separation except upon good and well-established grounds; and to run away would be to make him a social outlaw and to draw upon his head the animosity of the entire family into which he had married.

The local group was the next unit of organization after the domestic family. It was made up of several affiliated families, though blood relationships were not obligatory for membership in such a group. It was community of interest that drew members of a particular group together and, if mutually desirable, any person might attach himself to it. Such a community found that in union there was increased security and efficiency, both in economic and in warlike activities. A group was always known by some geographic name descriptive of the spot they chose for their settlement. The place might be a mountain, a canyon, a stronghold, or a spring. It might have been selected merely because it was a pleasant region in which to camp, with plenty of wood and water at hand, or because it offered unusual advantages for the storing of food and supplies, or because it was a good rallying point and easy to defend.

The local group was an ideal unit for any cooperative activity. So small that it could be instantly mobilized, and not too large to move rapidly and with perfect coordination, it constituted the nerve center for raiding and warfare. The closeness of families together permitted the maximum of social enjoyment, also; and while each family was economically independent of every other family, there were cooperative advantages that came to all from their proximity to each other. When the time came to lay in a supply of piñon nuts, or to gather and roast mescal, the women of half a dozen families found it to their advantage to go together and later divide up what had been secured on the expedition—to each family its due share. It was pleasant for the whole community to join in a great hunt. The women would all go along to take care of the meat and to perform all necessary menial tasks. However, after the hunt was over, there was a fair division of the game and each family was once more on its own.

In every local group several able leaders would develop. Such men came to the front by virtue of native ability and weight of personality. Though leaders, they had no claim to the title of chief, nor did they exercise any command over the group that had not been voluntarily conferred upon them. Such headmen could not bind their associates to any particular action or guarantee that they would stand by a treaty that might be made in their name. This is why, in the early days, it was so difficult for Americans ever to come to exact and enduring terms with Apaches. From among these men of mark in each group, when an emergency arose, one—the wisest, the wealthiest, the most capable—would be chosen as chief. He would speak for the group on great occasions and would lead them in time of war. Yet, while his words and his decisions would have much weight with his fellows, he possessed no authority over them except such as emanated from his superiority of personality. There was real democracy among the Apaches; it was for the rank and file to decide upon a given course of action.

So long as a chief was strong enough to protect his followers, courageous enough to lead them to victory against their foes, and sufficiently skillful to bring in the plunder, he held sway over them. When he failed to make good, an abler man took his place. A very brave and successful chief would win distinction for his group, would give it prestige so that ambitious young warriors would desire to join it, and so would force his organization into the forefront of the band to which it belonged. There was safety under his leadership, much plunder was assured, so the Apache nation as a whole came to know and honor his wisdom and prowess. It was thus that such chiefs as Mangas Coloradas, Victorio, and Cochise, who began as local rulers, rose to supreme influence in the tribe. When a chief of such honor and fame was killed or captured, it was an overwhelming loss to his local group and no effort was spared to avenge terribly his death.

The next higher coherent organization was the band. There were times when for purposes of hunting, raiding, or making war it was desirable for a number of local groups to unite in co-operative action. Tribal boundaries, and the limits within which such a particular band was supposed to wander in its search for food and plunder, were not strictly defined. Yet wide and vast as was the extent of the territory controlled by the Apaches and many as were the streams, mountains, and forests where they camped and hunted, regular supplies of water and food in that arid and crabbed Southwest were not easy to secure; and it was advantageous for each tribe to recognize its natural limits and for particular bands to seek their livelihood in well-recognized areas of country. A band would thus be composed of several local groups residing at well-identified places close enough to each other to make it possible for them to combine quickly and effectively for war. Indeed, the band was the largest manageable unit that could be relied upon for instant offensive or defensive action in time of need. From among the bold and able leaders in the various local groups that constituted the band, the strongest and most experienced would naturally be selected as chieftain. A chieftainship was never hereditary, either in the local group or in the band.

Finally came the tribal organization. An Apache when captured or required to give an account of himself would first name his tribe and then his band. But the tribal concept meant little to him as compared with the immediacy of his relationship with his local group and his band. The ties that bound him to these smaller units were close and realistic. Seldom did the tribe as a whole come into common action in an emergency. Yet there was, to be sure, real feeling of unity and a definite sense of territorial domain that held all the members of a tribe together. But the Apaches as a people were, in fact, very loosely united. They spoke the same language and possessed a basic unity of culture, but some tribes never came into contact with each other. Dr. M. E. Opler and Mr. Granville Goodwin, both of whom have lived for long periods in close association with the Apaches and have studied deeply their primitive characteristics and organizations, have adopted somewhat different tribal names and regional demarcations from those used in the past. They make the following divisions: the Mescalero, the Jicarilla, the Chiricahua, and the Western. Previous to the coming of the Americans, tribal boundaries were pretty well agreed upon among the Apaches and it was understood that the respective tribes were to keep within their own limits. The Mescaleros claimed as their domain New Mexico as far east as Hondo, as far north as Santa Fe, as far west as the Rio Grande, and on the south as far as northwest Texas—and indeed, some distance into Texas. The Jicarillas held a large section of northern and eastern New Mexico and even some contiguous portions of southern Colorado. The boundaries set for the Chiricahuas were the Rio Grande on the east, Laguna and Acoma on the north, the present eastern boundaries of the White Mountain and San Carlos Reservations on the west, and on the south as far as and a considerable distance into Sonora and Chihuahua. The Western Apaches occupied all that is now included in the White Mountain and San Carlos Reservations and a vast region in Arizona west of the limits of these two reservations.

Differences appeared among these various tribes in dress, in personal decoration, in the manner of erecting their dwelling places, and even in peculiarities of speech and vocabulary. Mr. Granville Goodwin, who has limited his studies to the Western Apaches, in a letter to me states that there are clans among them and that these clans are almost identical with those of the Navajo system. Dr. Opler finds that clans do not exist in any of the other three Apache tribes. Mr. Goodwin further says that "in dialect, culture, and tribal affiliations" some of the four tribes named above are "just as distinct from each other as any one of the Apache divisions is from the Navajo." Indeed, he holds that the Navajo originally were Apaches.

Notwithstanding what has been said above, the Apaches recognized themselves as one people and as distinct from all other peoples. One tribe as a whole never made war on another tribe as a whole. Often they were far from cordial toward each other, and members of one tribe might show open hostility toward members of another tribe. In the seventies and eighties there was always trouble when our Government tried to force separate tribes to live together on the same reservation, and the final conquest of the Apaches was due in great measure to the fact that Army officers were able to enlist volunteers from one tribe to fight against recalcitrants of a different tribe.

The Mescalero tribe was made up of two bands: the plains people on the east and the mountain people on the west. There were two bands of Jicarillas also: the Llanero, or plains people, east of the Rio Grande, and the Ollero, or sand people, west of the Rio Grande. Three bands constituted the powerful Chiricahua tribe: the red paint people to the north, a band that operated in northern Chihuahua and Sonora, and the band called the Chiricahua in the southwest—this band, under Cochise, becoming coextensive with the tribe. The Western Apaches consisted of four groups: the Coyotero, or White Mountain, the Tonto, the Cibecue, and the San Carlos. These designations are modern, although all these groups occupied the territory in primitive times that they now inhabit in our day.

The Apache economy was essentially an economy of war. War was the Apache's trade. A boy was instructed in the ways of the warpath almost from infancy. His earliest training was in the hands of his maternal grandfather and his father. While still small, he was given a bow and blunt arrows to play with. When he was large enough, he was taught to make his own weapons. It was a proud day in his life when he was taken on a hunt by his father and uncles; and then it was that his education in woodcraft began.

Since the local group was the basic fighting and raiding unit, it assumed responsibility for the training of the youth when he was ready for the warpath, as he was by the time he was fifteen or sixteen. Sometimes several boys were trained at once—usually in the early spring or in the fall. The youth was required to take dips in cold water, sometimes even to plunge into ice water. He had to take long runs over rough country with a load on his back. He must keep his mouth shut and breathe through his nose. By this time he was required to make his own weapons and to show skill in using them. Next, he was put through every hard exercise engaged in by men, including horseback riding. To test his will power and endurance, he was made to go without sleep for a long period, the vigil sometimes being extended to a period of forty-eight hours. Such intensive training went on for a long time, that is, until he was able to conduct himself like a real Apache, no matter how severe the test. The author was told by Jimmie Stevens, seventy-year-old interpreter at the San Carlos Reservation, whose mother was the daughter of a White Mountain Apache chief and whose father was one of the most influential American traders on the Apache Reservation in the seventies, that, as a climax to this Spartanlike training, the youth must go alone in the wilds for two weeks and live by his own skill and hardihood.

At last the novice might volunteer to go on the warpath. At this time a ceremony was performed in his behalf, and a helmet and shield were especially designed for him. A war dance accompanied this ceremony during which he must show his agility and endurance by leaping, twisting, and dodging with unwearied pep and strength. Then he was instructed in the language of the warpath by the ceremonial man in charge. He was not always able to perfect himself in these things at once; but as soon as he was well versed in it all, his request to go along with a war party would be granted. His novitiate was not complete until he had volunteered for four raids or war parties. During this apprenticeship on the warpath he must build the fires, prepare the food and cook it, look after the horses, stand guard at night, be constantly alert and observant, and never speak except in the language of the warpath. These four expeditions constituted his war college. During this period he was set in as harsh a strait jacket of behavior as the midshipman in the days of the sailing vessel. It was not until his fifth raid that he was allowed to take part in battle. But then, if he was made of the right stuff, he lost no chance to show his metal, and returned rich with the spoils of war and covered with glory.

The Apache armed himself in primitive times with the bow and arrow and the lance. The bow was a powerful weapon, strengthened as it was with layers of sinew on the back, laid on with such nicety that they could scarcely be seen. The arrows were more than three feet long. The upper part was made of cane or rush, but a shaft about a foot long, made of light yet hard and seasoned wood, was inserted into this. The point was of stone, bone, or iron. An Apache was able to shoot this arrow five hundred feet with fatal effect. If an attempt was made to pull the arrow from the body of the victim, the shaft came out of its socket leaving the point in the wound. Poisoned arrows were sometimes used. The lance was fifteen feet long, with a strong sharp point. An Apache horseman, in charging an enemy, held his lance above his head with both hands, controlling his horse with his knees. In battle he usually carried a shield. However, the Apache rarely fought in the open, and almost never against a large and well-armed force, unless completely taken by surprise. He was infinitely patient and skillful in ambush. He could so disguise himself with dirt and desert plants that the unwary traveler little suspected his presence until it was too late. Warriors kept watch from rocks and mountain lookouts across wide stretches of country, observing sometimes for days their intended victims before striking. They pounced upon solitary horsemen or small unarmed parties, but had a wholesome respect for large armed expeditions and soldiers. They crept up to lonely ranch houses and mines—killing, looting, and burning—and then quickly made their escape, driving stampeded herds before them. When a band was hard-pressed, or forced to do battle, it would scatter and disappear like a flock of wild turkeys, to reassemble at some preappointed spot.

The Apache was perfectly acquainted with the country that he inhabited for hundreds of miles around. He knew every spring, water hole, canyon, and crevice. There was no commissary or transportation problem for him. He could carry for days what little food he needed and could add some edible thing to his store, however arid the region. He could travel on foot, over the roughest terrain from fifty to seventy-five miles a day; and such was his endurance that he could keep up this pace for several days at a stretch. He had his own sign language, too, and his highly effective telegraph system. For him there were transmitted secrets, if not sermons, in stones and running brooks, and devilish possibilities in everything. His skill as a trailer was equal to that of the most erudite scholar who traces, reads, and translates the chirography of past ages in his cold, dark cubicle. The position of an overturned stone, the manner in which a twig or the branch of a tree had been broken, the way in which three sticks had been placed, the horse manure dropped in camp or along the trail, spoke to him in trumpet tones and taught him things well worth remembering. He had

APACHE SIGNAL FIRE

Drawing by Frederick Remington in the *Century Magazine.* Used by permission of D. Appleton-Century Company, Inc.

COCOSPERA CAÑYON, SONORA APACHES LURKING ABOVE

Courtesy of Harper & Bros.

APACHE INDIANS ATTACKING THE TRAIN AND PARTY

Reproduced from John R. Bartlett's "Personal Narrative"

GROUP OF APACHES

Reproduced from John R. Bartlett's "Personal Narrative"

perfected a system of smoke signaling over wide spaces that was swift and most effective. Both Cremony and White give details concerning the war craft of the Apache in trailing and communicating by smoke signals:

"Smokes are of various kinds, each one significant of a particular object. A sudden puff, rising into a graceful column from the mountain heights, and almost as suddenly losing its identity by dissolving into the rarefied atmosphere of those heights, simply indicates the presence of a strange party upon the plains below; but if those columns are rapidly multiplied and repeated, they serve as a warning to show that the travelers are well armed and numerous. If a steady smoke is maintained for some time, the object is to collect the scattered bands of savages at some designated point, with hostile intention, should it be practicable. These signals are made at night, in the same order, by the use of fires, which being kindled, are either alternately exposed and shrouded from view, or suffered to burn steadily, as occasion may require." [2]

Though the Apache devoted himself so diligently to the turning of live men into dead ones, he experienced the greatest horror when in the presence of a corpse. The Apaches buried their dead at the earliest moment practicable. Interment always took place in the daytime on the day of death if possible. The very unwelcome task of preparing the body for burial and of interring it fell to the nearest male relatives. Only a few assisted. Interment was made in some remote cave or crevice in the rocks if such a place of sepulture were available. If necessary, a grave was dug on low or level ground, and the deceased, together with all his personal effects, was placed therein. The body was then securely covered with brush and dirt and rocks so that coyotes could not get at it. Such burial mounds were often seen by the first American soldiers in Arizona. At the grave, before return-

[2] Cremony. *Op. cit.*, pp. 183–184.

ing to camp, the burial party would brush themselves all over with wisps of a green grass and then lay these tufts of grass on the grave in the form of a cross. Upon returning to the wickiup of the deceased, they would burn it up, together with everything that he wore or came in close contact with while alive. They would also burn everything that they wore while disposing of the body. They took pains, also, to disinfect themselves by bathing their bodies in the smoke of the sagebrush. The surviving family immediately moved from the locality where the death had occurred and made themselves new wickiups. The name of the dead was never again spoken among them, nor was the place of his interment ever visited or mentioned.

Very likely they were prompted by sanitary reasons in taking these extraordinary precautions; but back of all practical considerations was the superstitious fear that the spirit of the dead might return to haunt them and harm them. The nearer the relationship that bound them to the deceased, the more terrible this dread seemed to be. If a relative had kept anything that had belonged to the departed, he would fear that the ghost of the dead man would come back to claim it. They believed that they might arouse or anger the ghost of the dead if they spoke his name or made any mention of him or went near the spot where he was buried. There are on record many instances of "ghost sickness." It exhibited itself in the form of extreme nervousness and fright. It was most often brought on by the hooting of a near-by owl at night. The Apache had an excessive dread of the owl; and if an owl hooted near one's camp it was an omen of the most frightful import. They believed that the spirit of the dead entered into the owl and came back to warn or threaten them.[3]

Some writers assert that the Apache is destitute of the re-

[3] For an extended and exceedingly interesting account of the Apache attitude toward the dead, read Dr. M. E. Opler's article, "An Interpretation of Ambivalence," etc., in *The Journal of Social Psychology*, 1936, Vol. vii, pp. 82–116.

ligious sense. In fact the primitive Apache had an ever-present consciousness of the supernatural. There is not space here to discuss the myths of the Apaches that deal with the creation of the world or to record their stories of the birth and miraculous exploits of the culture hero; but assuredly they believed in some impersonal force, creator of the world, and source of all power, that influenced the affairs of men. This being was not thought of as wholly benign; but, whether for good or for evil, they recognized its sway over them. It was through the medicine men that this supernatural power worked for the good of man, or for his hurt, since there were among men those who sought through supernatural aid to do their fellow men harm as well as those who desired to help them. Those who trafficked with the supernatural for evil purposes were witches; and the Apache had a superstitious dread of a witch. These malevolent beings worked their evil spells through certain animals and natural forces—the bear, the owl, the snake, the coyote, clouds, lightning, etc.

John G. Bourke asserts that the medicine man was at once the most powerful and the most injurious influence in the life of the primitive Apache. He was the purveyor of fear, witchcraft, and idolatry. There was no particular family or clan set apart as supernatural practitioners. Any youth might aspire to become a medicine man. In order to succeed, he must, of course, convince his people that this higher power was willing to work through him. To become eminent he must be a dreamer of dreams, must give evidence of great spirituality, must fast, and keep lonely night vigils in the high places, must be able to interpret omens, and must master the art of swallowing fire, arrows, and spearheads. He might be a warrior as well as a shaman. Some very influential medicine men were blind and decrepit, and in some instances the function was exercised by women. The usual way to become a medicine man was to learn the art from a successful and renowned practitioner and to pay him well for his instruction and influence.

There were no set doctrines of practice. Each shaman did what he could do best. Some professed the power to bring rain; others to cure the sick; others to control snakes; and still others to recover lost or stolen property. Some there were who devoted themselves to the consulting of the spirits, but made no attempt to heal the sick or exercise miraculous power over the elements or over the animal world. All claimed to be able to work magic; but always with the qualification that witches, or some ghostly power, do not interfere. The most sacred and solemn of incantations was the spirit dance; but even in this highest of religious functions, all medicine men did not have recourse to exactly the same symbolism or make use of the same ceremonial dress.

It was the practice of medicine men to resort at times to secret and sacred caves. Apaches were exceedingly secretive concerning their religious ceremonials. Special virtue seemed to reside in the hair of the medicine man. He took care that no one should touch it. When in full regalia he no longer considered himself a mere man; he believed that he became the very power that he represented. Monotonous chanting, or beating incessantly upon a drum, seemed to have a sedative effect upon a patient and was much practiced. Medicine men held no free clinics. They demanded pay at time of treatment, either from the patient or his friends.

The sacred articles that the medicine man made use of were hoddentin, the medicine hat, the medicine shirt, and the medicine cord. Other charms and amulets of various sorts were employed, but these four were very important. Hoddentin was a kind of powder made of the tule. It was carried in a little buckskin bag and rarely was an Apache without such a bag. This powder he considered efficacious under almost all circumstances. It was regularly made use of by the medicine man. A pinch of it was applied to the breast or forehead of the sick; it was scattered on the path before a sick or wounded man; a pinch of it was thrown toward the sun at planting time, and when a war party set out; and it was sprinkled on the body of the dead. In cases of sickness it was eaten as a remedy; and the strength of an exhausted warrior was restored when it was placed upon his tongue. Among other supernatural powers inherent in the medicine hat and the elaborately constructed ghost-dance headdress were ability to cure sickness, and insight into the future, whereby a medicine man could see and forestall the coming of an enemy. The medicine shirt was an artistically ornamented shirt of buckskin. The decorations were symbolic of the sun, the moon, the stars, hail, rain, lightning, rainbow, and clouds, among elemental objects, and of the snake, the centipede, and the tarantula among animals. The medicine shirt also possessed the magical quality of providing security for the warrior against the arrows and bullets of his foe. One of the most efficacious yet mysterious accessories of the medicine man was the medicine cord. There were cords of one, two, three, or four beautifully decorated strands. Strangers were not allowed to look upon or talk about these medicine cords, so sacred were they. It was only with the greatest difficulty that Bourke was able to secure specimens of them. Only on the most solemn and important occasions were they in evidence on the person of the medicine man. They were believed to possess the very greatest efficacy. Only the leading medicine men could make them; and before a new owner could put one on, it must be sprinkled with "heap hoddentin."

BIBLIOGRAPHY

BOURKE, JOHN G. *Ninth Annual Report of the Bureau of Ethnology*, 1887–1888.

CREMONY, JOHN C. *Life among the Apaches.* San Francisco, 1868.

CURTIS, E. S. "Vanishing Indian Types—The Tribes of the Southwest." In *Scribner's Magazine*, May, 1906.

DELLENBAUGH, F. S. *The North Americans of Yesterday.* New York, Putnam, 1901.

GAY, DOROTHY FRANCES. *Apache Art.* Master's Thesis. University of Arizona Library.

GODDARD, PLINY EARLE. *Indians of the Southwest.* New York, 1921.

GODDARD, PLINY EARLE. *Myths and Tales from the San Carlos Apache.* Anthropological Papers of the American Museum of Natural History, Vol. XXIV, Part I.

GODDARD, PLINY EARLE. *Myths and Tales from the White Mountain Apache.* Anthropological Papers of the American Museum of Natural History, Vol. XXIV, Part II.

GOODWIN, GRENVILLE. "Clans of the Western Apaches." In *New Mexico Historical Review,* July, 1933.

HODGES, FREDERICK W. "The Early Navajo and Apache." In *The American Anthropologist,* old series, July, 1895.

HRDLICKA, ALES. "Notes on the San Carlos Apache." In *American Anthropologist,* new series, 1905.

LUMMIS, CHARLES F. *The Land of Poco Tiempo.* New York, Scribner, 1897.

OPLER, M. E. *An Analysis of Mescalero and Chiricahua Apache Social Organization in the Light of their Systems of Relationships.* University of Chicago Library.

OPLER, M. E. "The Concept of Supernatural Power among the Chiricahua and Mescalero Apaches." In *American Anthropologist.* Vol. XXXVII, No. 1.

OPLER, M. E. "An Interpretation of Ambivalence of Two American Indian Tribes." In *The Journal of Social Psychology,* Vol. VII, No. 1.

OPLER, M. E. "A Summary of Jicarilla Apache Culture." In *American Anthropologist,* new series, Vol. XXXVIII, No. 2.

ROBERTS, HELEN H. *Basketry of the San Carlos.* Anthropological Papers of The American Museum of Natural History, Vol. XXXI, Part II.

SMART, CHARLES. *Notes on the Tonto Apaches.* Smithsonian Report for 1867.

SMITH, DAMA MARGARET. *Indian Tribes of the Southwest.* Stanford University Press, 1933.

WHITE, DR. JOHN B., Surgeon in the U. S. Army and Physician to the Apache Indians under the Department of the Interior. *A Complete Vocabulary of the Apache and the Tonto Indian Dialect of Arizona Territory.* Bureau of American Ethnology. Manuscript Vault. (From photostat copy secured by Charles Morgan Wood, 1926.)

CHAPTER V

The Apache Confronts the American

THE first Americans who encountered the Apaches were soldiers and trappers. These first contacts were casual or accidental and happened in Mexican territory. The earliest report concerning this tribe from an American pen is that of Zebulon M. Pike, written in 1807, during his extended explorations in the unknown Southwest. Either purposely or "through an unintentional aberration from his prescribed route" he found himself (and was found by the Government of New Mexico) in Spanish territory. From Santa Fe he was sent under military escort to Chihuahua, Mexico, there to give an account of himself to the Commandant-General. It was during his long march from Santa Fe to Chihuahua that Pike got his first glimpse of the Apaches and made comments on the condition and habits of the Apaches as he saw them at that time. What Pike writes pertains to the relationship between these Indians and the Spanish; for as yet they knew nothing of the Americans, nor the Americans of them.

The earliest account we have of a clash between Apaches and citizens of the United States is to be found in *The Personal Narrative of James O. Pattie of Kentucky,* published in 1831. Late in February, 1825, a party of American trappers led by Pattie's father suddenly came upon a band of Apaches on the Gila River not far from the modern site of Fort Thomas. Surprised and alarmed, the Indians fled into the mountains. The trappers took pains to show themselves friendly, so no evil consequences resulted at that time. The party proceeded down the river, trapping along the way. The natives were occasionally seen skulking about, but not until several weeks later did they show an ugly temper. The Americans exerted themselves to get on good terms with a large band who made their appearance in the mountains above the river; but the Indians either could not, or would not, understand the friendly overtures of the intruders. Later it became evident that they mistook this party of white men for Spaniards.

A few days later this same band attacked the trappers on the San Pedro about six miles above its junction with the Gila. The Americans lost their horses and barely escaped with their lives; but the enemy suffered still more severely, ten of their braves being killed. The Indians found to their surprise that they were dealing with a type of white men they had never come in contact with before. When, months afterwards, young Pattie returned to the scene of the battle to recover the beaver skins that he had cached on the San Pedro, the band of Indians were again encountered. They had unearthed the beaver skins and made robes of them which they were then wearing. One of them was riding on the horse that Pattie's father had ridden. Pattie compelled the Indian to dismount and surrender the animal. The leader of the band then came forward and asked:

" 'Do you know this horse?'

" 'I do,' Pattie replied; 'it is mine.'

" 'Was it your party we took the horse and furs from a year ago?' the chief inquired.

" 'Yes, I was one of them; and if you do not give me back my horse and furs, we will kill your whole party here and now.' "

"He immediately brought me one hundred and fifty skins, and the horses," Pattie writes, "observing that they had been famished and had eaten the rest, and that he hoped this would satisfy me, for that in the battle they had suffered more than we, he having lost ten men, and we having taken from them four horses with their saddles and bridles. I observed to him that he must remember that they were the aggressors and had provoked the quarrel, in having robbed us of our horses and attempting to kill us. He admitted that they were the aggressors in beginning the quarrel, but added, by way of apology, that they had thought us Spaniards, not knowing that we were Americans; but that now, when he knew us, he was willing to make peace and be in perpetual friendship. On this we lit the pipe of peace, and smoked friends. I gave him some red cloth, with which he was delighted."

In 1828 a band of trappers in the employ of Ewing Young, a famous pioneer trapper, while on their way from Taos to the Colorado River for the purpose of hunting and trapping, were attacked by Apache Indians somewhere near the headwaters of the Salt River in Arizona. After a long, fierce fight the trappers were beaten and were compelled to return to Taos. Young was not an easy foe to deal with. His ire was aroused and his determination to carry out his enterprise stiffened. Enlisting a company of forty of the most daring and experienced mountain men, he led them in person. He set out with the purpose, first, of visiting vengeance upon the Apaches who had broken up the previous undertaking, and second, of carrying on a profitable trapping expedition. Kit Carson, though not yet twenty years of age, was accepted as a member of this veteran band; and it was during the next few months that he received his real baptism of fire.

It was April when Young and his men set out. In order to deceive the Mexican Government with respect to his destination he first marched a considerable distance northward; but when sufficiently remote from the settlements, he directed his course southwestward through the Navajo country and in due time, in the White Mountain region, came upon the Indians whom he desired to chastise.

The savages were no less eager for the fray than were the Americans; but they were not a match for these cool, hardened mountain men, either in strategy or desperate courage. To the jubilant Indians, Young, when he had shown himself in the open with what they judged to be a mere handful of followers, seemed to halt in fear. In reality, this experienced fighter was making use of his time to place the main body of the trappers in ambush. Seeing such a small company of Americans and mistaking the brief pauses of the leader for cowardice, as Young anticipated, the Indians swarmed over the hills and moved *en masse* against the few white men in sight. They paid dearly for their haste and indiscretion. When they had advanced to a position where the ambushed riflemen could subject them to a cross fire, the command was given to shoot.

Bullets were too scarce to waste; so the result of the accurate cross fire was withering. Fifteen Apaches were killed at the first volley, and many were sorely wounded. The Apache was never ashamed to run when he was getting the worst of it; and so it was in this case. When the trappers advanced into the open, the enemy scattered like autumn leaves in a gale.

Young and his party now busied themselves with their trapping along the Arizona mountain streams. The skulking Indians continued to harass them, stealing their traps and occasionally killing a horse or a mule. But never again did they dare to attack in the open.

About 1835, as the result of a most despicable act of treachery on the part of James Johnson, an American trader, and one Gleason, his accomplice, the friendly understanding that had hitherto existed between the Apaches and the Americans came to a sudden end. The leading Apache chief south of the Gila at that time, was Juan José, between whom and the Mexicans there was the most deadly enmity. Juan José was fairly well educated; had, indeed, been partly prepared for the priesthood in the Catholic Church, and was a very able chieftain—for strategic gifts and wisdom in council, however, more than for prowess in arms. His small but very aggressive force of staunch young warriors were more willing to risk death in executing his orders than they were to permit their leader to expose himself unduly to extreme danger.

So successfully had Juan waged warfare upon the Mexicans in Sonora that the Government was seeking at any cost some means of destroying him. Though it was against the law for American traders and trappers to operate in Mexico, Johnson, because he had married a Mexican wife, was allowed to come and go freely between the United States and Sonora. Juan José never lost an opportunity to do a good turn for American hunters, trappers, and traders; and, as Johnson often passed through his territory, a warm friendship existed between the two men; several times the chief had visited Johnson in camp near the frontier. Aware of the fact that Johnson enjoyed Juan José's confidence, the Government of Sonora offered the trader a large bribe if he would kill José.

Johnson soon found a chance to carry out his evil design. A party of ten or twelve Missourians, headed by a man named Eames, went into Sonora to purchase mules; but, as the Apaches had recently stripped the country, he was unable to secure the desired stock. Eames and his men when on the point of leaving Mexico fell in with Johnson and Gleason, and these villains, seeing, as they believed, just the opportunity they were seeking to betray the Apache chief and claim their reward, joined the Missourians on their return journey. As Johnson was very familiar with the region to be traversed, he assured Eames that the shortest and best route back to the United States was through the territory controlled by Juan José. Accordingly the whole party set out under Johnson's guidance.

Through his alert intelligence service Juan had heard of the approach of the Americans and also of the plot between the Mexican Government and the trader; so he met them on or near the Gila River several days after they left Oposura. Be it said to his credit that he refused to give credence to the report that Johnson was in complicity with the Sonoran Government. It was impossible for him to believe that Johnson, with whom he had long been on terms of intimate friendship, could consent to harm him. He met the Americans one evening as they were about to make camp and made known to Johnson the report that had been brought to him by his scouts. Johnson, of course, at once denied any connection with Juan's Mexican foes. The Apache chief then said:

"Don Santiago, you have never deceived me; and if you give me your word of honor that the report is false, I invite you to come to my camp with your men and pass the night with us."

Nothing could fit in better with Johnson's purpose, so the whole company went with the chieftain to his encampment. Upon their arrival the trader told Juan José that he had brought along a sack of pinole as a present for the women and children. The sack was taken from the back of the pack animal and a man was designated by the chief to take charge of the distribution. At once all the Indians—men, women, and children—gathered about the sack. That was what Johnson desired and expected. Concealed under an aparejo on the back of one of the trader's mules was a blunderbuss that had been brought for just this opportunity. It was loaded with balls, slugs, and bits of chain, not quite so serviceable as the machine gun of the modern American racketeer, but well adapted to its fiendish purpose. Meantime Gleason, under the pretext that he wanted to buy a fine saddle mule of Juan José's, had drawn the chief a little distance aside where the mule was standing. The plan was for Gleason to shoot the unsuspecting chief with his pistol at the same time that Johnson fired the blunderbuss into the crowd assembled about the bag of pinole. The scheme was instantly executed. The blunderbuss wrought cruel havoc among the crowd and Gleason shot Juan at the same moment. Wounded, but not unto death, the chief cried out:

"Don Santiago, come to my rescue!"

At the same time he clinched with Gleason and threw him to the ground, and now with drawn knife he was poised ready to stab him. Johnson came over, and Juan José said:

"For God's sake, save my life! I can kill your friend, but I don't want to do it."

In reply, Johnson shot him. He sank down dead on top of his prostrate foe.

"Thus perished that fine specimen of a man. I knew the man well, and I can vouch for the fact that he was a perfect gentleman, as well as a kind-hearted one." This quotation, and the whole account of the tragedy as related above, I have drawn from Benjamin D. Wilson's unpublished diary, *Observations on Early Days in California and New Mexico*. Wilson was a trapper in New Mexico at the time of the betrayal and murder of Juan José. He was near the scene of the tragedy at the time and met members of the Eames party who escaped. Wilson later moved to California, became the first American mayor of Los Angeles, was elected to the State Senate, and became so prominent in California that Mount Wilson was named for him, as were, also, civic objects in Pasadena. We must, therefore, accept his account of this terrible early outrage upon Apaches by Americans as authentic and trustworthy.

On August 14, 1846, with as little forethought as the dissolute father gives to his chance-begotten offspring, the United States Government assumed the wardship of the Apache. On that day, from the flat roof of a one-story house in the village of Las Vegas, New Mexico, General Stephen W. Kearny made the following proclamation:

"Mr. Alcalde and people of New Mexico: I have come amongst you by the orders of my Government to take possession of your country and extend over it the laws of the United States. We come among you for your benefit—not for your injury.

"Henceforth I absolve you from all allegiance to the Mexican Government. . . . I am your Governor. I shall not expect you to take up arms and follow me, to fight your own people who may oppose me; but I now tell you that those who remain peaceably at home, attending to their crops and their herds, shall be protected by me in their property, their persons, and their religion; and not a pepper, nor an onion, shall be disturbed or taken by my troops without pay or by the consent of their owner. . . .

"From the Mexican Government you have never received protection. The Apaches and Navajos come down from the mountains and carry off your sheep, and even your women, whenever they please. My Government will correct all this. It will keep off the Indians, protect you in your persons and property; and, I repeat again, will protect you in your religion." [1]

Never before nor since did Uncle Sam take into his strong awkward arms such a turbulent infant as this Apache nation. It was one thing for Kearny to declare himself military governor and that, if the people would go quietly on with their affairs and not oppose the new Government, they would be secure in all their civic rights and would be protected from the nomadic Indians; but it was a very different thing for the United

[1] Emory, W. H. *Notes of a Military Reconnaissance.* Executive Document No. 41. Washington, 1848.

States to make good these promises. Here, too, it should be stated that, in the Guadalupe Hidalgo Treaty, signed by the representative of the United States, February 2, 1848, and ratified by the Senate March 10, our Government formally and solemnly agreed to prevent Indians living in the United States from making raids into Mexico and from carrying Mexicans away into captivity.

These obligations were hard, indeed, to fulfill, were often impossible of fulfillment. For forty years the Apache problem was a festering thorn in the flesh of the American Republic and a source of desolation and death to thousands of individual citizens, both Mexican and American.

The following affecting account written by John T. Hughes, a soldier in the Doniphan Expedition, gives a good idea of the responsibilities and difficulties inherited by the Americans from the moment that Kearny raised the Stars and Stripes in Santa Fe. It is dated September 23, 1846.

"The chief of one branch of the Apaches, with about thirty of his tribe, came to hold a grand council with the Governor-General. The general made a long speech to him through an interpreter encouraging them to industry and peaceful pursuits, and particularly to the cultivation of the soil, as the surest and best mode of procuring an honorable subsistence; that they must desist from all robberies and the committing of all crimes against the laws of the territory; that if they did not, he would send his soldiers amongst them and destroy them from the earth; but if they would be peaceable towards their white brethren, he would protect and defend them as he would the New Mexicans and make them all brothers to the white people and citizens of the same republic and children of the same father, the President, at Washington City.

"To all these things the venerable Sachem replied in a spirit worthy of his tribe. He said, 'Father, you give good advice for me and my people; but I am now old and unable to work, and my tribe are unaccustomed to cultivating the soil for subsistence. The Apaches are poor; they have no clothes to protect them from the cold, and the game is fast disappearing from their hunting grounds. You must, therefore, if you wish us to be peaceable, speak a good word to the Comanches, the Yutes, the Navajos, and the Arapahoes, our enemies, that they will allow us to kill buffalo on the great plains. You are rich—you have a great nation to feed and clothe you—I am poor, and have to crawl on my belly, like a cat, to shoot deer and buffalo for my people. I am not a bad man; I do not rob and steal; I speak truth. The Great Spirit gave me an honest heart and a straight tongue. I have not two tongues that I should speak forked.

" 'My skin is red, my head sun-burnt, my eyes are dim with age, and I am a poor Indian, *a dog;* yet I am not guilty. There is no guilt there (putting his hand on his breast), no! I can look *you* in the face like a man. In the morning of my days, my muscles were strong; my arm was stout; my eyes were bright; my mind was clear; but now I am weak, shrivelled up with age; yet my heart is big, my tongue is straight. I will take your counsel because I am weak and you are strong.' " [2]

During the autumn of 1846, Lieutenant W. H. Emory, with the advance guard of the "Army of the West," passed through the Apache country from the Rio Grande westward along the Gila River. In his *Notes of a Military Reconnaissance* and in the *Journal of Captain A. R. Johnston, First Dragoons,* incidents are related that deal with the earliest contacts of soldiers of the American Army with the wild Apaches. Emory got his first view of the Apaches October 6 on the Rio Grande near Valverde. As he sighted some of them in the hills a considerable distance to the west, he thought they were trees or shrubs,

[2] *The Hughes Reprint of Doniphan's Expedition.* Topeka, Kansas, William E. Connelley, 1907.

but the trained eyes of Chaboneau, one of the guides, instantly made them out for what they were. He cried, "Indians! There are the Apaches." They came down to the American camp in a very friendly spirit, and after a council with the officers, "swore eternal friendship, as usual, no doubt, with the mental reservation to rob the first American or Mexican they should meet unprotected." They supplied the expedition with four young warriors as guides. Emory describes them as "smirking and deceitful looking." Even at this early period, some of them had firearms.

Kearny had made an appointment for a meeting with some of the leading Apaches farther west, near the Copper Mines; and there the great chief Red Sleeves (Mangas Coloradas) met him on October 20, with about a score of his people, both men and women. They were well mounted on small but active horses. Red Sleeves showed an eager desire to be on friendly terms with the Americans. One of the chiefs, struck with admiration at the soldierly bearing and peremptoriness of General Kearny, as the order was sounded for "boots and saddles" and the column moved out with promptness and precision, said with passionate vehemence: "You have taken New Mexico and will soon take California; go, then, and take Chihuahua, Durango, and Sonora. We will help you. You fight for the land; we fight for the laws of Montezuma and for food. The Mexicans are rascals; we hate and will kill them all." [3] They assured the General that "one, or two or three white men might now pass in safety through their country; that if they were hungry, they would feed them; or, if on foot, they would mount them. The road was open to the Americans, now and forever. Carson, with a twinkle of his keen hazel eye, observed, 'I would not trust one of them.' " [4]

November 2, not far from the junction of the San Pedro

[3] Emory, H. W. *Op. cit.*
[4] *Ibid.*

with the Gila, some Apaches made signals from the hills indicating that they wanted to talk with the strangers. However, they were so very timid that it was almost impossible to persuade them to come into camp. Finally, one by one, and warily, they risked it; and, finding that no harm was intended them, they promised to bring mules next day to a point six miles farther on, where they told the officers water was to be found. The high peaks above the river afforded fine lookout posts, and one of their number was "always seated, like a sentinel crow on the highest limb of the adjacent tree, watching over the safety of his thieving fraternity." [5] The Army was in desperate need of mules, for their animals were constantly breaking down; and they had high hopes that they could barter with the Apaches for fresh ones. Very few, though, were they able to get.

Major Swords had charge of the trading, and his lot was a hard one, though his discomfiture added greatly to the merriment of his fellow officers and the soldiers. One buxom Apache woman, somewhat advanced in years, was very talkative and took an active part in every bargain the major tried to strike.

"She had on a gauze-like dress, trimmed with the richest and most costly Brussels lace, pillaged no doubt from some fandango-going belle of Sonora; she straddled a fine grey horse, and whenever her blanket dropped from her shoulders, her tawny form could be seen through the transparent gauze. After she had sold her mule, she was anxious to sell her horse, and careered about to show his qualities. At one time she charged at full speed up a steep hill. In this, the fastenings of her dress broke, and her bare back was exposed to the crowd, who ungallantly raised a shout of laughter. Nothing daunted, she wheeled short round with surprising dexterity, and seeing the mischief done, coolly slipped the dress from her arms and tucked it between her seat and the saddle. In this state of

[5] *Ibid.*

nudity she rode through camp, from fire to fire, until, at last, attaining the object of her ambition, a soldier's red flannel shirt, she made her adieu in that new costume." [6]

The Apaches had with them a beautiful and intelligent Mexican boy about twelve years of age of whom they were very proud and to whom they were altogether devoted. Before closing a trade they would always consult him. He was very cheerful and contented; and when General Kearny offered to purchase him from his captor he said that the attempt would be useless. He was sure his master would not part with him, and he added that it had been so long since he had been taken from his home that he really had no desire to leave the Apaches. He was, nevertheless, much pleased, both by Kearny's offer to secure his freedom and the desire of his captors to keep him.

BIBLIOGRAPHY

EMORY, W. H. *Notes of a Military Reconnaissance.* Executive Document No. 41. Washington, 1848.

HUGHES, JOHN T. *Reprint of Doniphan's Expedition.* Topeka, William E. Connelly, 1907.

PATTIE, JAMES O. *The Personal Narrative of.* Cincinnati, Timothy Flint, 1831.

WILSON, BENJAMIN D. *Observations on Early Days in California and New Mexico.* Unpublished Manuscript. Berkeley, Bancroft Library.

[6] Emory, *ibid.*

CHAPTER VI

Uncle Sam and His Unruly Wards

W HEN Kearny was about to set out from Santa Fe for his march to California he appointed Charles Bent to act as Governor of New Mexico. By virtue of his office as Governor, Bent became also Superintendent of Indian Affairs. For many years he had lived in or near New Mexico, so he was well qualified to supply the Government at Washington with exact information concerning the various Indian tribes inhabiting the Territory. This he did in a condensed but illuminating report to William Medill, Commissioner of Indian Affairs.

First, Bent mentions the Jicarilla Apaches, numbering five hundred souls. He characterizes them as a wandering tribe without permanent home, lazy and cowardly, living almost wholly by thefts from the New Mexicans, since game had grown scarce in their region and they lacked the courage to compete with other Indians of the plains in the pursuit of the buffalo. Their only article of manufacture was a crude kind of pottery, capable of resisting fire. This ware was much used by the New Mexicans in cooking, and the Jicarillas gave it in exchange for the bare necessities of life. Because of their thieving habits these Indians were a great nuisance to the white settlers.

Bent next describes what he calls "the Apaches proper who range through the southern portion of this Territory, through the country of the Rio del Norte and its tributaries and westward about the headwaters of the River Gila. They are a warlike people, are about 900 lodges and from 5000 to 6000 souls; know nothing of agriculture or manufactures of any kind but live almost entirely by plundering the Mexican settlements. For many years past they have been in the habit of committing constant depredations upon the lives and property of the inhabitants of this and the adjoining territories and states from which they have carried off an incredible amount of stock of all kinds. The only article of food that grows in their general range is the maguey plant and that spontaneously and in very small quantities." [1]

In his reports Bent included facts about the other Indian tribes in New Mexico and pointed out that the United States, in taking over this portion of Mexico, had assumed responsibility for about forty thousand Indians. He made it clear to the Government that the control and management of these tribes presented an immediate and most serious problem; and, at the same time, offered certain wise and constructive suggestions, namely: the necessity of providing suitable presents for the Indians in all attempts at friendly communication with them; the establishing of stockade forts at crucial and strategic points; and the taking of representatives of each tribe to Washington so that they might gain some notion of the United States and come to see how unwise it would be to continue their predatory habits when opposed by so powerful a government. The real predicament in which our Government found itself at this early stage of its dealings with the Apaches must be studied in the light of the very complicated relationships of the Indian tribes among themselves and the animosity of each tribe toward the Mexicans; but I must, for lack of space, limit myself to the Apache aspects of the situation.

When the United States signed the Guadalupe Hidalgo

---

[1] Calhoun, James S. *The Official Correspondence of James S. Calhoun*, p. 6. Collected and edited by Annie Heloïse Abel. Washington, Government Printing Office, 1915.

Treaty in 1848, it entered into very grave responsibilities with respect to the control of the Apaches along the frontier of the two countries involved. We were not prompted to such action by motives purely humanitarian. It was forced upon our Government by the necessities of the case. It would have been impossible to frame a treaty with Mexico without guaranteeing that her border provinces should be safeguarded from Apache incursions. So, by Article 11 of the treaty, the United States bound itself to restrain the Indians from raids into Mexico, or, in case of failure to do so, to give full satisfaction for such breaches of the agreement, to forbid any American to acquire from the Indians either property or captives stolen in Mexico, to rescue captives brought into the United States from Mexico and return them to agents designated by the Mexican Government, and, finally, speedily to enact laws by which these agreements should be rendered effective. True, James Buchanan, American Secretary of State at that time, affirmed that we had "both the ability and the will to restrain the Indians within the extended limits of the United States from making incursions into Mexican territories, as well as to execute all the other stipulations of the eleventh article." Yet he must have realized, and many of our statesmen did realize, that it would be impossible for our nation to live up to the letter of these agreements. Indeed, this article did not pass the Senate without strong opposition; and very soon it was all too manifest that we were unable to keep these promises, much as our country desired to live up to its obligations.

The difficulties of the situation were stupendous. The territory involved was very remote; the savages were ever on the move, and were scattered over vast stretches of land, mountainous, unexplored desert country, where much of the time the heat was terrific. The American people knew almost nothing about the region or the Indians that inhabited it; Congress was as dilatory as it was uninformed; both civil and Army officers were left without adequate support or coordinated policy; and the whole country, citizens and statesmen alike, almost to the exclusion of other urgent national problems, was passionately absorbed in the struggle over slavery. At first the Army and the Department of Indian Affairs had to shoulder responsibility. But the number of troops sent to New Mexico was entirely inadequate to cope with the situation; especially were we deficient in cavalry. Infantry could not possibly meet the demands of warfare against a well-mounted wide-roving enemy in a terrain the roughest and most arid in America. Our soldiers were barely able to protect themselves, to say nothing about visiting punishment upon a proud and wily foe inured to this sort of warfare during three centuries.

It was most fortunate that the first Indian agent sent to New Mexico, James S. Calhoun, was an able and zealous officer. In March, 1849, soon after President Taylor took office, the Indian Agency at Council Bluffs was removed to New Mexico; and April 7 Calhoun received his commission as Indian Agent at Santa Fe. Though he set out at the earliest possible moment, he was not able to reach his new field until July 22. Two years and more had elapsed since Kearny took over the Territory in the name of the United States and things had been going from bad to worse. With intelligence and indefatigable energy Calhoun went to work to master the situation. Immediately he gathered an immense amount of valuable information concerning both the nomadic and settled Indians of his territory, and this knowledge he transmitted fully and promptly to his superior in Washington. Indeed, unprovided as he was with either money or troops, there was little he could do except gather facts and submit them to the proper officers in Washington. His recommendations from the first were wise and practicable.

October 1, 1849, he writes as follows to the Commissioner of Indian Affairs: "Numerous bands of thieving Indians, principally Navajos, Apaches and Comanches, are straggling in every direction, busily employed in gathering their winter supplies, where they have not sown. Not a day passes without hearing of some fresh outrage, and the utmost vigilance of the military force of this country is not sufficient to prevent murders and depredations and there are but few so bold as to travel ten miles from Santa Fe. How are these wrongs to be remedied? I answer, by a compulsory enlightment and the imposition of just restraints, both to be enforced at the point of the bayonet. It is now stated upon a more intimate knowledge of the various tribes of Indians in this region that a vast majority of the Apaches and Comanches live chiefly by depredations; that they look upon the cultivators of the soil with contempt as inferior beings, the products of whose labor, except in war, and in love, and the chase is degradation; and the man who has not stolen a horse, or scalped an enemy, is not worthy of association with these lords of the woods.

"The wild Indians of this country have been so much more successful in their robberies since General Kearny took possession of the country, they do not believe we have the power to chastise them. Is it not time to enlighten them upon this subject and to put an end to their ceaseless depredations?" [2]

In a supplementary letter sent to Commissioner Medill, October 5, 1849, Calhoun urges that the country be thoroughly explored and surveyed so that the more dangerous and evasive of the Apaches may be rooted out of their lurking places; insists that two more mounted regiments be sent into the Territory; advises the opening of military roads and the establishment of army posts and depots. Eager that the Commissioner shall have in hand the necessary information upon which Con-

[2] *Ibid.*, pp. 31, 32.

gress may act when it shall meet the following winter, he makes another long report, October 15. He writes: "It is not necessary to repeat to you that the Apaches, although frequently roving east of the Rio Grande, when at home are to be found on the west side of the aforesaid river and on both sides of the boundary lines between the United States and Mexico, as indicated by the maps, running west several hundred miles to, or near, the Pima Villages. How are these people to subsist if you effectually check and stop their depredations? How are you to comply with your obligations under the aforesaid 11th Article without invading foreign territory?

"To establish a proper state of affairs in this country, with the economy which the Government of the United States should, and will, ever observe, requires a strong arm—and a prompt arm, guided by an enlightened patriotism, and a generous spirit of humanity.

"Expend your millions now, if necessary, that you may avoid the expenditure of millions hereafter.

"The Comanches and Apaches, with all the adjacent fragments of other tribes, must be penned up; and this should be done at the earliest possible day." [3]

Calhoun stresses the fact also that unprincipled Mexican traders are a potent source of evil; and are disaffecting the industrious and well-disposed Pueblo Indians, by assuring them that the Americans are more greedy and cruel than the Mexicans.

Writing from Santa Fe, February 29, 1852, to Daniel Webster, Secretary of State, Governor Calhoun says: "Such is the daring of the Apache Indians that they openly attack our troops and force them to retreat or become victims of the scalping knife of the savages. Parties are being entirely cut off on the *Jornada* between Fort Conrad and Fort Fillmore; between

[3] *Ibid.,* pp. 54–56.

these points an escort affords no longer any protection. The mail from San Elizario, which reached here last evening, was attacked on the *Jornada* by the Apaches; an escort of ten men was furnished them from Fort Conrad, of which one man was killed and two wounded in the encounter. The San Antonio mail is entirely cut off, to a man; the only remains found of the bloody struggle were the irons of the carriage and the bones of the men in charge. Such, Sir, are the reports that reach us from day to day, and it is a lamentable fact that they are increasing rapidly, to such an extent that if such outrages continue much longer, our territory, instead of becoming settled with an industrious and thriving population, will be left a howling wilderness, with no other inhabitants than the wolf, and the birds of prey, hovering over the mangled remains of our murdered countrymen." [4]

On May 2, 1851, John R. Bartlett, United States Commissioner on the United States and Mexican Boundary Commission, arrived at the Santa Rita Copper Mines in New Mexico in the very heart of the Apache country and there established headquarters. As he was representing our Government in an international activity of no little moment and had under his authority a large and very diversified party consisting of a military escort, numerous scientists, and many other civilians of almost every rank and description, we may say that he was the symbol and epitome of the United States Government to these wild and warlike Apaches during the four months that he remained in that region. He came into close and frequent contact with the most powerful Apache chiefs of the west—Mangas Coloradas, Dalgadito, and Ponce. His dealings with these savages constitutes, therefore, a very important link in the story of American relations with the Apaches. Bartlett was a man of great ability and fine poise, honorable, humane, and cultivated; an

[4] *Ibid.*, pp. 485–486.

antiquarian, a trained observer, a good writer, and a skillful draftsman; and his account of the origin, dispersion, numbers, characteristics, and activities of the Apaches, including his own contacts and clashes with the powerful chiefs mentioned above, is extended and in some parts rich in details.

It was not until after Bartlett's party had been at the Copper Mines for six weeks that the Apaches presumed to visit the camp of the Americans. However, nothing that the Americans did had escaped their attention. Bartlett had just returned from a somewhat prolonged journey into Sonora, when on June 23, Mangas Coloradas, the most famous Apache of his generation, accompanied by Dalgadito and a dozen more of his band, presented himself before the Commission. Mangas informed Bartlett that his warriors had watched every movement of his, since he set out on his journey into Mexico up to the present time, and warned him that he ran great risks in traveling with so small a company into unknown territory where bad Indians roamed. He said that, as for himself, he was altogether friendly toward the Americans and that he and his tribe desired peaceful relations. Bartlett replied in a like amicable tone, explaining to him the results of the war recently carried on between the United States and Mexico and telling him that this party of Americans were now marking off the boundary between the two countries. He assured him that Indians living on the American side of the line would be protected by the United States Government, but that if they murdered either Americans or Mexicans or stole their stock they would be pursued and punished. Mangas Coloradas could not see why we should extend our protection to the Mexicans, but when Bartlett made it clear to him that our treaty bound us to do this, he said that his people would not harm either Bartlett's party or the Mexican Commission and promised that if any of Bartlett's horses or mules were stolen by his young men or were found astray, he would have them sent back to the American camp.

Simple presents were distributed to the Indians—beads, cotton cloth, and shirts—but the Commissioner not only refused to give them whisky; he assured them that he had none with him. It was as hard for the savages to understand how a party of Americans could be without whisky as it was for them to comprehend why we insisted upon protecting the Mexicans. They continued to be skeptical on this point, and whenever they saw bottles containing liquid of any kind, they would ask for a drink of it, supposing, of course, that it was whisky. "I one day handed them a bottle of catsup and another of vinegar," Bartlett writes, "and told them to ascertain for themselves. A taste put a stop to their investigations and they were afterwards less inquisitive."

Two or three times during their stay at the copper mines difficulties arose as a result of the obligations imposed upon our nation by Article 11 of the Guadalupe Hidalgo Treaty, and each time Bartlett with tact, but above all with firmness, stood by the terms of the treaty and made it clear to all concerned that the United States took its responsiblities seriously. The first difficulty arose in late June, 1851, when three New Mexican traders came to the headquarters of the Commission to secure provisions if possible. They had in their possession, secured by barter from the Pinal Apaches, a number of horses and mules and a Mexican girl about sixteen years old. The captive was a beautiful girl and it was their purpose to sell her wherever they could get the best price for her, which meant, of course, that she was to be doomed to a life of shame. The treaty with Mexico expressly forbade commerce in the states, whether in stolen animals or captive human beings, so when the facts were brought to Bartlett's attention, he without delay sent a note to the Commander of the military escort to obtain

Munitions Blag., Wash.

APACHE MOTHER AND BABY

PRESIDIO AT THE COPPER MINES

Reproduced from John R. Bartlett's "Personal Narrative"

VIEW IN COCHISE STRONGHOLD

the release of the girl at once and to hold the strangers until further notice. The order was promptly complied with; the young captive was held by the Commission and well cared for until Bartlett was able in person to restore her to her relatives in Santa Cruz, Sonora.

From the time that Bartlett arrived at the Copper Mines, the Indians and Americans had been on the best of terms. Mangas Coloradas and his people were encamped about four miles from the headquarters of the Commission, and men, women, and children frequently came in to see the Americans. The day after the release of Inez Gonzalez, the captive girl, there were many Indians at headquarters. Suddenly into the tent of Mr. Cremony, the interpreter, rushed two Mexican boys, the older one about thirteen years of age, the other perhaps two years younger, and begged him to save them from their captors. They were naked and their hair was cropped, but they were bright, fine lads. Mangas Coloradas and Dalgadito had learned that the boys had escaped and had sought the Americans for protection and these two chiefs were with Bartlett when the lads were brought before him. Mangas wanted Bartlett to buy them, but the Commissioner explained that Americans did not buy captives and at the same time reminded the chief that our Government was under obligation to protect captives found in the hands of the Indians and to return them to their own country. The Apaches either could not or would not understand the binding nature of our obligation under the treaty, or the repulsion of Americans, on grounds of humanity, to enslaving Mexican children and taking them away from their homes and parents. Talk was useless, and after a while the Indians went away in bad humor. Bartlett asked them to return the next day for further parley, for he was eager to keep on good terms with them, but they remained in a sulk for several days. As Bartlett had reason to believe that they would try to recapture the boys, he committed them to the hands of four brave and trusty men and, after providing them with good clothes, sent them off that night to the camp of General Condé, the head of the Mexican Commission.

After some days the chiefs and their followers came back to talk things over again, and with them came the former master of one of the boys. The arguments set forth by the Apaches were acute and eloquent. They ably made the best of their cause. They said the Americans had no right to take away their captives from them. Had they not long been on good terms with each other, coming and going openly to and from their camps, with their women and children and without any attempt to conceal their captives? They had believed that the Americans were sincere in their friendship, were their brothers. "Why do you take our captives from us?"

Bartlett replied that the actions of the Americans had been sincere and honest, explained that the dignity of our country compelled us to stand by our treaty with the Mexicans with whom we were now at peace. We had promised protection to the Mexicans and could not lie. We were eager to extend protection and friendship to the Indians likewise.

Said one of the Indians: " 'Yes, but you took our captives from us without beforehand cautioning us. We were ignorant of this promise to restore captives. They were made prisoners in lawful warfare. They belong to us. They are our property. Our people also have been made captives by the Mexicans. If we had known of this thing, we should not have come here.' " To all this Dalgadito added: " 'The owner of these captives is a poor man; he cannot lose his captives, who were obtained at the risk of his life and purchased with the blood of his relatives. He justly demands his captives. . . . Nor does the brave who owns these captives wish to sell them. He has had one of those boys six years. He grew up under him. His heart-strings are

bound around him. . . . Money cannot buy affection. His
heart cannot be sold.   He taught him to string and shoot the
bow and to wield the lance.   He loves the boy and cannot sell
him.' "

Bartlett answered: " 'I have no doubt but that you have suffered much by the Mexicans.   This is a question in which it is
impossible for us to tell who is right or who is wrong.   You
and the Mexicans accuse each other of being the aggressors.
Our duty is to fulfill our promise to both. . . . We feel for
our Apache brother and would like to lighten his heart.   But
it is not our fault.   Our brother has fixed his affections on the
child of his enemy.   It is very noble.   But our duty is stern.
We cannot avoid it.

" 'The captives cannot be restored.   The Commissioner cannot
buy them, neither can any American buy them; but there is
here in our employ a Mexican who is anxious to buy them and
restore them to their homes.   We have no objection that this
Mexican should do so, and if he is not rich enough, some of us
will lend him the means.'

"This last suggestion was accepted; and everyone concerned
went over to the Commissariat where the price agreed upon,
two hundred and fifty dollars worth of American goods, was
laid out and accepted by the Apaches." [5] And so the incident was
closed.

Once or twice again serious disturbances arose and it seemed
as if open warfare must ensue; but Bartlett's fairness and
ingenuity were always equal to the occasion.   However, as the
summer wore on, the Indians grew more and more insolent and
hostile.   Three different times they drove off the horses and
mules of the Commission.   The last time they also stampeded
the cattle of a Mr. Hay who was working a gold mine near by.

---

[5] Bartlett, John Russell, *Personal Narrative*, Vol. I, pp. 310–317, New York,
Appleton, 1854.

Colonel Craig was absent with the troop in pursuit of another party of marauders, but a volunteer company from the Commission followed the Indians and pressed them so hard that they had to scatter and leave the animals. Mr. Hay clearly identified Dalgadito as leader of this last thieving expedition. The time had now come for the Commission to move on westward to begin the survey so, late in August, the Copper Mines were deserted.

A more typical view of American ways and American ideals of honor than that presented by the high-minded Commissioner John R. Bartlett comes to us from the adroit pen of the pioneer wag, *bon vivant*, and diplomat Charles D. Poston. Poston had entered the Gadsden Purchase as early as 1854 and had then gone East to raise money for extended mining operations on the Santa Cruz River and in the mountains surrounding Tubac. In July, 1856, Poston was on his way back to Arizona with an ample supply of money and in command of a fairly tough outfit of frontiersmen "armed with Sharp's rifles, Colt's revolvers, and the recklessness of youth." At El Paso the party rested. Says Poston: "As the waters of the Rio Grande are rather sandy, champagne was used as a substitute, and it required a month to recruit the animals for a pitch into Apache land.

"First, I was provided with credentials from Washington. Dr. Steck, the Indian Agent on the Rio Grande, offered to go out with the company and introduce us to the Apaches. He sent four wagon loads of grain ahead for the Indians to make tiz-win with and appointed a rendezvous at the old Spanish fort near the Gila, called Santa Rita-del-Cobre, a triangular fort constructed with military skill.

"I camped the company on the Mimbres, taking only five men on horseback as an escort; and Dr. Steck was only accompanied by a Mexican boy, who had been a captive among the

Apaches, as an interpreter. There were about 350 Apaches in camp, the most noted being Mangas Coloradas (Red Sleeve) a fine looking chief. The Apaches were as friendly and civil as could be. We camped in the old triangular fort and they camped outside. In the course of nearly a week spent there we had many talks. They said they had always been friendly with the Americans and wanted to continue to be friends, but that the Spanish and Mexicans had treated them badly and that they would kill them and rob them as long as they lived. We exhibited our new fire-arms which were then Sharp's rifles and Colt's revolvers, shot at marks and drank tiz-win, roasted venison and made the Indians some presents. What they appreciated most was some matches which they wrapped carefully in buckskin.

"Before we took our departure there was a clear understanding between us: the treaty with the Apaches provided that they would not disturb the Americans coming into Arizona and that the Americans would not disturb the Apaches in their raids into Mexico. When we returned to camp on the Mimbres one old mule was missing, and when I complained to the chief about it, he said some of the boys had stolen it and he would have it sent back; and he did.

"In the camp at San Simon about fifty Apaches came along returning from a raid into Mexico, with plenty of horses and mules, and six captives, all girls. They were under a Coyotero chief named Alessandro, father of Natush, afterwards wife to little Steve. They made some bluster at first because we would not sell them ammunition; but finally consented to be friendly. Natush told me many years afterwards that they could have killed me many times from ambush, but they would not do it. After we became established at the old Presidio of Tubac, the Apaches came along on their way into Sonora and could easily have killed our *Vaqueros* and carried off the herd; but they refrained from doing so out of respect to the treaty. To give the devil his due, the Apaches kept the treaty more faithfully than the Government of the United States had kept the treaty with Mexico." [6]

From 1855 to 1860 Dr. Michael Steck was Agent for all the Southern Apache tribes. These included the Mescaleros, the Mimbres, the Mogollons, the Coyoteros, and the Chiricahuas. After 1856 both the Mescaleros and the Mimbres had shown a good disposition and had expressed their willingness to settle down and cultivate the soil, or to submit to any other plans that the Government might think best adapted to their permanent welfare.

The agent knew little about the Mogollons and Coyoteros and almost nothing about the Chiricahuas. Their habitat was so remote from his headquarters at Fort Stanton, and the region over which they roamed so wild, that no close contacts had ever been made with them. In Steck's report of August 7, 1857, we are supplied with accurate and adequate information concerning the state of affairs among the tribes under his care. It is true that the Mescaleros had been bad during 1855–1856, but their depredations were due to the fact that they were without food and had no way of securing it except by raids upon the white settlements. "There people are poor and very badly clad. . . . They devoured a dead mule with avidity, and eagerly eat up the leavings of dogs. They say there is not sufficient game in the country to keep them from starvation." [7]

With the exception of a few outlaws who had united themselves with the predatory Mogollons, the Mimbres band were eager for peace. They had shown an earnest desire to begin the planting of crops. As every other well-informed person had done since 1846, Steck makes it clear that the only hope

---

[6] From *The Scrapbook of Samuel Hughes.* Pioneers Historical Society, Tucson.
[7] Indian Affairs Report. House of Representatives, Executive Document No. 2, 35th Congress, 1st Session. Washington, 1857.

of protecting the property of the white people in Mexico, New Mexico, and Arizona, and the only means of improving the condition of these savages and building them up in the ways of civilized life, is to locate them on well-defined reservations, provide them with food and tools, and instruct them in the cultivation of the soil. He emphasizes the fact that the Government must allow some time to accomplish the desired end and must in the meantime supply the Indians with provisions.

Specifically Steck urges that new treaties be made with these Indians and that immediately the Mescaleros, Mimbres, Mogollons, and Copper Mine Apaches, all of whom at one time or another have looked to Mangas Coloradas as their chief, and all others of like language and inherited customs, be assigned a reservation on the Gila River west of longitude 109, where they shall have their permanent home. He advises that good agents be located among them to issue to them the necessary goods provided by the Government for their immediate needs and to advise and instruct them in their new manner of life. He recommends, also, that a military post consisting of four companies at least be established on the Gila to look after them and also to control Apache bands that roam the country still farther west. He insists that such steps be taken at once, as delay is sure to result in further destruction of property and consequent claims against the Government by those despoiled, the payment of which would cost ten times as much as the money required to carry out this plan, to say nothing of the suffering and loss of life sure to result from continued hostilities. He concludes with these wise and earnest words:

"There is no comparison, therefore, between the cost of a pacific policy and that of whipping them into subjection; besides, no permanent good is obtained by fighting them, as the survivors after every campaign will be less able to maintain themselves than before it. The department will be compelled, therefore, in the end to choose between the policy of feeding them and providing for their wants, and that of their total extermination."

During the summer of 1857 Colonel R. C. Bonneville in command of the Department of New Mexico carried on an extensive campaign against the Coyoteros north of the Gila, the most westerly of the Apache tribes. As a result of Bonneville's invasion of their territory, it became evident that, while a few of the bad men of the tribe had been guilty of depredations, the Coyoteros had never felt any fixed hostility toward the Americans but, on the contrary, now, as in the past when Pattie and Kearny had come that way, it was the desire of their chief men to be on friendly terms with the Americans.

September 2, 1857, just after their fight with Bonneville on the Gila, three Coyoteros, led by a chief called Chino Pena, visited Steck at the Indian Agency. Pena said that a grand council of the Coyotero tribe had just been held and that, after being in conference three days and three nights, the tribe unanimously sent him to ask for peace. He said he had been sent as spokesman for all the chiefs between the Pinal and Mogollon Mountains, to say that they would "offer all their mountains, waters, wood, and grass in exchange for peace." Colonel Bonneville and another officer, Major Simonson, were present at the Agency when the Indians arrived and they, as well as Steck, were convinced that the Coyoteros sincerely desired to live at peace with the Americans. Steck responded in the same amicable spirit, and sent them back to their people with the assurance that the Americans "wanted none of their wood, water, mountains, or their gold, but that we desired peace."

In his report of August 10, 1858, Steck says the Coyoteros have kept their promises and that, though as yet the Agency has no regular contact with them, his belief is that a good understanding could be reached with them if they were called into council, given presents, and supplied with implements for farming. He states further that though they are the largest and most powerful band in his territory, they are at the same time among the least warlike, even owning considerable herds and cultivating the soil to some extent, and raising crops of corn, wheat, beans, and pumpkins.

Steck's report of August 10, 1858, gives a sad picture of the effects of Government control over the savages who are near the white settlements. There has been much drunkenness and this has resulted in quarrels and deaths among themselves. The white people have not only made them drunk; they have swindled them out of their houses; and the Mexican people of Mesilla have even murdered them in cold blood. The tribes that have been brought into closest association with the white settlements have contracted the diseases of the white men and been poisoned by their vices and consequently have died in large numbers. From all these they were comparatively free in their wild state. They are now not only more liable to attack of diseases, but less liable to resist the inroads of such diseases when they fall a prey to them, so they die from diseases that ordinarily do not prove fatal.

Steck's report of August 12, 1859, is illuminating. At that time the Apache Agency extended from the Pecos River to the Colorado and included five distinct bands: the Mescaleros, the Gila Apaches (made up of the Mimbres and the Mogollons), the White Mountain Coyoteros, the Pinal Coyoteros, and the Chiricahua Apaches. The Gila Apaches "never have recovered from the effects of the campaign made into their country two years ago by Colonel Bonneville. They were then compelled to scatter in every direction for safety. Most of them ran into the republic of Mexico and there, exposed to the heat and malaria of the low country, many of them died. Before that war, they numbered over four hundred warriors and now the two bands united number less than one hundred and fifty.

"The Chiricahua Apaches . . . had very little intercourse with the Americans until after the establishment of the great overland mail, which runs directly through their country. In view of the importance of giving security to travel upon this great thoroughfare to the Pacific, the agent received instructions from Superintendent J. L. Collins to hold a talk and distribute presents to this band in December, 1858. An interview was accordingly held at Apache Pass, and since that time no traveller has been molested upon the road through their country. This band of Apaches rove about in small parties and have always been termed the Apaches Broncos, or wild Apaches. They are the most warlike band west of the Rio Grande, and the least reliable. They number about one hundred warriors and five hundred women and children. . . .

"The White Mountain Coyoteros is that portion of the Apaches living north of the Gila, upon the Rio San Francisco and head waters of the Salinas. They occupy a fine country, with many beautiful mountain streams and rich and fertile valleys for cultivation. This division numbers two thousand five hundred souls, of whom six hundred are warriors. In all their intercourse with the Government, their deportment toward travellers and traders, they have shown themselves to be the most reliable of all the bands of Apaches. . . .

"The Pinal Coyoteros occupy the country watered by the Salinas and other tributaries of the Gila. They take their name from the Pinal Mountain, in and around the base of which they live. Their country is also rich in timber and fertile valleys. They number about three thousand souls, of which seven hundred are warriors. . . . With a view of bringing about a proper understanding with these Indians, the agent was instructed to visit this band. A meeting was appointed at Cañon del Oro during the month of February, 1859. Ten of their chiefs were present and three hundred warriors. At this council it was agreed that peaceful relations should hereafter exist between the Pinals and our people, and up to this time they have acted in good faith. Colonel B. L. E. Bonneville, commanding department, has just returned from that country and reports all quiet. And Indian Agent, John Walker, referring to these Indians, and the interview he had with them, in a report to the Superintendent dated August 7, 1859, says, 'The result of these meetings was very satisfactory and, up to the present time, no well authenticated robbery has been committed by them. Many attempts have been made by interested and dishonest parties to create the impression that the Pinals are stealing, with the hope of inducing the department commander to send more troops to their territory. I know, however, that the country has never been so safe as at present.'

"The Pinal and White Mountain Coyoteros cultivate the soil extensively—raise wheat, corn, beans, and pumpkins in abundance. In this particular, they are far in advance of all the other Apaches. They have some game, mescal and tuna, and, as no settlements yet encroach upon their country, all they will need for a few years will be a liberal distribution of presents yearly and some hoes and spades to enable them to cultivate the soil more extensively." [8]

BIBLIOGRAPHY

BARTLETT, JOHN R. *Personal Narrative*, Vol I. New York, Appleton, 1854.

CALHOUN, JAMES S. *The Official Correspondence of James S. Calhoun*. Collected and edited by Annie Heloïse Abel. Washington, Government Printing Office, 1915.

HUGHES, SAMUEL. *Scrapbook*. Tucson, Pioneers Historical Society.

Indian Affairs Report. House of Representatives, Executive Document No. 2, 35th Congress, 1st Session, Washington, 1857.

Senate Executive Document No. 2, 36th Congress, 1st Session.

[8] Senate Executive Document No. 2, 36th Congress, 1st Session, pp. 712–715.

CHAPTER VII

Cochise: War Chief of the Chiricahuas

ON the Sonoita River, about twelve miles west of Fort Buchanan, in the early sixties, lived an Irishman named John Ward with Jesus Martinez, a Mexican woman, and her son— later known as Mickey Free, whom Ward had adopted. The boy was in the meadow watching Ward's cattle one day in October, 1860, when a band of Apaches raided the ranch and stole both the boy and the stock. Following the trail of the Indians as far as the San Pedro River, Ward became convinced that the raiders were Chiricahuas belonging to Cochise's band; so he rode to Fort Buchanan and reported his loss to the commanding officer, Colonel Pitcairn Morrison, Seventh Infantry, with the request that the troops assist him in an effort to recover the boy and the cattle.

Many weeks elapsed before any action was taken by the military. But on January 28, 1861, Morrison ordered Second Lieutenant George N. Bascom, Seventh Infantry, a West Point graduate in the class of 1858, to proceed to Apache Pass and vicinity with fifty-four men to recover the stolen boy and stock. If, as was expected, the trail led to the encampment of Cochise near the Overland Mail Station in Apache Pass, Bascom was to enter Cochise's camp and demand that the captive and the stolen animals be returned, using force if necessary to bring this about.

Bascom left Fort Buchanan, January 29, and arrived at

100

Apache Pass, February 3.[1] He marched eastward with his command, past the Overland Mail Station, halting there only long enough to supply his men with water and inform the station keeper that he was *en route* to the Rio Grande. He then moved on and went into camp about three quarters of a mile east of the station. Cochise had observed the passing of the soldiers, and the next day, February 4, he came down to the station to inquire why they were there. Some accounts state that Bascom had sent for him. He was told by the station keeper that the troops were on their way to the Rio Grande. With his wife and boy, a brother, and two nephews, he then proceeded down the canyon. Ward and an interpreter named Antonio were with Bascom; and Ward, recognizing Cochise as he approached said:

"There comes Cochise!"

At Bascom's invitation, the chief and his companions entered the officer's tent to partake of his hospitality. After Cochise had been seated, Bascom began talking with him through the interpreter. He explained the object of the expedition and demanded that Cochise deliver up the boy and the stolen stock. Cochise declared that he did not have the boy or the cattle, and that neither he nor any of his people had any knowledge of the depredation. He offered to make inquiry as to what band was guilty and, if possible, recover both the boy and the stock by purchase from those who held them, as was the custom among Indians. Cochise's statement that he was not guilty of the offense was later proved to be true. The raid had been made by Pinal Apaches, not by the Chiricahuas.[2]

Meantime, Ward had slipped out to inform the soldiers that Cochise was within the tent. They at once surrounded the tent,

---

[1] Wood, Charles Morgan. Extracts from Records in the War Department. November, 1856, to February, 1861.
[2] De Long, S. R. *The History of Arizona*, p. 29. 1905. Farish, T. E. *History of Arizona*, Vol. II, p. 31. 1915. Connell, Charles T. "The Apache Past and Present," Chap. 15. In *Tucson Citizen*, May 29, 1921.

and as soon as Bascom was informed of this fact, he told his guest that he and his people would be held as hostages until Ward's boy was surrendered. Almost before the words were out of the interpreter's mouth, Cochise had drawn his sheath knife, and with the spring of a tiger, had slashed the tent wall and leaped through into the midst of the soldiers, who were so astonished that they had not the wit to stop him, though they did recover sufficiently to send a fusillade of bullets after him. Another member of the party also tried to make his escape, but was knocked down and pinned to the earth with a bayonet. The rest remained quietly in the tent and were held as prisoners.

Once free and in his native canyons, Cochise collected a band of his followers and, coming out on the crest of the hill some distance above the station, called out to Culver the station keeper, Walsh the hostler, and Wallace a stage driver, none of whom as yet had any inkling of the scene of violence that had occurred at Bascom's camp and all of whom had been on friendly terms with Cochise, that he wanted them to come out and talk with him. They walked over to where he was, unarmed, and in their shirt sleeves. The Indians instantly made a rush and seized all three of them. Culver and Walsh broke away, and ran for the station, followed by a shower of bullets. Culver fell at the door of the house with a bullet in his back. Meantime, without the knowledge either of the employees or Cochise, Bascom had marched back to the station and occupied it with his men; and now, as the soldiers within heard the firing and, much excited, looked out and saw Walsh's head appearing over the outer wall as he sought safety within the inclosure, supposing him to be an Apache, fired at him and killed him. It was not until Bascom and some of the men ran to the door to aid the fallen Culver that the Indians knew Bascom had occupied the station.

The evening that Wallace was captured a wagon train went into camp two miles west of the mail station. About dusk Cochise surprised the party, bound two or three of the men to the wheels, and burned the wagons, the goods, and his human victims. Two Americans who were traveling with the wagon train he carried away. On the same day, or the following, the regular mail stage from the west drove into the canyon just after dark and was fired upon by Apaches who had concealed themselves in the rocks on each side of the road. The driver, King Lyons, was disabled by a shot in the leg and almost at the same moment one of the lead mules fell dead. The men inside the coach leaped out and cut the mule loose; William Buckley, Superintendent for the mail line, mounting the driver's seat whipped the remaining mules onward through a hail of bullets down the steep incline that led to the bridge across the ravine. Cochise had ordered that a part of the bridge be cut away and had supposed that his victims would be stopped there subject to his will. But, leaping the broken portion, the mules dragged the coach safely across, and on up the hill to the station. No sooner had the stage come to a halt that one of the wheel mules fell dead. Had this happened five minutes earlier, the entire company would have been at the mercy of the Apaches.

Buckley at once sent a messenger to William Oury at Tucson with an account of all that had happened at Apache Pass and the request that a courier be dispatched immediately to the troops at Fort Breckenridge on the San Pedro. Oury did as requested; and with a small party from Tucson set out as soon as possible for the scene of action. When he reached Ewell's Station, fifteen miles west of Apache Pass, he learned that Lieutenant R. S. C. Lord and Lieutenant Isaiah N. Moore, in command respectively of Companies D and F, First Dragoons, had preceded him. These officers marched from Fort Breckenridge, February 10. Oury overtook them at the rock tank, two miles west of the Pass, and they all arrived at the station in the evening, more than a week after Cochise made his escape. About the same time that word was sent to Tucson, Bascom dispatched a courier to Fort Buchanan for medical aid. This daring soldier led his mule up the mountainside in the dark, and reaching Dragoon Springs in the early morning, secured a remount and completed his journey before the end of the second night. Assistant Surgeon B. J. D. Irwin, together with James Grayson, a former soldier, and fourteen infantrymen mounted on mules, set out in a snowstorm to relieve Bascom and care for the wounded men at the Mail Station. It required two days to make the march. While Irwin's command was crossing the Sulphur Spring Valley, a party of Coyotero Apaches returning from a raid and driving a herd of cattle and horses before them were encountered and pursued in a running fight, during which thirty horses and forty cattle were recovered and three Indians captured. For gallantry in action on this occasion, Irwin was many years later awarded a medal of honor by Congress.

Meantime there was plenty going on at the Mail Station. On February 8 the soldiers and employees drove the stock to a spring some six hundred yards east of the corral to let them drink. Ever on the watch, Cochise had placed a number of his warriors in ambush in the canyon through which the animals had to be driven; and, as the men drove the stock before them on the return trip, the Indians fell upon the party, stampeding the stock, killing Mose Lyons, an employee of the station, and wounding two other men. The following day Cochise came out within hailing distance of the station, bringing Wallace along as interpreter, demanded the release of the prisoners held by Bascom and offered to free Wallace and the other two American prisoners he had taken. Bascom refused to make the exchange unless Ward's boy was also turned over. Again Cochise declared that he did not have the boy and that he knew nothing about his capture. Baffled once more in his effort to secure the release of his relatives, Cochise disappeared, taking Wallace with him.

Finally, a day or two later, mounted and horribly decked out in war paint, Cochise and his followers again appeared on the rocky slope, leading Wallace whose hands were tied with a rope, one end of which was attached to the saddle of Cochise. Once more Wallace, who spoke the Apache language, made known Cochise's demand for an exchange of prisoners. He said that he had already suffered greatly from cold, and torture at the hands of the Indians; and he pleaded with the Lieutenant to accept the proffered terms, as otherwise he and his companions would certainly be put to death. Sergeant Reuben F. Bernard, of Bascom's command, added his entreaties to those of Wallace, and so persistent was he in his opposition to the action of his superior that he was placed in arrest. All efforts on the part of Cochise to secure the release of his friends having now failed, he dragged Wallace to death behind his galloping horse, and, as later appeared, also put the other two Americans to a cruel death. When the command reached Fort Buchanan on February 23, Bernard was tried by the Commanding Officer for insubordination, but was released. Writing eight years later, Bernard, who had shown himself one of the bravest and most efficient Apache fighters in the Army and had risen steadily through the various grades to the rank of Lieutenant-Colonel, said he "knew personally of thirteen white men whom Cochise had burned alive, five of whom he tortured to death by cutting small pieces out of their feet, and fifteen whom he dragged to death after tying their hands and putting lariats around their necks." In conclusion he wrote: "This Indian was at peace until betrayed and wounded by white men. He now, when spoken to about peace, points to his scars and says, 'I was at peace with the whites until they tried to kill me for what other Indians did; I now live and die at war with them.' " [8]

And now comes the sequel of the horrible blunder made by Bascom. Irwin, Lord, Moore, and Oury, with the infantry from Fort Buchanan, the dragoons from Fort Breckenridge, and the civilians from Tucson seem all to have united at the Mail Station by February 15. After Cochise and his band dashed off dragging Wallace to his death, nothing more had been seen or heard of them. Well aware that a large force had now been brought together to punish them, the Indians had scattered and gone into hiding. The morning after the arrival of Oury and the dragoons, the soldiers were early in the saddle and off to search for Cochise among the Chiricahua Mountains. Cochise's village was found after a scout of two days and was destroyed; but the Indians easily eluded their pursuers. On the return march, when the troops were nearing the Mail Station, they rode into a small valley on the western side of the Chiricahuas where three bodies were found perforated with lance wounds. One of these bodies Oury was able to identify as that of Wallace. At the foot of a mound studded with oak trees, the three Americans were interred. The little valley led down toward the stage road. As the detachment proceeded toward the station a discussion arose among the men, which was soon taken up by the officers, as to the propriety of taking all of Bascom's hostages and hanging them to the trees that shaded Wallace's grave. Almost immediately it was decided that this should be done. Accordingly, Lieutenant Moore went to Bascom and informed him of this determination.

" 'No,' said Bascom, 'I am in control of the Indians, and I should incur censure if I disposed of them in that way.'

[8] Russell, Don. *One Hundred and Three Fights and Scrimmages.* United States Cavalry Association, Washington, 1936.

" 'Moore replied, 'I am the ranking officer, and I will assume all responsibility.' "

Irwin's version of the matter is as follows: "It was then and there decided to execute an equal number of the Indian warriors confined at the Mail Station. It was I who suggested their summary execution, man for man. On Bascom expressing reluctance to resort to the extreme measure proposed, I urged my right to dispose of the lives of the three prisoners captured by me, after which he then acceded to the retaliatory proposition and agreed that these prisoners and three of the hostages taken by him should be brought there and executed." [4]

So, early the next morning, February 19, the six Indians were marched out to the mound that sloped down toward the grave of Wallace and his companions, and were hanged upon the largest oak tree.[5] The two remaining prisoners, a boy and a woman, were placed in a wagon, taken to Fort Buchanan, and there released.

When Cochise learned the fate of his three relatives, his fury knew no bounds. He swore he would exterminate or drive out the entire white population of Arizona. From his impregnable strongholds he dispatched far and wide small bands of his picked warriors to plunder wagon trains, stampede cattle and horses, and murder unprotected settlers. They would rarely attack in the open. Concealed in some lofty lookout, the scouts would scan the valleys and mesas for small parties of careless travelers or unguarded wagon trains, and then, at a favorable ford or pass would ambush them—slay, burn, and loot, with little loss on their part. Or they would creep up to some isolated ranch—kill the men, plunder the house, destroy the crops, drive the cattle and horses before them into their mountain fastnesses, and carry the women and children into captivity. Pursuit was vain, since the Indians knew every trail,

[4] Irwin, B. J. D. "The Apache Pass Fight." In *The Military Surgeon*, October, 1933. Washington, D.C.
[5] The author has identified the spot and visited it more than once.

canyon, and cave for a hundred miles in every direction, could travel on foot fifty or even seventy-five miles a day over the roughest mountains and mesas, had a secret code of smoke signals by which they could communicate across wide reaches of country, could conceal themselves behind rocks, cactus, and tufts of bear grass, and pick off at will either soldier or settler who dared to risk himself in their retreats—vain, because in courage, energy, and intelligence Cochise was incomparable as a leader and a strategist.

The result was that by the summer of 1861 terror reigned supreme. Ranches, mines and small settlements were desolated and abandoned. Even the military was intimidated; and nowhere was there safety except in Tucson and two or three fortified mines and ranch houses where the embattled pioneers, armed to the teeth, would outface and outfight even Apaches. Raphael Pumpelly, metallurgist for the Santa Rita Mining Company, gives a vivid account of his own experiences during the spring of 1861, and also of the havoc wrought among his neighbors. For weeks at the Santa Rita Mine east of Tubac, Pumpelly had been in hourly danger of death. Two of his Mexican teamsters had been ambushed and slain, and his friend, Grosvenor, the superintendent of the Company, had met a like fate a few hours later. Pumpelly himself escaped only by chance.

A few days later, on his return from a trip to Fort Buchanan, whither he had gone to seek military aid, he was pursued and attacked by Indians. Riding to the *hacienda* of an American named Elliot Titus, Pumpelly found him and two of his men dead and mutilated. A watch belonging to one of the victims was still ticking, so recent had been the murderous assault. A few minutes later, riding like the wind with his single companion to escape the pursuing savages, he met a company of settlers burying a man who had been to the Fort to give notice of the slaughter of a neighboring family in the Sonoita Valley.

Pumpelly and Poston had made their plans to get out of the country as soon as they could. But on the night previous to the day they had set for their departure a Mexican herdsman galloped into Tubac with the news that he and a ranchman, named Bill Rhodes, had been chased by a large band of Apaches, most of them mounted, and that Rhodes had no doubt been killed. The next morning Poston and Pumpelly rode northward to see what had been the fate of Rhodes and two other Americans and a Papago Indian at the Canoa Inn on the road to Tucson. To their astonishment, they soon met Rhodes, his arm in a sling, but with spirit undaunted. When the Apaches were almost upon him, he had turned aside into a dense thicket, and there, buried in a dried up mudhole, he had single-handed stood off the whole band of Apaches, killing six or eight of them as, in single file, they attempted to thread the narrow passage to his lair. At the Canoa Inn, the bodies of the two white men and the Papago were found in terribly mutilated condition and pierced by scores of lance wounds. While some of the party kept watch, the others buried the three victims. Knowing that Mr. Richmond Jones, a superintendent of the Sopori Mining property, had come by Canoa the previous day, search was now made for his body. It was found, pierced by bullet and lance wounds, and was taken to Tubac for burial.

By early summer, word had reached Arizona that war had broken out between the North and the South, and in June orders came to the commanding officers of Forts Buchanan and Breckenridge to abandon these posts because of the advance of the Confederate forces, and to destroy all stores and supplies that could not be removed. All Federal troops that had not already been withdrawn were ordered to proceed to the Rio

Grande. There was, of course, great rejoicing among the Apaches; for, as they knew nothing about the death grapple in which the two sections of the nation were locked, they naturally assumed that the Americans were conquered and were withdrawing with terror. Very soon they were to learn how sadly they were in error; but the story of the Civil War period in the Southwest I leave for later treatment, as I desire to devote the rest of this chapter to an account of Cochise's character and personal fortunes to the end; for I consider him the most powerful and tragic figure in Apache history.

At this place in my story I must introduce the potent and unique figure of Captain Thomas J. Jeffords, who, in the long run, was to prove the beneficent resolving force in this bloodiest of Apache tragedies. Jeffords first came to Arizona in the summer of 1862, when he was thirty years old. He came as a Government scout, bearing dispatches from General E. R. S. Canby at Mesilla, New Mexico, to General James H. Carleton, in Tucson. He then returned as guide to the advance companies of the California Column on their march to Fort Thorn on the Rio Grande. He was a tall, erect, athletic man, more than six feet in height. Because he had rather long reddish hair and whiskers, he was known among the Indians by a name signifying "Sandy Whiskers." In the mid-sixties he was Government Superintendent of mails between Fort Bowie and Tucson; and for a time he drove a stage over the Butterfield route. While thus engaged, he was wounded by arrows shot from ambush by Apaches and to his death he carried the scars of these arrows on his body. He said that, to his knowledge, during the period of sixteen months that he was in charge of the mails between Fort Bowie and Tucson, fourteen of his men were killed by Apaches. At last, disgusted because the Government was unable to protect his carriers, he resigned his post, and went back to prospecting in the mountains.

But he made up his mind that he would first have a face to face talk with Cochise in order that for the future he might work on friendly terms with him. Having been so long among the Apaches as scout, trader, stage driver, and superintendent of mails, he had picked up some knowledge of their language, and had, of course, grown wise to all their ways. He found a friendly Apache who knew where Cochise was making his temporary camp and had him go with him part of the way and then send up a smoke signal indicating the approach of a solitary messenger on a peaceful mission. Then Jeffords rode into the encampment of Cochise, armed and alone. It had been seven years since any white man had come within the reach of Cochise's arm and escaped alive. The first thing Jeffords said was:

"I want to leave my arms with you or with one of your wives to be returned to me in a couple of days, after I have had a personal talk with you."

"Cochise seemed to be surprised, but finally consented to my proposition, took possession of my arms, and I spent two or three days with him, discussing affairs, and sizing him up. I found him to be a man of great natural ability, a splendid specimen of physical manhood, standing about six feet two, with an eye like an eagle. This was the commencement of my friendship with Cochise, and although I was frequently compelled to guide troops against him and his band, it never interfered with our friendship. He respected me, and I respected him. He was a man who scorned a liar, was always truthful in all things. His religion was truth and loyalty. My name with Cochise was Chickasaw, or Brother. The following will illustrate a point in Cochise's character: He said to me once, 'Chickasaw, a man should never lie.' I replied: 'No, he should not, but a great many do.' He said: 'That is true, but they need not do it; if a man asks you or I a question we do not wish to answer, we could simply say, I don't want to talk about that.' " [6]

To return to Jeffords' visit to Cochise: After he had been relieved of his arms, he calmly approached the wickiup of Cochise, and sitting down near him remained in silence for a considerable time, as was the Indian manner. Then he told Cochise that, as he trusted him, and believed that he was one who liked straight-speaking, he had come to see if some agreement could not be entered into so that he might pursue his work unmolested. Cochise, in his turn, sat for a good while in silence. Jeffords could not tell whether the outcome would be friendship or death on the spot. It was plain that Cochise, too, was in a quandary. However, having talked over the situation at some length, Jeffords' candor and courage won the day. He remained in camp with Cochise as long as he desired; and having come to a full and amicable understanding with his former enemy, when he was ready to go, his arms were brought to him and an escort was sent with him down toward the valley. Murder and ravage went on as usual, but he was never again disturbed by any member of Cochise's band.

By the end of 1871 President Grant's "Peace Policy" toward the hostile Indians was proving successful, throughout most of the tribes. However, the Apaches were still giving much trouble; and Cochise and his Chiricahuas, in particular, were a constant menace and source of anxiety. So far, no peace commissioner or other representative of the Government had been able to locate Cochise or get into communication with him. His scouts were on the lookout for a hundred miles in every direction, and by their smoke signals and swift runners they kept the great chief posted as he lay concealed in his favorite strongholds high in the inaccessible mountains. At last, the President requested the brave and discreet General O. O.

[6] Farish, Thomas Edwin. *History of Arizona*, Vol. II, p. 229. Phoenix, 1915.

Howard to go a second time as special commissioner to settle a number of distracting problems among the Indians of the Southwest. The chief object of his mission was to seek out Cochise and enter into terms of peace with him.

After striving fruitlessly for weeks to make some contact with Cochise, at a garrison in New Mexico, Howard had the good fortune to fall in with Jeffords who was then serving as guide to a troop of cavalry in their pursuit of a band of raiding Apaches. General Howard gives this account of his first meeting with Jeffords:

"The first tent I entered, a tall, spare man, with reddish hair and whiskers of considerable length, rose to meet me. He was pleasant and affable, and I was in the outset prepossessed in his favor. Giving my name, I asked:

" 'Is this Mr. Jeffords?'

" 'Yes, sir, that is my name.'

" 'Can you take me to the camp of the Indian Cochise?'

"He looked steadily and inquiringly into my eyes and asked: 'Will you go there with me, General, without soldiers?'

" 'Yes,' I answered, 'if necessary.'

" 'Then I will take you to him.' "

Something in his face and manner convinced Howard that he would do as he said, so he put himself completely into Jeffords' hands. First, Jeffords set out to secure as guides and intermediaries two young Apache chiefs in that part of New Mexico. One was a nephew of Cochise—Chie, by name—and the other, Ponce, was the son of Mangas Coloradas, who had been put to death by Union soldiers, as will be related in the next chapter. Both of these young warriors were dear to the heart of Cochise; so Howard's quest was half accomplished when they consented to go with him.

The party, consisting of six white men and the two Apaches, started westward toward Fort Bayard. The time was late

September. Jeffords had promised Howard that he would locate Cochise within a week. Four days had passed when they came to the foothills of the Stein's Peak Mountains. Chie sent up a peace signal, and then hurried ahead nearly a quarter of a mile. He stopped at a spring and imitated the bark of a coyote. A reply came back from the mountain. He ran up the steep slope and soon came back with another Indian who proved to be one of Cochise's scouts. He told Howard that he had looked into his last night's camp forty miles back. After having something to eat with them, he went back to his lookout, but in a short time returned on horseback, with his wife and child. Before dark, sixty Indians, men, women, and children, had gathered about the camp. Their horses and mules were left to graze with those of Howard's party, and the conversation was most friendly. Howard was told that he would have to cut down his escort, so he sent three white men over to Fort Bowie, there to await news from him.

The next morning the company, now reduced to five, continued their journey over the Stein's Peak Range and across the San Simon Valley. The September day was scorching hot and the route was waterless. But at twilight they reached a fine spring in the Chiricahua Mountains and made camp there. The following day they passed over the mountains and across the broad Sulphur Spring Valley to the spring that gives the valley its name. After eating and drinking, and resting a short time, they continued the march to the lower slope of the Dragoon Mountains, where they made a dry camp, though grass was found for the animals. Rising early the next morning, they pushed on until they came to a spring where they breakfasted and watered their animals.

The guides now informed Howard that they were nearing the camping place of Cochise. After resting for a couple of hours, they entered the Middle Pass of the Dragoons and wound their way through the mountains for fifteen miles to a point on the west side of the Dragoons. Again the Indians sent up smoke signals—this time to give notice of the number in the party and the purpose for which it came. Under an oak tree, on the bank of a clear stream, the mounts were unsaddled, and all but Chie gave themselves to food and repose. He, however, hurried off over the sharp rocks and steep hills to the fortress where Cochise was thought to be, though so far no sign of his whereabouts had been given. At night two Indian boys, both on one horse, came. They ate and drank but did not deign to make known their mission. At last, though, they delivered a message from Chie, and then led the way through a narrow canyon for seven miles, and brought them into a natural fortification of great extent and grandeur.

"There were canyons to enter by and canyons to leave by, but surrounded by a wall, varying in height from one hundred to two hundred feet. This wall incloses about thirty acres of swamp near the center, and many good natural springs and a fine stream of water. We encamped under a tree, and soon were surrounded by numbers of the wild Indians."[7] But no Cochise!

Next morning after breakfast a strange cry was heard at some distance, and therewith Ponce cried in excitement:

"He is coming!"

At once preparations were made for his entrance. The circle was extended and a blanket was placed on the ground for him to sit on. There was silence and solemnity throughout the assemblage as they waited. "In a few minutes there came riding rapidly down a ravine a single Indian, who looked very fierce as he approached, carrying a long lance in his hand. He was short, and thick-set and painted in that ugly way where ver-

---

[7] Howard, O. O. "Account of His Mission to the Apaches and Navajos." In *Washington Daily Morning Chronicle*, November 10, 1872.

million is combined with black paint. As soon as he reached us he dismounted and flew to Captain Jeffords, standing near by, and embraced him very warmly. Jeffords said, very quietly, 'This is his brother,' neither Captain Jeffords nor any of the Indians ever speaking the name of Cochise. . . .

"A mounted party following came in sight. This consisted of a fine-looking Indian, accompanied by a young man and two Indian women. I hoped it was Cochise. He dismounted and saluted Captain Jeffords like an old friend. He then turned to me, and I was introduced in this phrase:

" 'General, this is he, this is the man.'

"As I took his hand I remembered my impression. A man fully six feet in height, well proportioned, large, dark eyes, face slightly painted with vermillion, unmistakably an Indian; hair straight and black, with a few silver threads, touching the coat collar behind. He gave me a grasp of the hand, and said very pleasantly:

" 'Buenas dias.'

"His face was really pleasant to look upon, making me say to myself, 'How strange it is that such a man can be the robber and murderer so much complained of.' In my frequent interviews afterward I perceived that when conversing upon all ordinary matters he was exceedingly pleasant, exhibiting a childlike simplicity; but in touching upon the wrongs of the Apaches, in public council, or on horseback, in fact, when he considers himself to be specially on duty as the Chiricahua Chief, he is altogether another man. We walked together, and sat down side by side on the blanket seat beneath a fine spreading oak, which sheltered us from the scorching sun." [8]

Cochise now questioned Chie and Ponce as to how and why they came and as to their knowledge of Howard and his designs. After about ten minutes of such probing, he very

[8] *Ibid.*

pleasantly turned to the General and asked him through an interpreter the purpose of his visit.

" 'I came with the hope of making peace between you and the citizens, and of thus saving life and property.' "

Cochise replied: " 'I am as much in favor of peace as anybody. I have not been out to do mischief for the past year. But I am poor; my horses are poor and few in number. I could have taken more on the Tucson road, but have not done it. I have twelve captains out in different directions who have been instructed to go and get their living.' "

Howard then said: " 'I should like to make a common reservation on the Rio Grande for the Mimbres and Chiricahua Apaches.' "

" 'I have been there,' answered Cochise, 'and like the country and rather than not have peace will go and take such of our people as I can, but I am sure it will break my band. Why not give me a reservation here or at Apache Pass? Give me that and I will make peace, protect all the roads, and see that no property is taken by the Indians.' "

" 'Perhaps the Government would be willing to give you a reservation in that vicinity, but I think it much better for you and your people to go to Cañada Alamosa.' "

" 'How long will you stay?' Cochise asked at this point. 'Will you stay until I can get my captains in and have a talk with them? I cannot make peace without their advice.' "

" 'I came from Washington to meet you for the purpose of making peace, and I will stay as long as necessary.' "

Cochise said he would send out runners to call in his captains, but that this would require about five days. When mention was made of Apache Pass, Cochise's manner changed entirely. He said with bitterness:

" 'We were once a numerous tribe, living well and at peace. But my best friends were taken by treachery and murdered.

Apache Pass is the worst place. There six Indians were killed by Bascom and their bodies were left hanging until they were skeletons. The Mexicans and Americans kill an Apache whenever they see him. I have fought back with all my might. My people have killed many Mexicans and Americans and have captured much property. Their losses are greater than ours; yet I know we are all the time diminishing in numbers. Why do you shut us up on a reservation? We want to make peace, and we will faithfully keep it; but let us go wherever we please, as the Americans do.' "

Howard answered: " 'All this country does not belong to the Indians. It belongs to the Almighty, and all His children have an interest in it, so metes and bounds must be fixed in order to keep the peace. Such a peace as you propose would not last more than a week. If some rough prospectors for mines, always moving well armed, should fire upon and kill members of your band, or if some of your uncontrollable young men should take the property and lives of citizens—then this peace would be at an end.' "

During the eleven days that Howard was in his stronghold, Cochise did not again refer to the grievances of the Apaches. To his passionate declaration that the Americans had been the aggressors, Howard replied that many Americans thought what he said was true. " 'But now,' he continued, 'we want such horrid work as war, murder, and robbery to close.' "

At this Cochise, with a pleasant smile, said gravely: " 'I am glad you came.' "

"I then told him that it would be necessary for me in some way to notify the neighboring posts where I was and what I was trying to do, and to get some food, for we were out, and told him that Captain Sladen could go to Fort Bowie and do it for me. He shook his head and said he would like to have me go. The soldiers would listen to me. Captain Jeffords and

Captain Sladen could stay with him, and he would take care of them. Chie consented to go with me as a guide. We then all mounted and rode through a canyon to the outside of our handsome prison, Cochise and several of his Indians accompanying us. The view from this point on the western foot-hills is grand; mountains and valleys, rivers and canyons lie beneath you in plain sight. I did not wonder that the Indians delighted in their magnificent home. We stopped by a large flat stone under the shade of a tree. Cochise said:

"'My home.'"

Riding straight east, by a narrow trail at first, and then through rough canyons and along precipitous mountainsides, at great peril, and often in sore pain inflicted by the savage vegetation along the way, sometime before dawn Howard came out onto the Sulphur Spring Valley by way of the East Stronghold. At Sulphur Spring they were able to get a cart and two fresh mules to take them to the Fort, which they reached an hour after sun-up. They had traveled fifty-four miles during the night. Leaving the necessary orders at the Fort, Howard was back at Cochise's camp the second day.

Cochise and Sladen were watching for him from a high point in the mountains and came eagerly down to greet him. During Howard's absence some of Cochise's men came in and stated that they had killed five Americans. Said Cochise: "I do not think the troops can follow the trail of my Indians, but if they do, they will be in here tonight, and we will have a fight." Jeffords explained to Sladen that if the soldiers followed the trail, and there was a fight, the troops would be beaten. He told the Captain that if he preferred to leave, the Indians would conduct him in safety to General Howard. Like a sensible man, as well as a brave soldier, Sladen said he would remain.

Cochise moved his camp up among the rocks, and the Indians made a bed for Sladen and Jeffords. It was planned by Cochise that if the soldiers came in upon them the women and children would be taken out of the camp beyond possible danger. The braves, in the meantime, were placed in a position to resist any attack. When General Howard returned, he looked over Cochise's defensive arrangement, and said that no General in the Army of the United States could have made a better disposition of his men to resist an attack from a superior force.

Cochise now took Howard's party to a new camping place well up in the foothills, north of the entrance to his stronghold. Six miles away was a globular hill, rising symmetrically about three hundred feet above the plain. Here Cochise set up a white flag. After a few days, the chief captains and warriors having now arrived, a council was held. Cochise insisted upon a reservation in the mountains and valleys adjacent to their present meeting place. Here were his favorite strongholds, and from infancy this region had been his home. To this Howard finally agreed. One more firm demand was made by Cochise, namely: that Jeffords should serve as their agent. To this Jeffords stoutly objected. He had no taste for the office of Indian Agent, for no one better knew its difficulties. Besides, it would mean no small financial loss to him. But Cochise was inflexible; and, eager for the peace, Jeffords consented, with the stipulation that he was to have absolute authority in dealing with the tribe, without political interference of any sort.

A curious and solemn ceremony—what Jeffords called a prayer meeting—took place the evening after the council. On a little plateau near Howard's bivouac the Indians met to consult the spirits. First, there was "the muffled voices of many women, apparently imitating the low moaning of the winds. Then all —men and women—sang with ever-increasing volume of sound, and the women's voices rose higher and higher. It was a wild, weird performance. In due time a rough, tall, muscular Apache, his long hair hanging in braids down his back, came running

toward Howard, spoke gently, and invited all the white men
to join the band on the plateau. . . . When the singing ceased
the men kept on talking but without rising. Then an authorita-
tive voice silenced all the others. It was Cochise speaking in a
mournful recitative. The whole case was evidently being dis-
cussed and a decision reached." [9] These were anxious and
solemn moments for Howard and his friends, for they could
not tell which way the tide was flowing. But the spirits were
favorable to the peace, and the answer was rendered thus by
Cochise:

" 'Hereafter the white man and the Indian are to drink of
the same water, eat of the same bread, and be at peace.' "

"Word had been sent to the officers at Fort Bowie to meet
Howard and Cochise and their joint party at Dragoon Springs;
so the day after the conference everyone set out to conclude the
whole affair in cooperation with the local military authorities.
Cochise was hideous in fresh vermillion war paint, and as he
rode at the head of his mounted, excited, yelling, charging
warriors, his aspect was fierce and repellent. As the column of
blue-coated soldiers appeared in the plain below, marching
steadily toward them, suspicion and uneasiness was apparent
among the Indians. It was a critical moment. Any mis-step
might have set them in a panic. When he reached the appointed
place, Cochise stationed his warriors with consummate military
judgment—an evidence that he still suspected treachery." [10]
Howard wrote: "Cochise located his men with such skill that
everyone of them could, in two minutes, have been safely under
the cover of a ravine, and in three minutes more have escaped
behind a projecting hill, and so have passed to the mountains
without the least hindrance." [11]

[9] Howard, O. O. *My Life and Experiences among Our Hostile Indians.* A. D. Worthington and Company. Hartford, 1907.
[10] *Ibid.*
[11] *Ibid.*

But all ended happily. Every detail of the peace was completed. The reservation granted to the Chiricahuas was about fifty-five miles square, extending to the Sonora border and including the Chiricahua and the Dragoon Mountains, and the San Simon and Sulphur Spring Valleys. When the conference finally broke up, the Indians were very happy, talking and laughing as they gathered about the ambulance in which the officers had ridden from Fort Bowie. After all was over, and Howard was about to take his departure for Tucson, Cochise looked at him steadily a moment, then approaching, put his arms around him and said plainly in English, "Good-by."

Governor A. P. K. Safford published in the *Arizona Citizen* of December 7, 1872, a fine account of a visit he made to Cochise in the East Stronghold of the Dragoon Mountains two months after Howard had taken his departure. "Having been in the field of his bloody work nearly four years," the Governor writes, "and having at times endeavored to find him after the commission of dire crimes, but generally being compelled to travel in such condition that he was the last man I desired to meet, it will not be a subject of wonder that I had a curiosity to meet him and see who and what he is." Captain Jeffords conducted him into Cochise's presence. Indeed, Cochise in war paint, with a number of his warriors, rode out on the plain to meet the Governor's party. "He dismounted, and throwing his long, bony arms around Captain Jeffords, embraced him with the apparent fondness a mother would her child. His example was followed by each one of the party. Captain Jeffords then called me and said:

" 'This is the old man.'

" 'What old man?' I asked.

" 'Cochise,' he replied.

"When informed who I was Cochise cordially greeted me and we all sat down in a circle to have a talk. His height is about six feet; shoulders slightly rounded by age; features quite regular; head large and well-proportioned; countenance rather sad; hair long and black, with some gray ones intermixed; face smooth, the beard having been pulled out with pincers as is the custom of the Indians. He wore a shirt, with pieces of cotton cloth about his loins and head, and moccasins covered his feet. He is thought to be about sixty years old.

"I found him camped among the rocks at the foot of the mountains—a place evidently selected with care to prevent surprises, and from which with five minutes' notice he could move his band beyond the successful pursuit of cavalry. His lodge consisted of a few sticks set up in a circle, and skins placed around the base to break off the wind. Here he has about four hundred Indians of all ages. He has three wives. The last or youngest lives with him in his lodge and makes his clothes and does his cooking. Each of the others has a separate lodge and their respective children live with them.

"After breakfast, a cloth was spread upon the ground and the head men were gathered around in a circle. Cochise then said he would like to have a talk. He said he was glad to see me, and the fact that I had come among them unprotected was an evidence that I had confidence in his professions of peace. He then said that prior to the ill-treatment that he had received from Lieutenant Bascom, he had been a good friend of the Americans and that since that time he believed he had been their worst enemy; that the time was within his memory when the plains were covered with herds and the mountains were filled with Apaches, but now the herds are all gone, and the number of Apaches greatly reduced; that when he opened hostilities against the Americans he and his tribe made a promise to fight to hold the country until the last one was exterminated, but now he was determined to live at peace with everyone on this side of the Mexican line. He said that he liked General

Howard because he had the heart to come and see him, but for a long time previous the only friends he had were the rocks, that behind them he had concealed himself and they had often protected him from death by warding off the bullets of his enemies."

Governor Safford states that the Chiricahuas all told at that time numbered almost two thousand; [12] that they had been permitted to retain their property and their arms; and that they were well mounted and carried breech-loading guns. They declared at the outset that they would not place themselves under the military authorities, and, accordingly, were now under no control except that which they voluntarily conceded to the Agent, to whose requests they had always conformed since he had been placed over them. Armed and recuperated as they then were, Safford thought that they were more formidable than they had ever been, for they could live on the natural resources of the country, and in their native mountains, almost impassable for man or beast, could continue to resist such superior forces as could be brought against them, as Cochise had done for more than a decade. However, because of Jeffords' great influence over them, Governor Safford was hopeful that the peace with the Chiricahuas would be enduring. "Jeffords," the Governor writes, "is respected as an honorable man by all who know him. He had held interviews with Cochise for three years before peace was made by Howard, and was the only white man who had been in his camp for twelve years and had returned alive. . . . This act [of entering Cochise's camp alone] inspired Cochise with profound respect for his courage and sincerity. He brought Cochise to Cañada Alamosa in 1871, and led General Howard to his camp in 1872."

In 1874, only a short time before the death of Cochise, Al Williamson, a youth of eighteen, was a clerk in the trading

---

[12] This statement is in error. They numbered less than one thousand.

post run by Tully, Ochoa, and De Long at Fort Bowie. On several occasions Cochise came into the store and Al saw him, talked with him, and heard him talk. Williamson describes Cochise as tall, straight, with long hair bound about with a folded red flannel band, but without feathers. He had a Roman nose. Nachez, the younger son of the chief, was much like his father in build and appearance. But Taza, the oldest son, did not resemble him. He had a pleasant, smiling face, and was large. One day Al weighed Taza, and with nothing on but his serape of muslin and his loin cloth, he turned the scales at one hundred and ninety-nine pounds. Cochise never smiled. He was severe and grave of aspect. The officers would invite him in to drink with them; and he drank copiously. But he would never stay at the Fort after sundown, however much he might enjoy his drinking. He would mount his horse and be off; and he made it a strict requirement for his people that they should always leave the post before sundown. He rarely bought things at the store, but once he came in with a large, beautifully dressed elk skin to sell; and, when Al offered him ten dollars for it, he accepted the price without a quibble and turned back five dollars of this amount for a woolen shirt.

During these last months of Cochise's life, according to Williamson's report, a certain Señor Juan Luna came up from Frontéras with two ten-mule wagonloads of beans and corn that he wanted to sell to Tully and Ochoa at the Fort Bowie sutler's store. He was accompanied by a colonel and twenty of the most ragged Mexican soldiers that one could imagine. They were shown a camping place near by. Juan Luna said he would like to make a treaty with Cochise to come across his reservation regularly with goods to sell to the sutlers. Word was sent to Cochise and an appointment was made for a talk with Juan Luna, but he told him to bring no soldiers with him. They met in the presence of some of the Fort Bowie people, Cochise bringing with him his interpreter, Narbona, who had lived in Mexico, and Luna coming also accompanied by one of his men.

Cochise came in a flaming temper and fairly scorched Luna with sarcasm and fiery denunciation. "You come in here," he said, "and ask to make a treaty with me and to cross my reservation with your wagons and goods. You forget what the Mexicans did to my people long ago when we were at peace with the Americans, and you would get my people down into your country, get them drunk on mescal and furnish them with powder and lead and tell them to come up and get the big mules from the Americans. And when they would commit a depredation and steal mules and bring them back to your country, your people would get them drunk on mescal and cheat them out of the mules.

"Now you are asking for a treaty for safe conduct across my reservation to sell to Tully and Ochoa. Tully and Ochoa are friends of mine, and anyone who wants to bring their produce and trade with them are entirely welcome. But I want to warn you that you shall never cross the American line again with an escort of soldiers. You've got twenty soldiers, and what do they amount to! I can take five of my men and wipe them off of the earth and capture you. I've signed a treaty of peace with the United States and am living up to that treaty, so that no one need to fear to cross my reservation, for he will be perfectly safe." He went on further to say that he objected to having soldiers from a foreign country come in and ask his protection when he was carrying on no depredations.

While he was talking in such heat, one of his Indians got so worked up that he raised his gun and wanted to shoot Juan Luna. Cochise peremptorily stopped him with a motion of his hand, and the Indian was so mad and excited that, as reported by the Americans present, he sat down and wept.[18]

[18] The above items were carefully taken down by the author from interviews with Mr. Al Williamson, a well-known citizen of Arizona and a man of great intelligence and fine character, a few months before his death, October 19, 1934.

It will be seen from all that has been said above that, though born and bred a savage, Cochise was a man of distinction. His only home was a wickiup that could be constructed in half an hour and vacated, without leaving any of its furnishings behind, in half a minute; yet he had the same qualities of person, intellect, and decision that mark our leaders among the civilized nations of men. All public men who met him testify to a certain poise and dignity of character that was at once natural and masterful. His ways were not the ways of the white man; he was trained in the age-long school of savagery; yet, in physical prowess, force of character, and mental acumen, he was able to match whatever white foes were sent against him.

Cochise was a man of like passions with other men, of whatever time or race. He loved and he hated; he got drunk and beat his wives; he swore to his own hurt but changed not; he was subject to pride, cruelty, pity, and honor; he reflected deeply upon the probability of a life after death. His nature was not simple or shallow, but complex and passionate. The exhibitions of such a character are all the more interesting because they reveal themselves in both powerful and untutored ways. They are independent of civilized and conventional standards. Whatever movements of the spirit came to the surface in his wild and exposed career arose from the deeps of primitive human nature.

After the peace Jeffords, by authority of President Grant, had sole jurisdiction over the Chiricahua reservation. Neither soldier, civilian, nor Government official could come upon the reservation without his permission. The stolen horses and other ill-gotten property in the hands of the Chiricahuas at the time peace was declared were given back to their owners. During his lifetime, which extended only two years beyond the making of peace, Cochise sat always at Jeffords' right hand and his authority was always faithfully exerted for the preservation of peace. Emissaries from the White Mountain Apaches sought on more than one occasion to enlist the support of the Chiricahuas, but these efforts were in vain. To the end, Cochise was faithful to the terms he had entered into with Howard; and when he died, he advised his people never to go on the warpath against the whites. Before his death he requested Jeffords to continue to look after his own immediate group. Jeffords replied: "I am only one, and they are over three hundred, and they won't do what I ask them to do unless they want to." Cochise then called in the headmen of his own group, and in their presence selected his oldest son to be his successor and won their consent to do as Jeffords advised them.

Jeffords dealt with them as a friend and guardian. Their rights were safeguarded in every way possible and he did his best to see that they got justice. He made his reports directly to the Department of the Interior, and when another agent took his place, his accounts were audited in Washington. Though the usual amount for which an Indian agent was placed under bond was ten thousand dollars, Jeffords was under bond for five times that amount; yet, contrary to the usual slow procedure in releasing the bondsmen from their responsibility, Jeffords' audit was completed and his guarantors released three months after he turned over his office.

The final parting of Jeffords and Cochise was affecting. Cochise had been ill for a long time, was very weak, and knew that his end was approaching. Jeffords had provided the best medical aid possible and had stayed with him as much as he could. But the time came when he must go to the agency to issue rations to the Indians; and, as he was about to depart, Cochise said:

"Chickasaw, do you think you will ever see me alive again?"

"No, I do not think I will," Jeffords replied. "I think that by tomorrow night you will be dead."

Said Cochise: "Yes, I think so, too—about ten o'clock to-morrow morning. Do you think we will ever meet again?"

Somewhat taken aback, Jeffords answered: "I don't know. What is your opinion about it?"

"I have been thinking a good deal about it while I have been sick here, and I believe we will; good friends will meet again—up there."

"Where?" his friend asked.

"That I do not know—somewhere; up yonder, I think," pointing to the sky.

Sure enough, he died about ten o'clock the next morning. He was then in the East Stronghold, his favorite location. As the end drew on, he requested some of his braves to carry him up the slope a little way to the westward so that he might see the sun rise over the eastern ranges once more.

The accepted report as to his burial place, which derived from Jeffords, the only white man who knew the circumstances of his interment and who outlived him forty years without ever pointing out the exact spot, is that his body was buried somewhere on the mesa, near the entrance to the East Stronghold and that the Indians rode their horses back and forth over the grave many times so that the exact spot could not possibly be identified. There is another account of his interment that has impressed me very much, and seems to me more in keeping with Apache ways, and on the whole more probable.

On two occasions Al Williamson told me circumstantially that at Fort Bowie, a short time after the death of Cochise, Jeffords informed him that the sepulture of Cochise was after this manner: He was dressed in his best war garments, decorated with war paint and head feathers, and wrapped in a splendid heavy, red, woolen blanket that Colonel Henry C. Hooker had given him. He was then placed on his favorite horse, with one of his braves riding behind him to hold him in place. Followed by many Indians, the horse was guided to a rough and lonely place among the rocks and chasms in the stronghold, where there was a very deep fissure in the cliff. The horse was killed and dropped into the depths; also, Cochise's favorite dog. His gun and other arms were then thrown in; and, last, Cochise was lowered with lariats into his rocky sepulcher—deep in the gorge.

BIBLIOGRAPHY

CONNELL, CHARLES T. "The Apache Past and Present." In *Tucson Citizen*, May 29, 1921.

DE LONG, S. R. *The History of Arizona*. 1905.

FARISH, T. E. *History of Arizona*, Vol. II. Phoenix, 1915.

HOWARD, O. O. "Account of His Mission to the Apaches and Navajos." In *Washington Daily Morning Chronicle*, November 10, 1872.

HOWARD, O. O. *My Life and Experiences among Our Hostile Indians*. A. D. Worthington and Company, Hartford. 1907.

IRWIN, B. J. D. "The Apache Pass Fight." In *The Military Surgeon*, October, 1933, Washington, D.C.

RUSSELL, DON. *One Hundred and Three Fights and Scrimmages*. Washington, United States Cavalry Association, 1936.

WILLIAMSON, AL. Williamson interviewed by the author, June 10, 1934.

WOOD, CHARLES MORGAN. Extracts from Records in the War Department. November, 1856, to February, 1861.

CHAPTER VIII

Apache Activities during the Civil War

THE Civil War began April 12, 1861, with the Confederate attack on Fort Sumter, and ended April 9, 1865, with Lee's surrender to Grant. As has been set forth in the preceding chapter, the Apache War broke out in dead earnest a few weeks previous to the fall of Fort Sumter, as a result of the clash between Lieutenant Bascom and Cochise. A fiery whirlwind, leaving death and destruction in its wake, tore through the white settlements of Arizona.

There were only two military posts in the Gadsden Purchase at this time—Fort Buchanan on the Sonoita River, and Fort Breckenridge at the junction of Arivaipa Canyon and the San Pedro River. However, neither of these establishments could properly be called a fort. They were unfortified and it was as much as the soldiers stationed there could do to look after their own safety when the Indians grew hostile. Raphael Pumpelly, a man of keen observation and preeminent courage and ability, who was in the Gadsden Purchase at the time, writes: "Fort Buchanan consisted simply of a few adobe houses, scattered in a straggling manner over a considerable area, and without a stockade defense. The Apaches could, and frequently did, prowl about the very doors of the different houses. No officer thought of going from one house to another at night without holding himself in readiness with a cocked pistol. During the subsequent troubles with the Indians when the scattered white population of the country was being massacred on all sides for want of protection the Government was bound to give, the Commandant needed the whole force of 150 or 200 men to defend the United States property. . . . But now," as Pumpelly points out, "orders came from the abandonment of the territory by the soldiers. The country was thrown into consternation. The Apaches began to ride through it roughshod, succeeding in all their attacks. The settlers, mostly farmers, abandoned their crops, and with their families concentrated for mutual protection at Tucson, Tubac, and at one or two ranches." [1]

During the Civil War there was very little actual fighting between the Union and Confederate forces in Arizona and New Mexico; yet the troops of both armies were operating in these territories; and, in consequence, the Apaches were now and then caught between the upper and the nether millstone, though never without cost to soldier and white settler. As a matter of fact, both Federal and Confederate troops would have been glad to let the Apaches alone for the time being, for they had their hands full looking after each other. But the Apaches never remained idle long. They had to make their living; and, being no respecters of persons, they robbed and killed Rebel and Unionist indiscriminately.

Colonel E. R. S. Canby was appointed Commander of the Department of New Mexico, June 11, 1861. In July he reported that Apache depredations were frequent in Arizona. Two or three weeks later, in August, he wrote that the southern part of the Territory was in a very disturbed condition on account of Apache hostilities; and again on December 1, he reported "increasing Indian hostilities . . . Mescalero Apaches becoming more daring in their moods." As for Lieutenant-

[1] Pumpelly, Raphael. *Across America and Asia.* New York, Leypoldt & Holt, 1870.

Colonel John R. Baylor, Confederate Governor of Arizona and Commander of Mounted Rifles, C.S.A., his situation was still more annoying. Reporting to his commanding general from Fort Bliss, August 25, 1861, he wrote: "I regret to inform you that Lieutenant Mays, with a party of 14 men from Fort Davis, went in pursuit of Indians and attacked a village of Apaches, and after a desperate fight all were killed except a Mexican, who came in bringing the intelligence." September 24, 1861, Baylor reports that the Indians were very troublesome and that he had not enough troops to protect the citizens. However, on the tenth of October in response to a desperate call from unarmed miners at Pinos Altos in danger of extermination from the persistent attacks of the Gila Apaches, he sent a detachment of one hundred men under Major E. Waller to relieve the miners and protect the rich mines.

Each commanding officer, whether Union or Confederate, had his policy for suppressing the savages. In December, 1861, Colonel Canby wrote as follows to the Assistant Adjutant-General of the United States Army: "I have the honor to report that our relations with the Indians in this department are daily becoming more unsatisfactory. . . . The policy of settling them on reserves, removed from the Mexican population, protecting and assisting them until they are able to sustain themselves as heretofore—repeatedly recommended by the Superintendent of Indian Affairs and commanders of this department—is, in my judgment, the only policy that gives any assurance of success. It is recommended by considerations of humanity, economy, and experience."

Colonel Baylor's method was more direct. Writing from Mesilla, March 20, 1862, to Captain Helm, in command of the Arizona Guards, he issued this order: "I learn from Lieutenant J. J. Jackson that Indians have been in your post for the purpose of making a treaty. The Congress of the Confederate States has passed a law declaring extermination to all hostile Indians. You will therefore use all means to persuade the Apaches or any tribe to come in for the purpose of making peace, and when you get them together kill all the grown Indians and take the children prisoners and sell them to defray the expense of killing the Indians. Buy whisky and such other goods as may be necessary for the Indians and I will order vouchers given to cover the amount expended. Leave nothing undone to insure success, and have a sufficient number of men around to allow no Indian to escape."

Be it said to the honor of G. W. Randolph and President Jefferson Davis that when this order came to their attention, Baylor's career, both as military commander and Governor of Arizona, went to smash. On November 7, 1862, G. W. Randolph, Secretary of War, C.S.A., wrote as follows to Baylor's Commanding General, J. B. Magruder: "I have the honor to invite your attention to the inclosed copies of papers filed in this office, and request you to communicate with Colonel Baylor, and inform him in consequence of his order with regard to the Indians, that the authority to raise troops granted by the Department is revoked. The authority was to raise troops in Arizona Territory, and if deemed necessary it may be conferred on some other person. You will proceed as soon as practicable to take such steps as may be necessary to recover the Territory of Arizona. You will also inform Colonel Baylor that the President desires a report from him in reference to the inclosed order."

Brigadier General H. H. Sibley, in command of the Confederate Army in New Mexico, in a report to Adjutant and Inspector-General S. Cooper is less brutal and bloodthirsty than Colonel Baylor, but is favorable to the enslavement of the Indians. "During the last year, and pending the recent operations, hundreds of thousands of sheep have been driven off by the Navajos. Indeed, such were the complaints of the people in this respect that I had determined as good policy, to encourage private enterprises against that tribe and the Apaches, and to legalize the enslaving of them."

The policy of General James H. Carleton, Commanding the Department of New Mexico, is best stated in an order to Colonel Kit Carson, of October 12, 1862: "All Indian men of that tribe are to be killed whenever and wherever you can find them; the women and children will not be harmed, but you will take them prisoners and feed them at Fort Stanton until you receive other instructions about them. If the Indians send in a flag and desire to treat for peace, say to the bearer that when the people of New Mexico were attacked by the Texans, the Mescaleros broke their treaty of peace and murdered innocent people and ran off their stock; that now our hands are untied and you have been sent to punish them for their treachery and their crimes; that you have no power to make peace; that you are there to kill them whenever you find them; that if any beg for peace their chiefs and twenty of their principal men must come to Santa Fe to have a talk here; but tell them fairly and frankly that you will keep after their people and continue to slay them until you receive orders to desist from these headquarters; that this making of treaties for them to break whenever they have an interest in breaking them will not be done any more; that that time has passed by; that we have no faith in their promises; that we believe if we kill some of their men in fair open war, they will be apt to remember that it will be better for them to remain at peace than to be at war. I trust that this severity, in the long run, will be the most humane course that could be pursued toward these Indians."

May 15, 1862, the California Column was organized under command of Colonel James H. Carleton, and was ordered to make an expedition into Arizona and New Mexico for the purpose of recapturing all Federal forts in these Territories, of driving out or capturing the Rebel forces in that country, and of reopening the southern mail route. During the entire war this fine body of volunteers from California had only one engagement with the Confederate troops and that a very minor one.

However, the California Column from 1860 to 1865 became a scourge and a terror to the hostile Indians of Arizona and New Mexico. But the California soldiers did not go unscathed. June 15, 1862, General Carleton sent three couriers with dispatches for General Canby in New Mexico. On the eighteenth these messengers were attacked by Apaches, and two of them were killed. The third, John Jones, made an amazing escape and reached the Rio Grande. June 16, 1862, Colonel Edward E. Eyre was ordered by Carleton to make a reconnaissance in force toward the Rio Grande in advance of the main column. The command was unmolested by the Indians until it reached Apache Pass. Here about one hundred Indians appeared, but their leader declared they were friendly to the Americans. Later in the day, however, three soldiers, who had imprudently detached themselves from the main command, were found dead, stripped of their clothing and scalped. At one o'clock this same day, June 25, while Eyre was encamped two miles east of the pass, six or eight shots were fired into the camp by the savages, wounding Assistant-Surgeon Kittridge and killing one horse on the picket line.

July 8, 1862, General Carleton gave orders for Captain Thomas L. Roberts, of the First Infantry California Volunteers, to proceed eastward from Tucson to the San Simon accompanied by a wagon train with thirty days' rations for Colonel Eyre's men. The troops were to entrench themselves near the San Simon Mail Station and guard the train until the main column overtook them on its march to the Rio Grande.

Captain John C. Cremony, of the Second California Cavalry, with thirty-nine men was ordered to escort the Government train of twenty-one wagons, and to guard this train on its return trip to Tucson. During the next two weeks Roberts and Cremony and their troops saw service of the most dangerous and grilling kind, and gave proof of great bravery and skill in battle.

At Dragoon Springs the soldiers were deluged with torrential rains; but starting at five P.M. July 14, Captain Roberts' troops, who were in advance of Cremony and the train, marched all night and until twelve o'clock the next day and reached Apache Pass—a distance of forty miles. At Apache Pass, Mangas Coloradas with about two hundred warriors had joined forces with more than that number of Chiricahuas under Cochise. Roberts with proper precautions entered the pass with his almost exhausted troops, who had had only a cup of coffee during their nineteen-hour march. When they were about two-thirds through, the Apaches opened fire on them from behind rocks and trees and tufts of bear grass. The soldiers fought bravely, but to no avail, for their ammunition was wasted against the invisible foe. Roberts very wisely fell back to the entrance of the pass and reformed his men. He sent skirmishers into the hills so that they could command the road, and loaded and brought up his two howitzers. It was absolutely necessary for the troops to reach the springs, for both men and animals were almost famishing for water after their forty-mile march through July heat. Under a galling fire from the savages, they advanced steadily through the pass until they came to the abandoned stone station house of the Overland Mail. They were now within six hundred yards of the springs. They found shelter in the station house, but they could not pause there; they must reach the water. On two commanding heights above the springs the Apaches had made crude redoubts with loose stones. Through the openings between the rocks that formed their breastwork they kept up a hot fire on the soldiers below. Under such circumstances the guns of the troops were of little avail. But when the howitzers were gotten into position, the foe was treated to an effective and devastating fire such as they had never known before. The exact range was found and the shells burst among the rocks, doing terrible execution. Unable to stand in the face of these strange engines of destruction, the Apaches hastily abandoned their positions. Later, in speaking of this battle, one of the Indians said: "We were getting along well enough until you began firing wagons at us." Indeed, their loss was great. Three were killed by musketfire and sixty-three by exploding shells. How many were wounded, it was impossible to estimate. Strange to say, Roberts' loss during the entire six-hour battle under conditions so unfavorable was only two men killed and three wounded.

But the hardships of this sturdy band of soldiers were not yet over. After drinking and reenforcing themselves with a hasty supper, Roberts, with one-half of his men, started back to Ewell's station, fifteen miles east of the pass, to make sure of the safety of the wagon train, which Cremony was bringing along under guard of a comparatively small detachment. Several of Cremony's cavalrymen had been detailed to act with Roberts' advance company of infantry as couriers. At the earliest possible moment, Roberts had dispatched these cavalrymen under Sergeant Mitchell to inform Cremony how matters stood and to assure him that as soon as he and his men could get a cup of coffee he would come to Cremony's relief with a body of his infantry.

Upon reaching Cremony's encampment, the Sergeant hastily related what had happened to him and his comrades after leaving Roberts. No sooner had they gotten out of the pass than a company of mounted, well-armed Apaches appeared in pursuit. Three of their horses were killed under them and a rifle shot fractured the arm of Maynard, one of the cavalrymen, at the elbow. Worse yet, it was believed that John Teal, another private, had been cut off from his companions by fifteen of the enemy and killed. This last item of the report proved to be untrue, for at one o'clock in the night, bringing his saddle, saber, pistols, and blanket with him, Teal appeared at Cremony's camp.

What happened to this doughty warrior can best be related in his own words as set down in Captain Cremony's report. Said Teal: "Soon after we left the pass, we opened up upon a sort of hollow plain or vale, about a mile wide, across which we dashed with speed. I was about two hundred yards in the rear, and presently a body of about fifteen Indians got between me and my companions. I turned my horse's head southward and coursed along the plain, lengthwise, in the hope of outrunning them, but my horse had been too sorely tested and could not get away. They came up and commenced firing; one ball passed through the body of my horse. It was then about dark and I immediately dismounted, determined to fight it out to the bitter end. My horse fell, and as I approached him he began to lick my hands. I then swore to kill at least one Apache. Lying down behind the body of my dying horse, I opened fire upon them with my carbine, which being a breech-loader enabled me to keep up a lively fusillade. This repeated fire seemed to confuse the savages and instead of advancing with a rush, they commenced to circle around me, firing occasionally in my direction. They knew that I also had a six-shooter and a sabre and seemed unwilling to try close quarters. In this way the fight continued for over an hour, when I got a good chance at a prominent Indian and slipped a carbine ball into his heart. He must have been a man of some note, because soon after that they seemed to get away from me, and I could hear their voices growing fainter in the distance. I thought this a good time to make tracks and I have walked eight miles since."

It was later learned that the Indian whom Teal shot was the famous Mangas Coloradas. He was severely wounded but later recovered.

About two o'clock in the night, Roberts and his detachment reached Cremony's camp. After a three-hour rest, and without breakfast, for there was no wood to cook with, Roberts and Cremony proceeded with the wagon train to Apache Pass. Roberts and his men, in a period of less than forty-eight hours, had marched seventy miles and taken part in two battles, almost without food and sleep. It would seem that human endurance and resolution could scarcely go further than this. Roberts and Cremony reached the pass about noon, July 16. After a good dinner, the soldiers again fought off the Apaches from the spring. Careful guards kept watch throughout the night, and at eight in the morning, skirmishing with the Indians as they went, they marched out of the pass into the open country to the east. In his report to his superior officer, Roberts wrote: "Very few of us had ever been under fire before, but I do not know a case of flinching. When we got through and out into the open country, I called in my skirmishers, saying that all who could not walk might step to the front, and I would provide a place for them to ride. Of the entire company only two stepped to the front."

Because of the wily and deadly hostility of the Chiricahua Apaches, General Carleton found it absolutely necessary to establish a post in sinister Apache Pass. It was impossible to move troops either eastward or westward with safety unless they could have assured access to the springs in this canyon. For years it had been the practice of the Apaches to lie in ambush here and kill travelers who came to drink and to water their animals. Colonel Eyre, with the advance column, had lost three men here. As has just been stated, Captain Roberts, following with the wagon train, had fought for six hours to gain possession of the spring and had succeeded only after losing four men killed and wounded. Accordingly, July 27, as General Carleton was on the march from Tucson to the Rio Grande, he issued orders to establish Fort Bowie and garrison it with one hundred men under command of Major T. A. Coult, Fifth Infantry, California Volunteers. The fort was supplied from time to time by passing troops with tents, ammunition, and rations. The Commander of Fort Bowie was instructed to attack the Apaches whenever he found them near his post, to escort all trains and couriers through the pass and well out into the mesa, and to take the liberty of sending out detachments strong enough to give protection to soldiers and settlers when he deemed it wise to do so.

The defenses were completed by August 4; and in a dispatch to Carleton dated August 17, 1862, Coult gives interesting details concerning the erection of this fortification. The defenses were four in number. "Alcatraz (I give the names applied to them by the men who built them) is on the left flank of the camp, 150 feet in length, and commands every point within musket-range in the Canyon toward the road and camping ground of trains. Fort Point, on a slight elevation, covers the rear of the camp and the wagon road up the hill. It is 95 feet in length. Bule Battery overlooks the country and the approaches to the hill on the southwest, or right flank, of the camp. It is 97 feet long, and effectively covers and protects the cattle corral and picket rope of the cavalry detachment. Spring Garden (guarding) overlooks the spring and commands the ravine in which it is situated and every point within musket-range around the spring. This wall is 70 feet long. The total length of wall around the post is 412 feet, the height 4 to 4½ feet, and thickness from 2½ to 3 feet at bottom tapering to 18 inches to 2 feet at top, and built of stones weighing from 25 to 500 pounds. The works are not of any regular form, my only object being to build defenses which could be speedily completed, and at the same time possess the requisites of sheltering their defenders, commanding every aproach to the hill, and protecting each other by flank fires along the faces."

Captain E. D. Shirland, Company C, California Volunteer Cavalry, reported a sharp engagement with a large band of Apaches late in August, 1862. He was returning from an expedition to Fort Davis when six mounted Indians approached him with a white flag. They seemed to have nothing particular to say for themselves when he talked with them, and as twenty-five other mounted men had appeared, and behind them a large body on foot, Shirland became convinced that the enemy was trying to get him into a trap. He began a running fight, hoping in this way to outdistance the Indians, supposing that the mounted Apaches would, of course, pursue him. They did so for a time, but the soldiers made it too hot for them and they dropped back. The Indians left four dead on the field, and Shirland believed that twenty more were wounded. There were two soldiers wounded.

No important conflicts with the Apaches are reported during the remainder of 1862. General Carleton's grim order concerning the extermination of all Apache warriors issued to Kit Carson, October 12, and also to Captains N. J. Pishon and William McCleave, did not result in much bloodshed. McCleave and Pishon made diligent efforts to catch and kill the troublesome Mescaleros but without success. These Apaches did not approve of the policy of extermination except as applied to the white. There was, however, another aspect of Carleton's policy toward hostile Indians which he had also stated clearly—namely, concentration upon reservations. This ultimatum became effective as a result of the vigorous campaign he had ordered. In a report to the Adjutant-General of February 1, 1863, he writes: "The Mescalero Apaches have been completely subdued. I now have 350 of that tribe at Fort Sumner and *en route* thither. These comprise all that are left of these Indians, except a few who have either run off into Mexico or joined the Gila Apaches. I shall try to settle what have come in on a reservation near Fort Stanton and have them plant fields for their subsistence the coming year."

The activity of the Army against hostile Indians during 1863 was almost unremitting; yet the results were disappointing. General Carleton states that "not over one scout in four which was made against the Indians" in 1863 was at all successful. To describe in detail the many petty combats and futile expeditions of 1863 would make very dull and barren reading. However, there were a few thrilling events of lasting historic importance during this year, and these I now proceed to relate.

In a letter to the Adjutant-General of the Army, dated January 2, 1863, General Carleton announced his intention of organizing an expedition to send against the constantly hostile band of Apaches around the headwaters of the Gila River, in the region of the famous Copper Mines. Mangas Coloradas was their chief. Carleton stated that it was his intention after whipping this murderous band to establish a fort near Pinos Altos gold mines (in this same locality), both to furnish protection to the miners and for its moral and restraining effect upon the Apaches. January 11 General J. R. West, commanding the District of Arizona, issued an order for four companies of the California Volunteers under Captain William McCleave to take the field against these Gila Apaches, and so important was this expedition considered that the General himself accompanied it.

January 14 Captain E. D. Shirland was detached from the main command, with twenty men, and sent to capture Mangas

Coloradas, if possible, who was known to be in the vicinity. In four days Shirland returned with the captive chief. Mangas Coloradas in his talks with Shirland asserted that he was supreme in the region of the Copper Mines and had authority over all of this tribe. But when a member of the band was brought before him red-handed for punishment, the chief declared that he himself was innocent and could not be held responsible for the deeds of another. It was made clear to him that no subterfuge would now avail; that his plea for peaceful intention was only an attempt to escape the punishment that he now saw about to be inflicted upon his band. As he had voluntarily placed himself in Shirland's hands, West felt that he would not be justified in executing him, but decided at once that he should not be allowed to go free to continue his atrocities. He was told that he would be held a prisoner the rest of his life; that his family would be allowed to join him; and that, if he made any attempt to escape, he would instantly be killed. He was then turned over to a military guard.

In the night West was aroused from sleep and informed that Mangas Coloradas had attempted to escape and had been shot dead by the guards. The accounts of the capture and execution of this famous Apache are confusing and contradictory. More than one soldier who was present at the time has left on record the assertion that the captive was tormented and enraged beyond endurance, and when forced to angry complaint, was shot. I give West's own account of the event. He says that he investigated the death of Mangas Coloradas at once and found that he had made three attempts to escape between midnight, when he was placed under guard of a sergeant and three privates, and one o'clock when he was shot while, for the third time, attempting to escape. It seems too likely that General West had so deeply impressed the guard with the common feeling of himself and his command, that the rascal deserved death, that the soldiers believed they were carrying out the real desire of the commanding officer with respect to him. It is probable that the old chief was improperly treated in order to arouse his fury and give the guard an excuse for shooting him.

When Shirland took Mangas Coloradas, it was understood that the chief was to be permitted to return to his people at a certain time. The troops now marched to Pinos Altos and upon arriving there were approached by the followers of Mangas Coloradas. They were attacked by order of Captain McCleave, and eleven Indians were killed and one wounded. This affair was on January 19, 1863. The following day the troops came upon an Indian *ranchería*, and in a surprise attack killed nine of the Indians, wounded many more, destroyed the *ranchería*, and captured thirty-four animals—some of them Government mules previously stolen by the Indians. January 29, at Pinos Altos Mines, two hunting parties of the California Volunteers were attacked by the Apaches, and a sergeant and a private were killed. The Indians were driven off with severe punishment, losing twenty killed and fifteen wounded.

February 22, 1863, McCleave moved with his four companies to the site recommended for Fort West. The post was occupied that spring, but General West instructed McCleave not to erect buildings until further orders. On March 22 the Gila Apaches ran off sixty head of horses from the grazing ground near Fort West. Within three hours Captain McCleave was in pursuit, with one hundred poorly mounted men and five days' rations on pack mules. The Indians had a good lead and they made fast time. Their trail led in a westerly direction. Following it for seventy miles, McCleave found that it continued down the Gila for five miles, and then across a divide to the Black River. By the time McCleave reached the Black River, the soldiers had been in the saddle more than three days, almost without sleep, and many of the horses were giving out. Signs indicated that they were now near the marauders. In the twilight they moved noiselessly up the stream two miles and made camp in the darkness and rain. At eight the next morning, just four days to an hour after the chase began, thirty men under Lieutenant Latimer, mounted on the only horses that were still fit for service, and thirty on foot led by McCleave started out to find a *ranchería* which they were sure was near by. Lieutenant French with the remainder of the command stayed behind to guard the broken-down horses, the pack animals, and provisions. McCleave climbed a mountain on the west side of the stream and proceeded twelve miles, without success. He then rested with his men in a heavy rain from one o'clock until daybreak. When daylight came, McCleave was able to make out from an elevated position the *ranchería* for which they were searching. Latimer was ordered to go in advance and charge the Indians with his cavalry. This was gallantly done. Part of the dismounted men began at once to catch and guard the stolen horses, while the others, from the bluff, took part in the battle. In twenty minutes the Indians were routed and the *ranchería* destroyed. Twenty-five were killed. All the Government horses that could be found, as well as a good many Indian horses, were secured. Private James Hall was mortally wounded, and on the return trip, when the soldiers were attacked by the Indians from the walls of a canyon, Lieutenant French was wounded. For alacrity and endurance in pursuit and bravery in attack, this expedition is perhaps unsurpassed in the history of Apache warfare.

In the *Overland Monthly* of September, 1870, there is a vivid account of this campaign by one who took part in it. Says the writer: 'Our sole sustenance, four days and nights, had been hard bread and raw pork, with but four hours' sleep during that time. . . . Out of one hundred horses with which we started, but thirty remained alive; and of these, but fifteen were capable of further service. . . . Most of the men had performed two days' journey on foot, with all their accoutrements."

There was, perhaps, no more completely successful expedition against the Apaches than that conducted by Thomas T. Tidball in early May, 1863. It was difficult, indeed, for an American officer to outwit and outmarch a band of Apaches; but in this instance the Indians were outdone both in craft and celerity. It was known to Colonel David Fergusson, in command at Tucson, that there was a very hostile and cruel band of Apaches who rendezvoused at a *rancheria* in Arivaipa Canyon. May 2, 1863, Fergusson gave Tidball orders to start that very night to chastise these dangerous Indians. He was to select twenty-five men from Companies I and K of the Fifth Infantry California Volunteers and was to be accompanied by ten volunteer American citizens, thirty-two Mexicans under Jesus Maria Elias, and about twenty Papagos from San Xavier, commanded by their brave and discreet governor, José Antonio Saborze. Nine tame Apaches were also to go along as guides. Tidball was to be in full command of this mixed force. It was the purpose to surprise the *rancheria*. They were to kill as many warriors as possible, but were to bring women and children back to Tucson as captives.

The party traveled five nights in utter silence, resting and concealing themselves by day. Not a gun was fired; never was a fire lighted. The *rancheria* was taken completely unawares. The evening and night before the battle, the company had traveled sixteen hours over frightful precipices, through gloomy canyons and chasms heretofore untrod by white men. At dawn they fell upon the encampment, numbering more than twice their own force, killed more than fifty Apaches and wounded as many, took ten prisoners, and captured sixty-six head of stock. Thomas C. McClelland was the only man killed in the attacking party.

October 23, 1863, by a General Order, Carleton created the new military District of Northern Arizona. He did this because the discovery of gold in the region of modern Prescott was attracting many prospectors from the Pacific Coast, Mexico, and the East. Previous to 1863 there were no white settlers in northern Arizona. But now Carleton thought it necessary to place a military force in this region to protect the miners from the Apaches and to insure order among the prospectors and adventurers until a civil government should be organized. He ordered the following officers and troops to proceed to the new gold fields without delay: Major Edward B. Willis of the California Volunteers; Captain Herbert M. Enos, U. S. Army; Dr. Charles Lieb, acting-assistant surgeon; and Companies C and F, First Infantry California Volunteers, under Captains Hargrave and Benson; and Captain Pishon, with thirty, rank and file, of Company D, First Cavalry, California Volunteers. A board of officers were named to fix the site of a military post, to be named Fort Whipple, and to submit a plan for it. During the coming winter the troops were to live in huts. The site first chosen was about seventy miles south of the San Francisco Mountains on Rio Verde. As soon as the site of the territorial capital was selected, Assistant-Inspector General N. H. Davis and Governor Goodwin recommended that the location of the post be changed; so, May 27, 1864, Major Willis wrote to Carleton to inform him that the site for Fort Whipple "is a mile and a half northeast from the town now being built on Granite Creek [Prescott]."

King Woolsey, Arizona's great Indian fighter, had a famous encounter with the Tonto Apaches in the early winter of 1864. This affair has always been alluded to as "The Massacre at Bloody Tanks" or "The Pinole Treaty." During the winter of 1863–1864, the Indians had been very busy running off the stock of the settlers in Peeples' Valley and thereabout. In January Woolsey led a company of the settlers against these marauders. The official report of the engagement is very brief: "On January 24, 1864, a party of thirty Americans and fourteen Maricopa and Pima Indians, under King S. Woolsey, aide to the Governor of Arizona, attacked a band of Gila Apaches sixty or seventy miles northeast of the Pima Village and killed nineteen of them and wounded others. Mr. Cyrus Lennon of Woolsey's party was killed by a wounded Indian."

But the account of the battle as it has come down to us from Arizona pioneers is much more detailed and colorful. First the party struck into the Tonto Basin in pursuit of their enemies. A few miles from the present site of Miami, they found that they were encircled by Indians on the hills above. There was with Woolsey's party an interpreter Jack, a young Yuma Indian who had been a captive among the Apaches for a time. He persuaded about thirty of the leading Apaches to come down without arms for a council. He told them that he and his white friends were there to make peace and bring gifts. Leaving the main body of his men about two hundred feet in the rear, with instructions to open fire on the Apaches when he should give the signal by putting his hand up to his hat, Woolsey went forward with three others (each one with two revolvers secreted under his coat) to hold council with the chiefs. As they were seated in a semicircle, so the story goes, an Apache entered the group drawing two lances at his heels, while another one appeared and secretly distributed a handful of knives to the Indians. Then came an Indian boy almost out of breath to announce that the Big Chief ordered them all to leave the conference, as it was his intention to wipe out all the whites and their Indian allies. Woolsey now gave the prearranged signal, and at the same time shot the chief seated at his side. The others who were with him used their pistols in like manner. The men at the rear, who were armed with rifles,

made havoc among the Indians who had remained on the mountains. So severe was the punishment administered to the Tonto
Apaches that they did not trouble the settlers again for a long
time. The reason that this affair is always spoken of as "The
Pinole Treaty" is the fact that a widespread report has per-
sisted to the effect that the gift of pinole that was given to the
Indians had been treated with strychnine and that about forty
Indians died of poison. The writer does not give credence to
this sinister story.

No sooner was the Territorial Government set up in 1864
than Governor John N. Goodwin went to work to acquaint
himself with the wide wild domain over which he was to rule.
He visited the mining settlements that had sprung up about
Fort Whipple, traveled eastward as far as the Verde and Salt
Rivers, and in March visited Tucson. From Tucson, April 4,
he wrote a long personal letter to General Carleton at Santa Fe,
giving an account of his explorations and making recommendations concerning military protection for the settlers and the
officers of Government. Two weeks earlier than this, Assistant-
Inspector General N. H. Davis had made a very lucid report
to Carleton concerning the same matters. He had inspected
Fort Whipple and had visited the many locations recently settled and had then joined Governor Goodwin on his journey
southward. All of the best-informed prospectors and Indian
fighters agreed with Goodwin and Davis as to the necessity of
locating a strong permanent post east of the Verde or at the
junction of the Verde and Salt Rivers.

Governor Goodwin said in his letter: "The Indian difficulties
are becoming very serious, and unless vigorous measures are
taken, the new mining regions will be deserted. I think that
this is a very critical period in the history of this Territory.
If the people who have come into northern Arizona are driven
out, the settlement of the Territory will be retarded for many

years; but if the Indian difficulties are speedily settled, a large emigration will come in here during the next year. The people here will do all in their power. I think that three effective companies of rangers can be raised for service against the Indians, who will serve without pay, requiring food only, and to some extent ammunition."

Colonel Davis writes in his report to Carleton: "I am satisfied, General, from reliable information gained from a variety of sources, and from the character and disposition of the Indians in this territory, who are, with few exceptions, bitterly hostile to the whites and apparently disposed to combine for a general war against them [that our only true policy] is to put forth every effort in a vigorous and decisive campaign against the barbarous tribes. . . . The condition of affairs here must be looked in the face and the Indians subdued and rendered harmless, or the country deserted by whites, its mines and agricultural resources undeveloped, and the Territory given up to the savage and the coyote.

"The advantages of a large and permanent military post north of the Gila, east of the Rio Verde or San Francisco, and perhaps along the Salinas, are impressed upon my mind more strongly than ever . . . if you would give the heaviest blow to the Apache Nation and best promote the interests of Arizona."

General Carleton was moved to prompt action by the recommendations of these two able men, Goodwin and Davis. He set in motion at once the best-planned and most far-reaching campaign against the Apaches ever yet inaugurated by the United States Government. Within two weeks a comprehensive General Order was issued that affected every military unit in the department. The order required that all Apache males capable of bearing arms should either be removed to a reservation or exterminated. A post was to be established on the Gila north of Fort Bowie, the site to be determined by Colonel Davis, and the fort to be named for Governor Goodwin. A combined force of five hundred infantry and cavalry under Colonel Edwin A. Rigg was to take post there. From this point parties whose numbers were to be determined by Colonel Rigg were to march in every direction where the enemy could be found. On scouts of seven days or less the soldiers were to carry their food in their haversacks. On longer scouts pack mules were to furnish transportation. The rations on these expeditions were to consist of meat, bread, sugar, coffee, and salt, and nothing more. Each soldier was to be allowed only one blanket for bedding. "To be encumbered with more is not to find Indians," wrote the General.

At the same time that these operations were in progress from Fort Goodwin, detachments were to move northward from Tucson through Cañada del Oro and on to the San Pedro; from Fort Bowie, toward the south into the Chiricahuas; from Fort Whipple, southeastward toward the Salt River; from Fort Canby, into the western Mogollons; from Fort Wingate, toward the head of the Gila by way of the Sierra Blanca Mountains; and from Forts Craig and McRae westward to the head waters of the Mimbres River and also to the southward in the direction of Pinos Altos and Cooke's Canyon. Parties were to scour the country toward the south from Fort Cummings and toward the north from the camp on the Mimbres. These numerous expeditions were all to take the field May 25 and were to remain out two months if possible.

In addition to this formidable activity on the part of the military, Governor Goodwin was asked to have parties of miners in the field at the same time; and it was arranged to send out four bands of Pima and Maricopa Indians, with fifty in each party, to smite their ancient enemies. Moreover, notice of these combined and simultaneous movements was sent to the

Governors of Sonora and Chihuahua, with the warning that, when hard-pressed, the Indians would cross into Mexico, and with the request that these two exposed states put companies of militia into the field to cooperate with the Americans against the common foe.

The General gave this parting counsel to his troops: "Every party, in energy, perseverance, resolution, and self-denial, must strive to outdo all other parties. Dependence must be placed on the gallantry of small numbers against any odds. This covering of so much ground by detachments of determined men, moving simultaneously from so many different points, must produce a moral effect upon the Indians which it is hoped will convince them of the folly long to hold out against us." Surely such grim and extensive preparations for the wholesale destruction of their tribe must have made even Apache devils tremble —if they comprehended the scope and intensity of the plan!

Now what came of all this masterly preparation and whole-hearted cooperation? Very little—so far as either the extermination of the fighting Apaches was concerned or the location of them on reservations. There was earnest effort on the part of soldier, civilian, and Indian allies. Energy, resolution, and military skill were exhibited by both the officers and men put into the field, but, somehow, the Apaches were indisposed toward either imprisonment on reservations or extermination. The total results of the year may be summed up as follows: Two hundred and sixteen Indians were killed and a great number wounded; seventy-five horses and cattle, and one hundred and seventy-five sheep, were recovered. But on the other hand sixteen whites were killed and one hundred and sixty-two horses and cattle, and three thousand sheep were taken. Thirty Western Apaches were placed on the reservation at Bosque Redondo. The outcome was seen by all to be a pitiful failure. It is true that the whites had destroyed many acres of growing crops that the Apaches were raising in the fertile and sheltered little valleys; but, as a result thereof, hatred of the whites was increased and suspicion and lack of confidence on both sides was more apparent than ever.

The Apaches were too shrewd for the white man, and their hiding places too rough and remote for soldier or civilian to attack with success. They were perfectly at home in these canyons and mountain hideouts, and every movement of the detachments that were sent out against them was observed and reported by their ever vigilant scouts. Time and again the soldiers would come upon the *rancheria* they had been hunting for so diligently, and with such great hardship, to find that it was deserted and no Indians in sight. When they were successful in locating a band of Indians, almost always the savages would approach with a flag of truce desiring to talk with the officer in command; but usually there was such suspicion of bad faith on both sides that these parties would break up in a battle—the Indians, in almost every instance, fading away and escaping without much loss, but more than ever determined never to yield to their pursuers.

In a few instances, however, whether by virtue of extraordinary foresight, energy, and military prowess, or by trickery and treachery, the Indians were taken by surprise and suffered heavy losses. Some of the most successful of these scouts I here describe in detail. On the fifteenth of March, 1864, even before Carleton's order of May 1, a large band of Indians, probably Chiricahuas, ran off the Government herd from Cow Springs. March 24 Colonel G. W. Bowie ordered Captain Whitlock to pursue the Apaches and punish them. Leaving the camp on the Mimbres, March 27, Whitlock kept up the chase until the morning of April 7. In his command were thirty-five mounted men and thirty-six on foot. Whitlock displayed great judgment, as well as rare persistence and resolution. Previous experience in chasing Indians had taught him that it was not wise to follow directly the trail over which they had stampeded stock. Whitlock, therefore, followed the direct trail only about thirty miles in order to determine its general direction. When he had made sure of this he turned north to the Gila so that his pursuit could not be suspected. Five days he traveled down the river, sending out a scout the third day to find the trail of the Indians again. It was found and it still continued straight westward. After being out nine days, always traveling by night and never lighting fires, he made camp, and leaving twenty men on guard, started with the rest to intercept the trail and follow it once more. Soon fresh tracks and other signs indicated that the Indians were not far away. March 7, at four A.M., the campfires of the marauders were located. This word was brought to Whitlock and his command, ten miles in the rear, just at dawn; but by rapid marching he was able to reach the encampment and make the attack just as the Indians were rousing from their slumbers. Thirty Indians were killed, many were wounded, and the stock was captured, except two mules and one pony. Following so soon after Captain Tidball's devastating battle in Arivaipa Canyon, this victory was most depressing to the Indians of that region. The Army mules had been run by the savages more than eighty miles without water over rocky mountains and through canyons of frightful character. The trail could have been followed for the first thirty-five miles by the dead carcasses of horses and mules from which the fleshy parts had been cut by the Indians. Whitlock on this remarkable scout did not lose a man or an animal.

Scarcely less brilliant than the expeditions of Tidball and Whitlock was that of Lieutenant Colonel N. H. Davis in May while he was in search of a suitable location for Fort Goodwin. After marching about ten miles down the canyon of the Gila from the mouth of the San Carlos, Davis made camp in an arroyo a short distance from the river. He heard that, across the high, stony Mescal Mountains, there were some *rancherías* of Indians. After a long night march he divided his command, part under Captain Tidball and part under Captain Burkett, and succeeded in attacking the Indians at daybreak, and in killing forty-nine and taking sixteen captive. Two famous chiefs perished in this battle—one, mortally wounded, thrust his own spear into his body and so expired. Fields of corn and wheat were destroyed and much booty was recovered. It was evident from articles found in the *ranchería* that it was this band who had slain Messrs. Mills and Stevens on the Santa Cruz in December, 1863, and had attacked Mr. Butterworth. One pistol that was captured had Mill's name on it and a shotgun was identified as the property of Stevens. The Diary of Mr. James was found, also. Among other articles recovered were two saddles, two fine pairs of saddlebags, and more than six hundred dollars in gold.

In his message, delivered to the First Legislative Assembly of Arizona at Prescott, September 26, 1864, Governor Goodwin had this to say about the Apaches: "But for them, mines would be worked, innumerable sheep and cattle would cover these plains, and some of the bravest and most energetic men that were ever the pioneers of a new country, and who now fill bloody and unmarked graves, would be living to see their brightest anticipations realized. It is useless to speculate on the origin of this feeling, or inquire which party was in the right or wrong. It is enough to know that it is relentless and unchangeable. They respect no flag of truce, ask and give no quarter, and make a treaty only that, under the guise of friendship, they may rob and steal more extensively and with greater impunity. As to them, one policy only can be adopted. A war must be prosecuted until they are compelled to submit and go upon a reservation."

The Legislative Assembly drew up a Memorial asking that Arizona be placed in the Military Department of the Pacific and submitted it to the Governor for his approval, supporting the desirability of this action (among other things) by the charge that the campaign of 1864 against the hostile Apaches was a failure. Governor Goodwin refused to approve the Memorial but in his communication to the Legislative Assembly concerning it he implies that he, too, considered the campaign a failure. He writes: "The principal causes of the failure of that campaign to accomplish its purposes were ignorance of the country and the lack of competent guides."

BIBLIOGRAPHY

Arizona History. Elliott.

BANCROFT, HUBERT H. *History of Arizona and New Mexico.* San Francisco, 1889.

DUNN, J. P. *Massacre of the Mountains, A History of the Indian Wars of the Far West.* New York, Harper, 1886.

FARISH, THOMAS E. *History of Arizona,* Vol. II. Phoenix, 1915.

Journals of the First Legislative Assembly of the Territory of Arizona. Prescott, 1865.

LOCKWOOD, FRANK C. *Pioneer Days in Arizona.* New York, Macmillan, 1932.

Miscellaneous Documents of the House of Representatives, 38th Congress, 2d Session. Washington, 1865.

PUMPELLY, RAPHAEL. *Across America and Asia.* New York, Leypoldt and Holt, 1870.

The Overland Monthly. San Francisco, 1870.

War of the Rebellion. Official Records of the Union and Confederate Armies. Prepared under the direction of the Secretary of War, by Bvt. Lieutenant-Colonel Robert N. Scott. Washington, 1880. Series I: Vols. I, IV, IX, XV, XXVI. Part 1, XXVI; Part 2, XXX; Part 1, XXXIV; Part 3, XLI; L; Part 1, L; Part 2.

CHAPTER IX

Soldiers, Citizens, and Savages

CARLETON had done his best to conquer and control the Apaches, but had failed after all. It is natural that an enlightened American who coolly reads today the events of the past should suppose that with the close of the Civil War our Government would have turned its attention seriously to the solution of the Apache problem in the Southwest. But it did not do this. There were pressing and clamorous postwar issues that absorbed the attention of populace and officers of government alike. New Mexico and Arizona were very remote; the white population scant; and knowledge of the condition and needs of the people in that region meager indeed. As a result, Apache hostilities went on unabated.

It seems to us now that the failure of the Government at that time to devise some clear, firm policy for the disposition and control of the wild Apaches was stupid and reprehensible. The untold loss of life and destruction of property on the part of whites as well as Indians, and the unimaginable sufferings that came to individuals of both races during the next seven years, must be laid squarely at the feet of the Federal Government. Both soldiers and citizens did the best they could; and, as for the savage, he struggled in primitive darkness to maintain his existence and his hitherto free domain in the only way he knew—by murder and plunder, the A B C of his education and that of his ancestors.

It should have been as plain to the United States Government at that time as it is to us today that the only policy to pursue was that finally enforced by General George Crook: settlement of the Apaches upon reservations under Government protection and supervision, or steady and stern extermination. The only humane course was to allow the Apache to choose between restraint and wise educational direction by the Government, on suitable reservations, or death at the hands of United States soldiers. Necessarily, these alternatives would have to go hand in hand. At the close of the war the United States should have garrisoned New Mexico and Arizona with an active army of ten thousand soldiers, if that many had been necessary, for the stern and prompt. subjugation of willful Apache murderers and marauders, and at the same time should have made it unmistakably clear that all Indians who desired to give up warfare and live at peace with the white men would be settled upon honestly and humanely administered reservations set aside for them in their own favorite haunts.

Instead of pursuing such a course, what did Washington do? The Government committed itself to no policy, but allowed confusion to grow worse confounded. Neither soldier, savage, nor citizen was able to say how he should conduct himself. In the absence of any other fixed policy, killing was, of course, continued as the only common and familiar method of dealing with the situation. Meantime, by a reorganization of military forces, January 20, 1865, Arizona was detached from New Mexico and made a district of the Department of California. At this time there was neither telegraph, railroad, nor other means of rapid communication between headquarters on the Pacific coast and commanding officers in wide, wild, rough Arizona.

During the spring of 1865 authority was given to recruit a regiment of Arizona Volunteers for service against the Apaches.

By November 3 five companies had been mustered in, namely: Companies A, B, C, E, and F. These Companies together numbered three hundred and fifty men. Companies A, E, and F were made up wholly of native Arizonians, so were, of course, men of Mexican birth. Company B consisted of Maricopa Indians, and Company C of Pima Indians. The officers were all Americans, except Lieutenants Gallegos and Cervantes who were Mexican born. These Arizona Volunteers were mustered out at the end of one year; but civil and military officers alike speak in very high terms of their effectiveness during their period of service.

It was the opinion of General John S. Mason, who commanded the District of Arizona at the time, that "native troops, Papagos, Pimas, Mexicans, and also volunteers of our own race, were more effective in the Indian warfare than were two or three times the number of regular troops." He recommended that two or three companies of mounted scouts be enlisted from "men who have been raised on the Sonora frontier, and have been fighting Apaches for years—men who are accustomed to travel for days with a little pinole and dried beef, and who can follow a trail with the certainty of an Indian. . . . Such companies would, in my judgment, do more effective service than thrice the number of regulars." In like vein, General Irvin McDowell, in command of the Department of California, in his report of 1866 to the Secretary of War, writes: "Until very recently there were also several companies of Arizona Volunteers. . . . They were the most effective troops for the service in that country that we have had. . . . In fact it is not too much to say that *they* only within the past year have inflicted any considerable injury on the hostile Apaches."

These Arizona Volunteers had spent most of their time actively scouting for Indians. Company F had operated from its station in Skull Valley; Companies B and C from Fort

McDowell; and Companies A and E from Camp Lincoln. Though these volunteers came from the hot parts of Arizona and took their stations at higher altitudes in the middle of a very severe winter, when the ground was covered with snow, and in spite of the fact that they were barefooted and only half-clothed and half-fed, and for half of the time had, indeed, "been compelled to remain inactive for want of necessary food and clothing," during their short enlistment under the conditions described, they killed or captured more than one hundred Apaches.

January 20, 1865, Arizona was made a district of the Department of California, and General John S. Mason was placed in command of the district, February 20. It was May before he reached Yuma, June by the time he took active command of the troops in Arizona, and November before he was prepared to undertake a campaign against the Indians. He was not responsible for these delays. He was a good officer, though entirely unfamiliar with the district under his command. Upon reaching Arizona he made a tour of the Territory in company with Governor Goodwin. He writes: "At the time of my arrival in the district, I believe every ranch had been deserted south of the Gila. The town of Tubac was entirely deserted, and the town of Tucson had but about 200 souls. North of the Gila, the roads were completely blockaded; the ranches, with one or two exceptions, abandoned, and most of the settlements were threatened with either abandonment or annihilation. . . . The district is immensely large, the distance over which supplies have to be hauled very great, requiring strong escorts to guard the trains, and with the very small number of men in the different companies, and but one officer with each company, most of the posts, for the present, can do but little more than hold their posts and escort their supply trains."

At the time Mason assumed command there were twenty-eight hundred troops in Arizona; but there was a great lack of officers to command them. Sometimes there was not a single commissioned officer in a company; and at one time a subaltern was in command of a post consisting of two companies, and, besides, he had to do duty both as quartermaster and commissary. The following posts were occupied during the time Mason was in command in Arizona, as points of activity against the Apaches. They were in reality not forts, but mere cantonments. Fort Bowie, in Apache Pass; Camp Crittenden, near the Mexican border; Camp Lowell, at Tucson; Camp Grant, on the lower San Pedro; Fort Goodwin, near the Gila; Fort McDowell, on the Verde; Fort Whipple, near Prescott; Camp Date Creek, south of Prescott; and Camp Lincoln, on the upper Verde.

Mason concluded that the only certain hope of securing peace, eventually, was to occupy the region where the fighting Apaches had settled their women and children and had gathered and stored their provisions, and by destroying their *rancherías* and food supply in midwinter force them to seek peace. He was greatly hampered in his plans by delays in the bringing up of supplies, by the mustering out of volunteers just at the time the campaign should have been at its height, and by the great severity of the winter, with the thermometer sometimes far below zero and the snow one or two feet deep on the ground. But, in spite of all this, a number of successful scouts were made, and he proved a faithful and intelligent commanding officer.

In March, 1865, before Mason's arrival in Arizona, numerous Indians in the region about Fort Goodwin came in with a flag of truce and asked the commanding officer, Major James Gorman, to accept their surrender, as they were no longer able to hold out against the warfare of the whites. They were promised security and provisions. Then came the transfer of Arizona to the Department of California, with a long interim of confusion and uncertainty. Gorman wrote: "I was placed in the position of the man who drew the elephant in the lottery: with nothing to feed them, no transportation to send them to the reservation, and no orders to do so if I had. I made the best of it and told them they could go until I heard from the great chief." They did not leave, but others continued to come in. General Mason wrote in a report dated April 29, 1866: "I am satisfied that the only true policy is that at present adopted. By pressing the Indians from all points, and giving them a reservation where they can be protected and fed, we will succeed in the end. Already we have near nine hundred Indians on the reservation at Fort Goodwin, and they are reported as coming in daily."

In his report of 1866 to the Secretary of War, General McDowell refers to the fact that Apaches in the territory around Fort McDowell and Camp Lincoln had been punished so severely by the troops that they begged for peace. They were told that their petition would be granted if they would go to Fort Goodwin where well-disposed Indians were being cared for. But they said they could not do that, as they and the Indians already assembled at Fort Goodwin were enemies. Under these circumstances McDowell, uncertain whether they were sincere in their desire for peace, and too short of troops to chastise them further, granted their petition and ordered that they be brought in as prisoners to the vicinity of Fort McDowell, with the understanding that they were to plant crops and "keep the peace with the whites and their allies, the Gila Indians, the Pimas, and the Maricopas."

In the light of conditions described above, it is scarcely necessary to point out how citizens, soldiers, and Indians would have been relieved from much suffering and embarrassment if the Government at Washington had promptly and intelligently at this time both doubled the military forces operating in Arizona and set aside ample reservations in suitable locations, under wise and humane supervision, for the reception, care, and education of the Apaches whenever and wherever they sued for peace and desired to place themselves under Government supervision; for the same views held by Mason and McDowell were advocated and practiced by succeeding military commanders in Arizona (to the limited extent made possible by the Government) up to the time of General Crook, who finally actually made effective the policy of severe and persistent punishment of hostiles who choose to continue their trade of plunder and murder, rather than live peaceably on ample Government reservations provided for them.

In May or June, 1866, Mason was superseded, and in his place came two commanding officers—Colonel H. D. Wallen for the north, and Colonel Charles S. Lovell for the south. Conditions remained unchanged during the few months these officers were in command. Nor was anything of importance achieved during the incumbency of their successors, General J. I. Gregg and General T. L. Crittenden, who came early in 1867. Apache hostilities continued as usual.

The military situation in Arizona in 1867 is made clear through three military reports: that of Assistant-Inspector Roger Jones to General H. W. Halleck, commanding the Division of the Pacific, dated July 15, 1867; that of General Irvin McDowell, commanding the Department of California, commenting on the recommendations made by Colonel Jones; and that of General Halleck in his annual report, dated September 18, 1867.

After a tour of all the posts in Arizona Jones, in the report referred to above, recommended the following changes: first, the organization of Arizona into a separate Department; second, instead of the policy then in operation whereby small commands were dispersed widely over the Territory in small posts, the concentration of troops at a few large posts; third, provision for more mounted men; and fourth, the erection of storehouses, hospitals, and comfortable quarters for the men. The reason for each recommendation are set forth by the inspector with clarity and emphasis. Always, he says, it requires weeks to transmit orders from San Francisco to the distant and scattered commands in Arizona. As to the disposition of troops in the Territory, he maintains that the dispersing of soldiers into small commands entails both great waste and loss of military efficiency. He points out that it is impossible to cover so wide an extent of country with the small number of troops available. At each post many men are taken from active service because a good many men must be left to perform routine duties and to protect the post itself. Besides, these numerous posts provide soft berths for incompetent commanders and disbursing officers. The change suggested would surely be in the line of economy. He asserts that, as things are now, life and property were never so insecure on the roads and around the settlements. In support of his third point, he shows that effective operations against the Indians are impossible without more mounted soldiers. He thinks that infantrymen should be supplied with mounts and armed with the Spencer carbine; and that when on escort duty, mounted infantrymen should be armed with both revolvers and carbines. Finally, as to storehouses, hospitals, and quarters for the men, he contends that if the comfort, health, and welfare of the soldiers are not provided for, they grow discontented and inefficient. He asserts that money annually appropriated by Congress for such purposes is squandered by incompetent officers; and he drives home his criticisms by saying that in a region where the heat is more oppressive than in any other place he has ever known, soldiers are left to endure such misery as no Southern Negro or Irish peasant has ever been left to suffer. General McDowell's reply is no less vigorous and illuminating than the Inspector's charges. He states that he has not been unaware of the unsatisfactory conditions stressed by the Inspector; but he makes it clear that these conditions are not due to the causes set forth. The first two recommendations made by Jones had already been tried, but without success, as he would know had he been acquainted with the region for a longer time. When Arizona came under his command, McDowell says, he made it a District, appointed a general officer with full authority to command it, sent a brigade, numbering at one time thirty-six companies, more and better men than had ever served in Arizona before, and, for the most part, better officers than those now on duty in that Territory. The posts were then larger even than now recommended by the Inspector. Seven companies were stationed near old Fort Buchanan, four at Camp Grant, five at Fort Goodwin, four at Fort Whipple, and, at one time, six at Camp McDowell. The general in command had his headquarters "at Yuma, Prescott, and at the very place suggested by the assistant inspector-general, Sacaton." Two of his successors had their headquarters at Sacaton. Were conditions any better then than now? They were not.

McDowell proceeds to explain lucidly the real difficulties that had to be met in the war against the Apaches. First, "the Apache kills and robs as a means of livelihood. It is his normal condition." Second, "there is no confederation or alliance between the several tribes, frequently none between the bands of the same tribe." Third, "the hostile Indians all live in the most remote and inaccessible parts of the Territory, to which it is difficult for whites, under the most favorable circumstances, to penetrate." Fourth, the parts of the "Territory inhabited by the whites are seamed with mountain ridges, which, like the plains between them, are bare of trees, and from which the roads and the settlements are as plain to the sight of the stealthy Apache as is the pit of a theatre to the spectator in the gallery."

Fifth, the Apache is thus able "to make a sure calculation what to do, and what to avoid. He can from his secure lookout in the mountain side or top, see for miles off exactly how many persons are moving on the road, and how they are moving; he knows exactly where they must pass, where only they can get a drink of water; he never has occasion to take any risk, and it is the law never to take any." Sixth, "having been in this business for years, and having an exact knowledge of every ridge, pass, and ravine, and being entirely unencumbered with any luggage, camp or garrison equipage, and being able to go for days on an amount of food on which a white man would sink from exhaustion, he can strike and escape before anyone but the one stricken has knowledge of his presence; and if he is too hard pressed to carry off his booty, he has only to abandon it and gain one of the inevitable mountain ridges, and he is safe from any pursuit that a white man either on foot or horseback can make."

After giving examples of the difficulties listed above, and explaining how impossible it is for a large body of troops to practice the necessary secrecy and celerity to make successful attacks on the savages under such conditions, McDowell shows the unfairness of the assertion made by Jones that life and property in Arizona have never been so insecure as at present and that he had never known the roads so dangerous since he traveled through the Territory in 1857 and 1859. McDowell asserts that even if this statement were true, the reason would not be that offered by Jones. Rather, it would be due to the fact that then there were "fewer hostilities to guard against, and fewer, much fewer, points to guard." For when the Americans first came into Arizona the Apaches were friendly toward them and remained so until the time of the Civil War. There were then only two military posts in the region—Forts Buchanan and Breckinridge; and north of the Gila there were no white settlements. The Indians, at present constantly on the warpath against the whites of Arizona, were then ravaging and murdering in Sonora and Chihuahua.

McDowell reiterated his belief that nothing would be gained by mounting infantrymen; and, as to the inadequacy of storehouses, hospitals, and quarters for troops in Arizona, he declared orders had been given that under the direction of their officers "and by their own labor, for which they would receive extra pay, they were to make themselves comfortable, just as miners and prospectors were accustomed to do, by building huts of stone, wood, adobes, poles placed upright and filled in with clay, turf, sods, reeds, willows, etc." The reason that more permanent quarters were not built, McDowell explains, was because "it was not known, nor could it be ascertained at once where permanent posts would be required."

Reference to General Halleck's annual report dated September 18, 1867, written with Assistant-Inspector Jones' report and General McDowell's reply to it before him, enables us to round out the picture of military and civil conditions in Arizona at that time. Halleck states his belief that, while operations against hostile Indians would be more effective if "troops could be concentrated in larger posts, so as to have available a greater number for active campaigning in the country where they leave their families and obtain most of their supplies," to do this with the limited forces at hand would make it necessary "to withdraw all protection to many small settlements which have heretofore been often broken up, but are now in a more flourishing condition. . . . It has, therefore, been found that local military protection to the small agricultural districts in Arizona has not only reduced the Government expenses in such districts, but has had a most beneficial effect upon the Territory generally." So he approves McDowell's disposition of troops, and at the same time emphasizes the fact that more soldiers are needed in Arizona. "With an additional force of, say, one regiment of cavalry and one or two regiments of infantry in that country, which are really required there, we would be able to accomplish the double object of affording local protection, and, at the same time, of penetrating into the mountain homes of these savages."

In his report to the Secretary of War one year later, September, 1868, Halleck states that there are located in Arizona two full regiments of infantry and nine companies of cavalry; yet, both in his report of 1867 and in this one, he recommends that the military forces be increased by one or two regiments of infantry and 200 enlisted Indian scouts. He writes: "Officers are unanimous as to the value and usefulness of these scouts in the field."

In another part of his report Halleck says: "It is useless to try to negotiate with these Apache Indians. They will observe no treaties, agreements, or truces. With them there is no alternative but active and vigorous war, till they are completely destroyed, or forced to surrender as prisoners of war." Then he hits the nail squarely on the head: "But what is to be done with these Indians when captured or surrendered as prisoners of war? The agents of the Indian Bureau, as a general rule, refuse to receive them, and the military have no funds or authority to establish special military 'reservations' for them. To keep and to guard them at military posts will require the whole force of the garrison, and prevent the troops from operating in the field. We have no available funds with which to purchase seeds and agricultural implements, so that they can be made to contribute to their own support; and to keep them in idleness for any length of time has a most injurious effect. If permitted to hunt and fish for their own support, they are certain to desert and resume hostilities. It is hoped that some steps may be taken to modify our Indian system, at least in Arizona, so as to obviate these very serious difficulties in the reduction of the Apaches and the pacification of the Territory."

Early in 1868 General Thomas C. Devin assumed command in Arizona. He was an able and active officer and carried on vigorous and most difficult scouts into the very heart of the Apache territory south of the Mogollons, north of the Gila, and throughout the Salt River regions; but, in spite of his best efforts, he rarely found any Indians, though the troops came upon numerous deserted *rancherías*. He also broke new trails into hitherto almost inaccessible Apache haunts and made maps for the guidance of future expeditions. Sometime in 1868 General Devin broke up the temporary reservation at Fort Goodwin, established in 1866, because the Indians would not give up known murderers among them nor promise to settle down permanently. Also a temporary reservation at Camp Grant for Pinal Apaches was abandoned for the reason that these Indians would not agree to the required terms. Between April and September, 1868, the troops in Arizona made forty-six scouting expeditions; almost every Apache-infested part of the Territory was covered, but with meager results. Only thirty Indians were killed and seven captured in the course of these costly and difficult expeditions.

It was a very different story during the year 1869. Early in 1868 General E. O. C. Ord succeeded McDowell as Commander of the Department of California. His attitude toward the hostile Apaches was grim and forceful. He instructed his "troops to capture and root out the Apaches by every means, and to hunt them as they would wild animals." In his report of 1869 he states that his orders were carried out "with unrelenting vigor. . . . Over 200 have been killed, generally by parties who have trailed them for days and weeks into the mountain recesses, over snows, among gorges and precipices, lying in wait for them by day and following them by night. Many villages have been burned, large quantities of arms and supplies of ammunition, clothing, and provisions have been destroyed, a large number of horses and mules have been captured, and two men, twenty-eight women, and their twenty-four children taken prisoners; and though we have lost quite a number of soldiers, I think the Apaches have discovered they are getting the worst of it."

Sad to relate, the whites were far from getting the best of it. In Pima County alone, according to lists published in the newspapers during the year that ended July 17, 1869, more than fifty whites were slain by Apaches, and nearly a score wounded; and during the following year forty-seven were killed and six wounded.

The Apache situation is revealed in the clear light of day in the following moving story. It is taken from the report of General Ord to the Adjutant General of the Army, dated September 27, 1869. This is the same General Ord who had instructed his troops to "capture and root out the Apaches by every means and to hunt them as they would wild animals." Here is the extract: "Colonel John Green . . . in a recent scout into the White Mountains, a country of which we know but little, after destroying some villages, killing a number of warriors, and destroying a large quantity of corn, etc., having heard of a village thirty miles north, where the Indians were reported friendly, and anxious to appease the troops, sent Captain John Barry . . . to examine the matter, and if he found them concerned in hostilities, to destroy them." Thus he describes the result: "On the night of August 1, Captain Barry returned with his command, and reported that when he reached Miguel's village [Miguel was the Apache chief who voluntarily led the way to his *rancheria*] there was a white flag flying from every hut and every prominent point; that the men, women, and children came out to meet them, and went to work at once to cut corn for their horses, and showed such a spirit of delight at meeting them, that the officers united in saying that if they had fired on them they would have been guilty of cold-blooded murder; even my chief scout, Manuel, who has no scruples in such matters, and whose mind was filled with taking scalps when he left camp, said he could not have fired on them after what he saw. . . .

"Miguel reiterated that he wanted to go on a reservation where he could be protected, and Captain Barry repeated what I had previously told him—that he must go to Camp McDowell and see the district commander. He also gave him a letter for that purpose. Miguel promised to start on the following day and commenced to make preparations at once. . . . The Apaches have but few friends, and, I believe, no agent. Even the officers when applied to for information cannot tell them what to do. There seems to be no settled policy, but a general idea to kill them wherever found. I, also, am a believer in that, if we go for extermination, but I think, and I am sustained in my opinion by most of the officers accompanying my expedition, that if Miguel and his band were placed on a reservation properly managed, and had a military post to protect them, they would form a nucleus for the civilization of the Apaches, as they seem more susceptible of it than any tribe I have seen. I even believe that, if the Apache is properly managed, he could be used against the Apache, and so end the war in a short time. Miguel said that he had soldiers, and would place them at my disposal whenever I wanted them."

Be it said to the honor of General Ord that he instructed the district commander to send Colonel Green into the White Mountain Country to see whether it was fitted for a reservation for the friendly Apaches. General Ord in his report makes the following pertinent comment: "The earnestness with which the troops make war on the hostile Apaches is in proportion to the good will shown toward the inoffensive or friendly Indians. Many border white men, especially those that have been hunted,

or lost friends or relations by them, regard all Indians as
vermin, to be killed when met; and attacks upon and murder of
quiet bands, who in some instances have come in to aid in
pursuit of more hostile savages, is nothing unusual in Arizona.
One citizen is now in confinement, arrested by the troops, for
an attempt to murder a friendly Hualapai near Camp Mohave,
and dozens of them are at large now who have tried it and
succeeded. These citizens are not proceeded against by the
civil authorities of the country. Reservations to be at all safe
from such attacks in that country must be forbidden ground
to all white men, save the troops sent there to watch the Indians and guard them and officers of the Indian Bureau."

It seemed that the conscience of the nation was, at last, being aroused in protest against the injustices and cruelties so
long practiced against the Indians. The wise and humane
action of Colonel Green and General Ord related above was
only one indication among many that the people, both civil
and military, were awakening to a sense of their responsibility
toward the savages whom we first ruthlessly dispossessed of
their native heritage and then shamelessly oppressed and mistreated. The Apaches were the wildest, least known, and least
encountered, but now, even they, because of their fierce resistance and the awful atrocities of the inhuman war now being
waged between the white man and them, were attracting the
sympathetic attention of humanitarians, statesmen, and soldiers
alike. The dawn of peace and good will was not far off, but
there were still to be devastating storms and deluges of blood.

April 15, 1870, the new Department of Arizona was created.
The citizens of Arizona had long desired this action and were
hopeful that the military would now be able to curb the Apaches.
May 3 General George Stoneman was appointed department
commander, and early in July he set up his headquarters at
Fort Whipple. Stoneman had passed through Arizona in 1846

with the Mormon Battalion, and though just out of West
Point, had discharged his duties with distinction. Later he won
the rank of Brevet Major General for long and gallant service during the Civil War. A brave, capable, humane officer,
he was highly qualified for his new post. Yet within a few
months he was the most unpopular, bitterly criticized commander Arizona had ever had; and during the preceding six
years she had had many. The awakened East censured Stoneman for killing wild Apaches wherever found, whether good
or bad; he was denounced and reviled in Arizona because he
did not proceed more swiftly with the business of extermination—the only policy at that time at all popular with Arizonians. To make matters worse for the new commander, the
Government had just inaugurated a program of severe retrench-
ment in Army expenses. General J. M. Schofield, Commander
of the Division of the Pacific, in his annual report gave notice
that the meager appropriations for the quartermaster department would require great reduction of expenses in Arizona, the
withdrawal of a portion of the troops, the abandoning of unnecessary posts, the breaking up of expensive depots that could be
spared, and general economy in administration wherever possible.

What Stoneman actually did during his brief year of command was: to continue the policy of placing Indians who showed
a friendly disposition upon reservations and supplying them
with food, blankets, and instruction in the ways of civilization;
to build permanent military roads into the wilds inhabited by
the Apaches; to abandon, or recommend the abandonment of
ten of the eghteen posts in the Territory; to discharge as many
employees as could be dispensed with, reducing the number
"from thousands to as many hundreds"; to cancel contracts by
which the Government was deliberately being bled; to set the
soldiers at work at Camps Bowie, Date Creek, Yuma, Hualapai,

TYPES FROM ARIZONA

Drawing by Frederick Remington. From *Harper's Weekly*, Aug. 21, 1886.
University of Arizona Collection

GENERAL GEORGE CROOK ON THE TRAIL

Drawing by Frederick Remington, in the *Century Magazine*. Used by permission of D. Appleton–Century Company, Inc.

LIEUTENANT ROSS'S ATTACK

Drawing by Frederick Remington, in "On the Border with Crook." Used by permission of Charles Scribner's Sons

Verde, and Thomas building quarters; and, finally, to carry on vigorously the main work required of him, the chasing and killing of recalcitrant Apaches. The troops were kept constantly on the move, trying to forestall attacks of the enemy and pursuing and punishing marauding Apaches with relentless vigor. Most daring and resourceful among a score of officers, indefatigable in energy and courage, who distinguished themselves during this period were Bourke, Ross, Winters, Sanford, Russell, Carrol, Almy, and above all, Lieutenant Howard B. Cushing who died in desperate action, May 5, 1871. No man during this period had done so much as he to quell and chastise the militant Apaches. Indeed, in view of the fact that up to this time the policy of killing Indians was the supreme test of a commander's success, Stoneman deserved a high rating; for by October, 1870, in the numerous deadly expeditions led by the officers named above, two hundred Apaches had been slain.

Nevertheless, before the beginning of the year 1871, the attacks upon Stoneman and the Army by citizens and the newspapers were scathing, scornful, and bitter in the extreme. Bare facts alone cannot make clear the state of mind in Arizona at this time. The modern reader must view the situation with a sympathetic and imaginative mind if he would know the whole truth. No one was wholly to blame except bad white men and bad Indians. The suffering and death inflicted upon the settlers of Arizona had driven them to frenzy, fear, and fiery hatred. During the year that Stoneman was in command, the Apaches had renewed their attacks with the most deadly intent. They struck simultaneously at points far apart. The stage stations, both east and west of Tucson, on the San Pedro, at the Cienega, and near the Picacho were attacked; Pete Kitchen's ranch near the border was raided and his boy killed in the field; Tucson itself was taken by surprise and a large number of beeves and work oxen were driven into the mountains; a mail carrier was killed near San Xavier; the Paymaster's clerk and one of his escorts were killed on the road between Camp Reno and Camp McDowell; A. J. Jackson was murdered at San Pedro; and a Mexican was killed and scalped near Fort Wallen. On Portrero Creek six Mexicans were attacked and killed; the ranch of Gardner, near Sonoita, was raided, his herd of cattle was stampeded, a Mexican boy was captured, and David Holland killed; at Davis Springs, not far from Camp Crittenden, Peter Riggs, Thomas Venable, and a Mexican were killed and goods valued at six thousand dollars were burned; a Mexican wagon train was attacked on the road between Phoenix and Wickenburg, one teamster was killed and three wounded, and a horse and thirty-two cattle were stolen; in an attack upon a wagon train near Camp McDowell, George King was killed, two men wounded, and twenty-five mules stolen; two prominent men, Kennedy and Israel, were killed about twenty-five miles northeast of Tucson by a large party of Apaches, their teams captured and their wagon train and valuable goods burned; and, finally, most tragic of all, a party of Mexicans returning to Sonora after a visit to relatives in Tucson, were massacred near the border. A beautiful young Mexican girl, Doña Trinidad, was one of the victims. The above is a typical, but only partial, list of the atrocities visited upon the inhabitants of Arizona during the incumbency of General Stoneman.

In order to form a rounded and correct picture of conditions in Arizona at this time it is necessary for us to consider some very prevalent sins and shortcomings of the white population. There were staunch and honest citizens in Arizona at that time —but their number was all too few. On the other hand, there were numerous cruel and depraved men. Some of the finest, most honorable Americans in Arizona at this period were Army officers, and they, as well as other honest and decent white men, have made it clear to us that innumerable worthless citizens of that day exceeded in vileness and brutality any outrage ever traced to an Apache. Residents of Arizona—especially politicians, corrupt contractors, and some of the Indians agents—regularly robbed the Government and cheated the Indians.

In his report of September 28, 1869, General Ord states that "at one post inspected by me, I found that its garrison of eighty-six men had lost fifty-four men by desertion, and every deserter had carried off a good horse and repeating rifle, worth together from $150 to $300 at the post. These horses and arms are generally sold to citizens in the vicinity for half or a third of their value, so that the citizen finds more profit in encouraging desertion by buying the deserter's arms, horse, and clothing than in arresting him for the small reward of about $20 in gold. . . . If the paymasters and quartermasters of the army were to stop payment in Arizona, a great majority of the white settlers would be compelled to quit it. Hostilities are therefore kept up with a view to protecting inhabitants, most of whom are supported by the hostilities. Of course, their support being derived from the presence of troops, they are continually asking for more." Stoneman affirmed when he reduced the number of posts in the department that the only hardship involved was the money loss to the people in the vicinity of the deserted posts, as they would "be unable, as heretofore, to dispose of their hay, etc., to the Government at the usual and exorbitant prices." At Fort Thomas a citizen had contracted to furnish five hundred tons of hay at eighty-two dollars a ton in gold. When Stoneman took command, this agreement was canceled, and a contract entered into for two hundred tons at forty-four dollars in paper money.

Joseph Fish, an Arizona pioneer, in his well-known unpublished manuscript, writes: "Of all the contractors of early days, it is hardly possible to find one who remained in the Territory. As soon as they made their money, they went east or to San Francisco to live. Not one of this patriotic fraternity cared a fig for Arizona. The people were taught to oppose agencies where the Apaches worked and were fed. They feared that it would reduce the military force for one thing, and that it would suspend campaigns and lead to an inactive state of war."

As a climax to the whole situation described in this chapter came the Camp Grant Massacre of April 30, 1871. The story of this deed constitutes the blackest page in the Anglo-Saxon records of Arizona. In February, 1871, one hundred and fifty Arivaipa Apaches led by Eskiminzin, their chief, came to Old Camp Grant and expressed an earnest desire to live at peace. They declared that they were not hostile to the whites; that for five years they had been living in the mountains like wildcats, in fear of the troops; and that many of their number had perished from exposure and starvation. Now they were very poor, without food or clothing, and many were old and sick. Here in the fertile Arivaipa Canyon, near its junction with the San Pedro, before the coming of the Americans, they had for many years built their wickiups, planted their crops of corn, and lived happily. They begged that they might return to their native fields under the protection of the troops.

Lieutenant Royal Whitman, who was then in command at Camp Grant, was convinced that they were in desperate straits and had a sincere desire to live at peace. He had no authority to receive them or to deal with them, but told them he would consult his superiors to find out what could be done, and, meantime, that they should settle down in their old fields near the post where he would supply them with food and blankets. March 1 they came back to the spot that had been their home for generations—sixty warriors poorly armed, and ninety children, women, and old men. Whitman was a drunkard and, no doubt, was crooked in his dealings with the Government, but he had a warm heart and a genuine interest in these good, well-disposed Indians. He rode over to their camp frequently; he knew them by name—men, women, and children; and he won their complete confidence and friendship. The influence he exerted over them was really remarkable. Other Arivaipas, singly, and in small bands, gradually came in and settled near the post, and they were all regularly cared for and supervised by Whitman. Among them there may have been some hostiles who used this improvised reservation as a safe rendezvous before and after a raid; but it has never been proven that there were such; and the other white men at Camp Grant, as well as reliable pioneer writers of that day, give it as their opinion that these Indians were sincere and peaceful.

Meantime, bloody and destructive raids were constantly occurring near Tucson, around Tubac, and in other parts of southern Arizona. At each new outrage the settlers grew more frantic. They had never approved of this irregular settlement of Indians near Camp Grant. They declared that renegades were continually slipping away from this reservation, committing some new outrage, and then returning to be fed and protected by Whitman until they were ready for another outbreak. Late in April a small band of Indians drove off a number of horses and cattle from San Xavier and killed a man. The people of Tucson and San Xavier declared that the outlaws were from Eskiminzin's band. Excited crowds in Tucson came together in public meetings demanding vengeance; and a committee of three or four leading citizens was sent to interview General Stoneman, then near Florence, with the demand that the Arivaipa Indians be punished and that the settlers be given protection. General Stoneham replied that he had a very limited number of troops at his disposal; that they were constantly in the field in pursuit of bad Apaches; that Tucson was the most populous center in the department; and that its citizens would have to protect themselves as best they could.

This answer supplied oil to the fire of their rage. A secret movement was at once set on foot to destroy, root and branch, the Indians on the Camp Grant Reservation. Extermination —nothing less—was the end and aim of these "leading citizens," all of whom had always held that club and gun only could end the Apache menace. The two men who took the initiative in the infamous affair, Jesus M. Elias and W. S. Oury, were two of the most militant and influential pioneers in Arizona.

The expedition left Tucson secretly in small parties in order to avoid suspicion on the part of the military. Some miles out of Tucson on the road to Camp Grant guards were stationed to turn back any rider who might be sent to warn the troops at Camp Grant of what was afoot. The party rendezvoused, April 28, in the Pantano wash, east of Tucson. There were one hundred and forty-six in all: five Americans in addition to W. S. Oury, the leader; forty-eight Mexicans; and ninety-two Papago Indians. A wagonload of arms, ammunition, and provisions had been supplied by the Adjutant-General of the Territory. Leaving the Rillito at four P.M., the company went by Cabadilla Pass, between the Rincons and the Santa Cruz, and lay hidden most of the next day on the San Pedro. Marching all night they reached the encampment of the Indians just at dawn; and with clubs, rifles, and revolvers fell upon the Indians before they were fully awakened from their slumbers. The camp was unarmed and most of the men were away hunting in the mountains; but men, women, and children, utterly dazed and surprised, were brained by the Papagos with clubs, or shot down as they ran by Mexicans and Americans. One hundred and eight Arivaipas were slaughtered during the course of a few minutes. Only eight of this number were men. Twenty-nine children were "spared" and taken by Tucson citizens or sold by the Papagos into Sonora as slaves. Two of these children escaped and five were later recovered from Arizonians. The fate of the rest was never known.

From the point of view of the avengers the expedition was a great success. The "red devils" had all been killed or captured; the army had been outwitted; and not a man in the punitive expedition had been hurt "to mar the full measure of the triumph," in the words of Oury. The deep damnation of the deed cried out trumpet-tongued to the people throughout the nation. In his report of that year General Schofield referred to this ferocious incident as "no less barbarous than those which characterize the Apache." Captain John G. Bourke writes: "The incident, one of the saddest and most terrible in our annals, is one over which I would gladly draw the veil." Historians who were residents of Arizona in the middle seventies—for example, Joseph Fish and John P. Clum—with bitter indignation, stamp the outrage upon their pages in all its gory horror. President Grant, in a letter to the Governor of the Territory, declared that he would place Arizona under martial law unless those who engaged in the massacre were promptly brought to trial before a civil court. One hundred and four of those who took part in the affair were indicted and tried before a Federal judge in Tucson. After being out only twenty minutes, the jury exonerated them. The majority of leading white men in Arizona at the time approved, or at least condoned, the action of their fellow citizens. No Arizona judge or jury would have convicted a white man for killing an Apache.

BIBLIOGRAPHY

Annual Reports of the United States War Department, 1868, 1869, 1870–1871.

Arizona Daily Star, June 19, 1910.

BANCROFT, H. H. *Arizona and New Mexico. Works*, Vol. XVII. San Francisco.

BOURKE, JOHN G. *On the Border with Crook.* New York, Scribners, 1891.

Chronological List of Actions with Indians in Arizona and New Mexico. January, 1866 to January, 1891. A.G.O., War Department, Old Records Section. Washington, D.C. Supplied by Charles Morgan Wood.

CLUM, WOODWORTH. *Apache Agent.* Boston, Houghton Mifflin, 1936.

FARISH, THOMAS EDWIN. *History of Arizona*, Vols. V and VIII. Phoenix.

HAMMOND, GEORGE P. *After the Civil War, Wanted—A Policy.* Unpublished ms. supplied by Charles Morgan Wood.

HAMMOND, GEORGE P. *General Stoneman in Charge.* Unpublished ms. supplied by Charles Morgan Wood.

House of Representatives, Executive Documents, I, Part 2, 41st Congress, 2d Session.

House of Representatives, Executive Documents, 42d Congress, 2d Session.

House of Representatives, Miscellaneous Documents. Nos. 18 and 19, 38th Congress, 2d Session.

Journals of the Third Legislative Assembly, Territory of Arizona. Prescott, 1867.

Journals of the Fifth Legislative Assembly, Territory of Arizona. Tucson, 1869.

SCHMECKEBIER, LAURENCE F. *The Office of Indian Affairs.* Baltimore, Johns Hopkins Press, 1927.

CHAPTER X

Crook, the Terrible and the Just

THE Camp Grant Massacre forced the Apache situation in Arizona upon the attention of the nation. No sane and sensitive mind could longer ignore or look with complacency upon such a state of affairs as was blazoned to the world by this shocking incident. For a long time the cruel treatment of the Apaches in Arizona had caused stirrings of conscience in the souls of good and informed citizens throughout the nation; and now there was a widespread belief that the Apaches were not having a square deal. It was becoming more and more apparent that the Government itself was responsible for deeds that were a stench in the nostrils of the civilized world. The result of this aroused feeling among people of humanitarian instincts was the creation at Washington (with the strong approval of President Grant) of the Permanent Board of Peace Commissioners, the object of which was to put an end to the injustices and cruelties visited upon the Indians and to introduce a sane, uniform, benevolent plan for the improvement of the red man.

Very prominent among Christian citizens who favored the Commission and the objects it sought to attain was Vincent Colyer—a Quaker, an ardent friend of the Indian and a believer in his inherent goodness. He was one of the members of the Peace Commission; and him President Grant sent to New Mexico and Arizona with plenary power to locate the nomadic

Indian tribes in New Mexico and Arizona upon suitable reservations, to place them under the control of the properly designated officers of the Indian Department, and to supply them with such food and clothing as they might need. Letters from Grant instructed both the Secretary of War and the Secretary of the Interior to clothe Colyer with such enlarged powers as would enable him to carry out the object of his mission as stated above. Already Congress had appropriated seventy thousand dollars "to collect the Apache Indians of Arizona and New Mexico on reservations, furnish them with subsistence and other necessary articles, and to promote peace and civilization among them."

Colyer reached the Apache country in late August. First he interviewed Colonel Nathaniel Pope, Superintendent of Indian Affairs in New Mexico, and with his aid and approval located the Southern Apaches, who inhabited the region about Ojo Caliente, on a reservation adjacent to the Tulerosa River. Next he proceeded to Camp Apache, Arizona, where he was cordially received by Colonel John Green, the commanding officer. Here, September 7, 1871, he established Camp Apache Reservation. September 8, he set out for Camp Grant, where he arrived the thirteenth. He approved the reservation already established there and extended and carefully defined its limits. In consultation with Colonel N. A. M. Dudley in command of Camp McDowell, he established a temporary reservation five miles square at that post. At Camp Verde, October 3, he set aside a reservation for the Apache-Mohaves. With the approval of General George Crook, who had recently been placed in command of the Department of Arizona, he established a mile-square temporary reservation at Beale Springs for the Hualapai Indians, and one of like extent at Camp Date Creek for the Apache-Mohaves of that region.

Though Colyer came with authority direct from the Presi-

dent of the United States and carried credentials from the
Secretary of the Interior and the Secretary of War, Governor
A. P. K. Safford thought it necessary for him to issue a proclamation to the people of Arizona, under date of August 15,
1871, in which the following astonishing sentences occur:
"I . . . call upon the officers and citizens of the Territory to
receive said Commissioners with kindness and hospitality; to
give them all the aid and information . . . within your power
and knowledge. They have been selected with a view to their
integrity and humanity of purpose, and sent here in the legal
performance of duty. If they come among you entertaining
erroneous opinions upon the Indian question and the condition
of affairs in the Territory, then, by kindly treatment, and fair,
truthful representation, you will be enabled to convince them
of their errors."

The two leading papers of the Territory, the *Tucson Citizen*
and the *Arizona Miner*, viewed Colyer's mission with bitterness and contempt. John Marion, editor of the *Arizona Miner*,
in editorials written previous to Colyer's arrival, referred to the
Commissioner as "a cold-blooded scoundrel," "a red-handed
assassin," and printed other endearing terms concerning him
of like import. He wrote: "We ought, in justice to our murdered dead, to dump the old devil into the shaft of some mine,
and pile rocks upon him until he is dead. A rascal who comes
here to thwart the efforts of military and citizens to conquer
a peace from our savage foe, deserves to be stoned to death, like
the treacherous, black-hearted dog that he is. . . ." The
editorials in the *Citizen* were similar in tone, though they fell
a little short in vituperative eloquence. There is small wonder
that Mr. Colyer, after reading many editorials and articles of
this kind, showed no great eagerness to interview the citizens
of the Territory with respect to his mission. He tells us that
he was invited by gentlemen from Prescott to address a public

meeting in that city on the Indian question, and that they assured him they would "protect him with their rifles and revolvers." He wrote to the Prescott committee that, since his official duties were wholly with the Indians and the officers of the Government who had them in charge, he saw no sufficient reason why he should address a public meeting in which he "should have to be protected with rifles and revolvers."

To tell the truth, Colyer was as contemptuous toward leading citizens of Arizona as they were full of scorn for him. He was a partisan—committed heart and soul to the cause of the Indians. The proved evils that he had uncovered looked so gross and wicked to him that he did not desire to talk with white men who had committed or defended them. He was in Arizona merely to carry out officially the instructions of the President, conveyed to him by the Secretary of the Interior— that is, "to locate the nomadic tribes upon suitable reservations," to bring "them under the control of the proper officers of the Indian Department," and "to supply them with necessary subsistence, clothing and whatever else" they needed. Everywhere he went he was received in a very friendly and sympathetic spirit by the Army officers in command of the various posts. In reality, some of these officers had been among the first to urge upon their superiors and the Government just and humane action in dealing with these wild but bewildered tribes they had been ordered to exterminate. Moreover, they, too, had borne the abuse of the citizens and been cut with the vindictive lash of public scorn.

Colyer was honest in purpose and a true philanthropist, but he was prejudiced and intolerant, and his knowledge of the situation he was set to remedy was inadequate. He showed in his report that the Apaches in Arizona, even those to whom rations had been issued, were in an almost starving condition, with no alternative but to steal or die. One-half of all the savages who had been at war with the Americans, through his efforts, were gathered upon reservations. They numbered about four thousand and included most of the Tontos, many of the Coyoteros and Pinaleños, and all of the Apache-Mohaves and Apache-Yumas.[1] Those who were still hostile and were determined to fight to the end were a small number of Mescaleros and Pinaleños, the Apache-Mohaves under Del Shay, and the Chiricahuas.

Colyer's decisions and adjustments were approved by Grant; and General Sherman, in command of the Army, gave orders that they should be permanent. However, some of them soon had to be set aside by General Howard, who came to Arizona a little later with plenary powers from President Grant as a Peace Commissioner to rectify mistakes that had been made and to make peace with Cochise, chief of the Chiricahuas. Howard was a broader and more experienced philanthropist than was Colyer, and was able to achieve more lasting results.

As has been noted above, Crook assumed command of the troops in Arizona only two or three months previous to the arrival of Colyer. He came unannounced and unknown, "without baggage and without fuss." Not even the stage driver knew who this lean, quiet, muscular passenger was. He took up his task as unobtrusively as a Pinkerton detective. First he talked with his friend Governor Safford. Before sunset of the June day on which he arrived in Tucson, orders had been issued to every officer in the southern division of his Department to report to him at once in Tucson. He listened much, but said little. He drew full and minute information from the Governor, from Army officers, and from the citizens of Tucson. He listened attentively and reflected deeply, but gave no inkling whatever of his own plans or policies. His supreme policy (and habit) was to listen to everything and say noth-

---

[1] Detached members of the Mohave and Yuma tribes living with the Apaches.

ing. His reticence was always superb—to some it was exasperating.

Crook was every inch a soldier. He knew no such thing as ease. "The flinty and steel couch of war" was his "thrice-driven bed of down." He was always fit for march, battle, or bivouac. No soldier ever surpassed him in energy, endurance, and indifference to exposure. He used neither liquor nor tobacco, and no soldier ever heard a profane or obscene word from his lips. He was as little given to show and outward insignia as was Grant. He rarely wore a uniform when it was not obligatory that he do so. In Arizona, no matter how hot, in duck suit and white canvas helmet, he rode everywhere on horseback or on his powerful mule "Apache." On one of his terrible northern marches, he wore Government boots, corduroy trousers, a heavy woolen shirt, an old style Army blouse, a brown felt hat, and an old Army overcoat with red lining and a wolfskin collar. He was a shade over six feet in stature, erect, spare, sinewy, and muscular. His head was clean-cut and his features sternly chiseled; his bluish-gray eyes were deep-set; his nose prominent; his mouth large and firm, but not hard; his complexion ruddy; and his hair light brown. Decision, sagacity, tenacity of purpose were written in every feature. He was modest and reticent to a fault—somewhat too severe and brusque in speech, also. But he was not unkind. Children were not afraid of him; and there was no man—soldier or savage—so poor or ignorant that he could not gain access to him. Under all the quietness and unpretentiousness of his exterior, "manifesting itself even to a stranger, there was the power, the awful force of a man who *does*."

By July 11 Crook was on the march at the head of a force consisting of five companies of cavalry and a large body of scouts, trailers, and packers. The immediate objective was not battle, but a strenuous practice campaign. Crook desired to study the country, harden his men, create *esprit de corps,* and build up a pack-train service that could follow at the heels of the fighting men anywhere. The line of march was to be by Fort Bowie, to Fort Apache, thence over the Mogollons to Camp Verde, and finally on to Fort Whipple and Prescott— a distance of about seven hundred miles through the country of the enemy, over burning mesa, through dense forests, and over uncharted mountains.

This long, hard march served its purpose well. It was a true school for soldier and officer alike. Crook came to know his command—its strength and its weakness—and the command came to know and respect its leader. He made it clear to his subordinates that he wanted them to take note of everything; and on his part he was ever alert to learn all that he could about the trend of the mountain ranges, the source and direction of each stream, the location of water holes, the quantity and quality of grasses to be found, the meaning of the smoke signals they saw now and then, and the names, characteristics, and possible uses of the plants and animals native to the region. Picket duty was a constant requirement; for not only did the smoke signals indicate the presence of hostile Apaches, but twice during the march cavalry detachments came upon the embers of campfires of raiding bands that had been disturbed in the midst of their feasting; and once Crook and some of his officers who were riding in advance of the cavalry were shot at by Indians in ambush.

Humor, romance, and tragedy go with the mule wherever he plods his weary way. The mule never had a better friend than Crook. He has been called "the daddy of the army mule," and his men were fond of saying that he was "pack-mule wise." No other military leader ever gave so much time and thought to the perfecting of his pack train. He knew that when the final test came, victory or defeat would lie in his transportation system; for, just as water can rise no higher than its source, so men in the field can advance and fight only as food and ammunition are delivered to them at the front. The pack train he had made one of the chief studies of his life. He had familiarized himself with the good results achieved by the highly organized transportation systems of Spain, Peru, Mexico, and the mining communities of the Southwest; and now, at the beginning of his campaign in Arizona, he set about the task of bringing his pack train to the highest possible state of efficiency as patiently and intelligently as the scientist carries on an experiment in his laboratory. Nothing was too good for his pack train; in the interest of economy he saw to it that every article used was of the best material. Drunken and cruel packers were removed, and sober, decent men put in their places. Mules must be of uniform size and proved fitness for the particular country in which a campaign was to be carried on. Raw-boned, sore-backed, abused, and nondescript animals were not to be tolerated. Every mule must be properly shod and fed and groomed; and each mule was to have his own pack saddle specially fitted to him. Crook spent much of his time in close observation of the pack train; and he often talked with the packers on the march and around the campfire. As a result of all this, his pack trains were the best to be found in the army. A Government circular stated that the average burden for a mule should not be more than one hundred and seventy-five pounds. But the animals in Crook's command carried an average of more than three hundred pounds; and they suffered less, throve better, and bore up longer in hard campaigns over the rough Arizona trails than any other mules in the service.

In the lovely region about Camp Grant in the White Mountains many Apaches under such well-behaved chiefs as Miguel, Pedro, and Alchise, hunted, raised corn, lived happily, and gave every evidence that they desired to walk in "the white man's road." Crook called the leading men about him and talked to them in very simple, straightforward words, about his plans and purposes for them. He told them that he never spoke with a divided tongue, and urged them to listen with both ears. His object was peace, not war; it was simple wisdom for all the Indians to live at peace with the white man, for white people were sure to come in increasing numbers. The best thing for the Apaches to do was to plant crops and raise cattle, sheep, and horses, as the country would soon be full of white people, and there would not be enough game to supply everyone. He assured them that so long as they behaved themselves they would be protected by the soldiers; and he requested them to carry his words to the Indians who were living wild and raiding the white settlements. He wanted to treat everyone alike. The past would be forgotten and a fresh beginning would be made. There were good Indians and bad Indians, good whites and bad. After this Indians and white men were to be treated alike. The good were to be protected and the bad punished. He explained that it was important for peaceable Indians to help control the bad ones, for when there were Indians on the warpath, there was constant danger that the innocent might be mistaken for the guilty and punished. So, just as white men do, the well-disposed Indian should help run down and bring to justice the wicked ones. He was now doing his best to find out who were eager for peace and who were determined to remain hostile. Everyone must decide now. After this it was to be either peace or war; and those who refused to come onto the reservations and remain there quietly, he would hunt down and kill. He would see that all had a chance to work. They could grow their own crops, raise their own flocks and herds, and if they raised more than they needed, he would see to it that they got a fair price for what they had to sell. In this way they would become well-to-do, like the white man, and would be able to send their children to school. He told them it was best, in order to make sure there would be no misunderstanding, that all of his words and theirs should be written down. He said, too, that since the Indians did not know the white man's ways, it would be better for the soldiers to remain with them on their reservations to explain things and protect them. To the wise, friendly White Mountain chiefs and their people, these simple and sincere words seemed "good medicine."

It was just at this time, while Crook was making his march from Tucson to Prescott and getting ready to strike a decisive blow, that President Grant, as previously related, was trying to find a peaceful solution to the Indian troubles in Arizona through the labors of Vincent Colyer of the Indian Peace Commission and General O. O. Howard, his own special representative. Crook cooperated courteously and fully with both Colyer and Howard, though he had little confidence that the outcome of the peace negotiations would be satisfactory. Meantime, he had continued to make quiet preparations for a stern campaign against incorrigible hostiles.

By the autumn of 1872 it had become apparent to everyone that nothing but force could put a stop to Apache outrages in Arizona, and that Crook was the man for the hour. Within a year from the time that Colyer had entered the Territory the Indians had made more than fifty new raids and had killed more than forty citizens. The Wickenburg massacre in which Loring, a brilliant young scientist, and a number of other stage passengers were attacked and murdered in the most cold-blooded manner, was the most sensational of these raids. At the Date Creek Agency not far from Wickenburg the Government was feeding about a thousand Apache-Yuma Indians, together with a few Apache-Mohaves. These Indians were not altogether trustworthy. Now and then some of them would raid and steal. Crook satisfied himself that the terrible Wickenburg massacre was the work of bad Indians from the Date Creek Agency and with grim determination he set about ferreting out the criminals.

The task he had undertaken was not an easy one to accomplish, as even the well-disposed members of the band were, of course, loath to report on their own kin. For weeks and months Crook kept watch and followed every clue. Some of the Date Creek Indians were related to the Hualapais, and through this tribe Crook received a friendly warning that the next time he visited Date Creek he and his escort were to be killed. Owing to the sudden death of the officer in command at Date Creek, Crook made a trip to that post sooner than he had intended or the Indians had expected. Word was sent to the Indians that he would have a talk with them at a time and place fixed by him. He appeared at the appointed time, unaccompanied by soldiers. But along with him, in a casual sort of way, came a dozen of his packers—hardy, seasoned fighting men of the West—armed with knives and revolvers, and ready for instant action in case of treachery. The guilty Indians had laid their plot carefully. After the talk had gone on for some time in the most friendly manner, the leader, who sat in the middle of the semicircle opposite Crook and his party, asked for some tobacco; and when it had been given to him he began rolling a cigarette. As the General knew, this was the prearranged signal for an attack on him and his men.

At the first puff of the cigarette the fellow next to the leader raised his carbine and shot at Crook. Lieutenant Ross, on the alert, struck the rascal's arm; so the bullet missed its mark. There was a deadly set-to. Hank Hewitt, a powerful man, seized the chief conspirator by both ears and beat his head against the rocks until he was unconscious. Some of the band were killed and a number were wounded; but most of them made their escape and came together later at the head of the Santa Maria River where five canyons unite. Crook sent word to them that unless they all came in he would be compelled to hunt down and destroy the whole band. No reply came back; so plans were made to pursue and punish them. They naturally expected the attack from the direction of Date Creek, but "the Gray Fox" let a considerable time pass; and then just as they were beginning to think they were safe, a command led by Hualapai scouts attacked them from an unexpected quarter, killing, wounding, or capturing more than forty.

Since hostilities were bound to continue, it was a good thing that the Wickenburg murders and the attempt on Crook's life were spectacular; for the East now woke up and saw conditions as they really existed. In the fall of 1872 Crook received orders to bring all the renegade Indians onto the reservations and to guard them closely. So he began the closing-in and wiping-up campaign that he had long been preparing for. Concerted action was to begin about November 15. A number of separate commands, each one to be directed by an experienced officer, were to set out from widely separated posts and all move toward the Tonto Basin. Each command was to find and fight the Indians wherever possible until they submitted or were destroyed. The hostiles were to be kept constantly on the the move, so that if they escaped death in battle they would perish from privation, fatigue, or cold among the snow-clad mountains where they were to be driven. Crook himself, while leaving each unit free to act upon its own initiative, was to move from point to point along the front as occasion demanded. Major Randall was to operate from Camp Apache, Major Price from Date Creek, Major MacGregor from Fort Whipple, Major Mason from Camp Hualapai, Captain Burns from Camp McDowell, Colonel Carr from Camp Verde, and Major

Brown from Camp Grant. Each expedition was to have its own scouts and its own pack train, made up of picked and hardened men. After reaching the Tonto Basin, the common objective, the various columns were to radiate in every direction, and thus from new angles cover again the country already traversed. Crook gave orders that women and children should be protected wherever possible; that prisoners should be well treated and, if possible, enlisted as scouts. Every trail was to be followed to its end; there was to be no falling back; if the enemy could not be pursued on horseback, the men were to proceed on foot. No sacrifice was to be considered too great.

The campaign arranged for, Crook set out at once for Camp Apache where he enlisted a force of Apache scouts. From Camp Apache he went to old Camp Grant by long and most difficult marches. At once he dispatched the column at Camp Grant under Major Brown to harry the Mescal, Pinal, Superstition, and Matitzal Mountains, with Camp McDowell as a terminal. Major Brown led two troops of the Fifth Cavalry and thirty Apache scouts. With this command went Captain Taylor and Lieutenants Bourke, Almy, and Ross—officers unsurpassed for bravery and endurance. General Crook had given personal attention to every detail that might enter into the success of this expedition. He had secretly gathered minute information from the Apache scouts who knew the whole region the troops were now about to enter. The first object was to find the *rancheria* of the brutal chief, Chuntz, and wipe it from the earth. A short time before this Chuntz had killed a little Mexican boy at Camp Grant in cold blood. After finding and destroying the stronghold of Chuntz, Major Brown's force was to ferret out the *rancheria* of Del Shay in the region of the Matitzal range. Brown's way was through the roughest and rockiest mountains—now over ridges and through defiles of granite and porphyry, and again through thickets of cholla,

Spanish bayonet, scrub oak, and manzanita. There was snow on the mountains, and the cold was intense. The scouts were kept far in advance of the soldiers, and it was apparent at once that they were brave and trustworthy. The *rancheria* of Chuntz was found and destroyed, but he and his band escaped. No trace was found of them; they had fled the region. December 25 Brown's troops united with Burns' command that had left Camp McDowell a week before and had scoured the Matitzal range, killing six Apaches, capturing two, and destroying the *rancheria* where these Indians were in hiding. Those who escaped fled to a cave in the Salt River Canyon where a few days later one of the most terrible battles in Apache history was to be fought by the combined command of Brown and Burns.

Major Brown, on the evening of December 27, 1872, first made known to his officers and men that Crook's chief object in sending out this expedition was to find the cave alluded to above. Nanteje, one of the Apache scouts, had known this stronghold from his boyhood. He was willing to lead the troops to it; but he explained that the march would have to be made by night and that if their approach was discovered not a man could escape. Only the hardiest soldiers were permitted to take part in the attack. All the rest were ordered to remain with the pack train and keep strict watch for hostiles. The party was to start at eight o'clock and go on foot across a rough projection of the Matitzals into the Salt River Canyon. Food and equipment were reduced to the smallest possible compass, but an abundant supply of extra cartridges was carried by each soldier in the blanket that he had slung about him. The command moved slowly and cautiously forward during the long night; and as the first gray tinge of dawn appeared, twelve or fifteen of the best sharpshooters were sent a little way in advance. These men had descended the precipitous face of the canyon several hundred feet when, in a small open space in front of the cave, they came upon a band of Apache warriors who had just returned from a raid on the Gila River. They were dancing around a little fire where several squaws were crouched in the act of preparing food for the hungry raiders. Ross and his men fired on the camp and killed six braves. The survivors, in consternation, rushed for the cave; and Major Brown, apprised by the terrific noise that a serious action had begun, hurried Bourke forward with forty men who were close at hand. Down the dangerous face of the cliff they went, and just as soon as Brown could bring up the rest of his force he, too, pressed forward. Bourke was not to bring on a fight if he could avoid doing so, but was to find shelter for his men and then to watch the cave and make sure that the enemy did not slip away. Bourke's men and those under command of Ross came together—nearly sixty in all—and hid themselves behind rocks and boulders where they could command both sides of the cave. Almost immediately Brown brought his men up and placed them a little in the rear of this first line. After making sure that his whole force was safely disposed, he had his interpreters demand an unconditional surrender. The reply was a wild howl of rage and defiance. The Apaches did not know what a strong force confronted them and they felt sure of their prey. A renewed call to surrender brought only shouts of scorn. Brown now gave the Indians a chance to send out their women and children with the assurance that they would not be harmed. The Apaches answered with defiance that they would all fight to the bitter end.

Meantime, the savages used every device to get the soldiers to expose themselves. It was all in vain. Then they shot arrows high into the air, hoping they would fall upon the men in the rear. Little harm was done, however. The cave was protected in front by a smooth wall of rock about ten feet high.

To surmount this in the face of the foe was impossible. Sharp-shooters were now placed at advantageous points, but the Indians were no less wary than the soldiers. The men in advance were next ordered to fire against the sloping wall of the cave back of the warriors, who were massed at the front, behind the stone rampart. The deflected bullets did considerable damage and so galled the Apaches that they returned the fire, and in so doing, necessarily exposed themselves somewhat. Cries of women and children gave evidence that the firing of the soldiers was doing its deadly work; so again Major Brown called upon the Indians to surrender or at least to send out their women and children. There was a short silence and then came the death chant and a desperate charge over the rampart.

Under cover of this bold assault about a dozen of the braves slipped down and then off through the rocks toward Brown's right flank. Half a dozen of them were shot down before they had gone ten yards, and the rest were driven back wounded into the cave. One daring fellow broke off toward the left flank and got behind the first line of soldiers, but he was immediately shot to pieces by the men in the rear line. It was now manifest that the Indians intended to die in the cave, unless reenforcements should arrive to relieve them. Burns had been sent early in the morning with Company G and the Pima guides to follow the trail of the horses that the raiders had brought from near Florence. As he was returning from a long detour through the mountains, he heard the heavy firing in the canyon. He approached the scene of battle on the canyon rim, directly above the cave and quickly took in the situation. He had two of his men harnessed so that they could lean far over the edge of the precipice; and from this point of vantage, held securely by their comrades, they fired at the Indians below. But the exposed savages lost no time in retreating under the cliff. Burns now gave orders to roll huge boulders down

APACHE INDIAN SCOUTS

Munitions Bldg., Wash.

Munitions Bldg., Wash.

GERONIMO

Munitions Bldg., Wash.

ESKIMINZIN WITH HIS SON AND DAUGHTER

at the mouth of the cave. Immediately havoc was wrought by this frightful bombardment. The roar made by the falling and bursting masses of rock was appalling. Up to this time one or two of the survivors had continued to fire with cool desperation. But at last the shooting ceased. Brown now signaled to Burns to stop rolling down the boulders and also silenced his own guns. At noon, not knowing what to expect, he ordered his men to scale the wall and enter the cave. A frightful scene of carnage met their gaze. Thirty-five of the Indians were still alive, but many of this number were dying and about half of them did expire in the cave. In all, about seventy-five met death. The stronghold was amply supplied with arms and provisions. Some of the squaws who had been seen about the campfire at dawn had escaped; and as they would undoubtedly carry news of the attack to a neighboring *ranchería,* Brown deemed it urgent to withdraw from the canyon at once.

One desperately wounded warrior in the cave was overlooked by the soldiers. He later crawled out from among the dead and was able to intercept and turn back a large band from his tribe who were coming to join the Indians in the Salt River Canyon. They were not so much rescued as reprieved, for though they reached another stronghold, Turret Butte, almost as unassailable as the cave, Major Randall's column pounced upon them here and meted out grim punishment. This band had been surprised redhanded in a marauding expedition. They had attacked, tortured, and slain a small party of white men near Wickenburg; and while attempting to make their way into the Tonto Basin, were vigorously pursued by the cavalry detachments operating on the western front. Though they had been followed so hard, they thought they had made good their escape when they reached this mountain fastness, hitherto considered impregnable. But Crook's strategy was here triumphantly demonstrated. There was no spot on mountain or mesa or in deepest canyon where a hostile Indian could rest in safety. Major Randall took up the chase where the column from the west had had to drop it. In the night, on hands and knees, Randall's men crawled up the steep mountainside until they saw the campfires of the savages on the rocky summit. At dawn the attack was made, and it was so sudden and determined that some of the warriors in their panic jumped to their death over the precipice. The rest were slain or captured.

By the end of the winter the most warlike savages had had enough. Early in April messengers were sent to Crook at Camp Verde to ask for terms of peace. They were told to bring in all their leading chiefs for a conference. Soon the mountains surrounding the Tonto Basin were everywhere alive with swift runners and signal fires. So far as possible the fighting was halted at once. In a short time Chalipun came with three hundred representatives of the leading tribes and offered to surrender. H said he was spokesman for all the hostile Apaches. Captain Bourke, the gallant and magnanimous soldier and fascinating historian, upon whose writing I have relied throughout this account, gives this graphic picture of the closing scene in this stern campaign of pacification:

"At Camp Verde we found assembled nearly all of Crook's command, and a dirtier, greasier, more uncouth-looking set of officers and men it would be hard to encounter anywhere. Dust, soot, rain, and grime had made their impress upon the canvas suits which each had donned, and with hair uncut for months, beards growing with straggling growth all over the face, there was not one in the party who would venture to pose as an Adonis; but all were happy, because the campaign had resulted in the unconditional surrender of the Apaches and we were now to see the reward of our hard work.

"Crook took Chalipun by the hand and told him that, if he

would promise to live at peace and stop killing people, he would be the best friend he ever had. Not one of the Apaches had been killed except through his own folly; they had refused to listen to the messengers sent out to ask them to give up the warpath and come in; and consequently there had been nothing else to do but go out and kill them until they changed their minds. It was of no use to talk about who began this war; there were bad men among all peoples; there were bad Mexicans as there were bad Americans and bad Apaches; our duty was to end wars and establish peace and not to talk about what was past and gone." [2]

For his distinguished service Crook was made a brigadier general. General Schofield, Commander of the Military Division of the Pacific, in a general order wrote: "To Brevet Major General George Crook, commanding the Department of Arizona, and to his gallant troops, for the extraordinary service they have rendered in the late campaign against the Apache Indians, the Division Commander extends his thanks and congratulations upon their brilliant successes. They have merited the gratitude of the nation." There was ardent rejoicing throughout Arizona. For the first time in three hundred years the trails and mountains were free from marauding Apaches. For two years under the strong, wise administration of this great soldier and philanthropist peace prevailed and civilization grew apace. Crook was not only an Indian fighter and manager; he was a builder and planter as well. Under his regime, unhealthful posts were transferred to better locations; he improved the quarters of the officers and men, constructed good wagon roads from Army post to Army post, and had maps made of the hostile regions and of the Territory. He built a telegraph line seven hundred miles in extent, encouraged his officers to study the ways, ideas, rites, and cere-

[2] Bourke, John G. *On the Border with Crook.* New York, Scribner, 1896.

monies of the Indians under their control, and made plans to secure and set out on the various military reservations of Arizona such vines and fruit trees as were best suited to the climate and location. It was a misfortune for Arizona and the Apaches when, March, 1875, he was transferred to the command of the Department of the Platte.

BIBLIOGRAPHY

BOURKE, JOHN G. *On the Border with Crook.* New York, Scribner, 1896.
CROOK, GEORGE. *Résumé of Operations against Apache Indians from 1882 to 1886.*
DAVIS, BRITTON. *The Truth about Geronimo.* New Haven, Yale University Press, 1929.
Reports of the Commissioner of Indian Affairs, 1883–1886.
Reports of the War Department, 1883–1886.
Senate Executive Document No. 117, 49th Congress, 2d Session.

CHAPTER XI

Sowing the Wind

THERE was great rejoicing in Arizona when, on April 6, 1873, at Camp Verde, the hostile Apaches surrendered unconditionally to General Crook. Much had been accomplished, to be sure. Yet very much remained to be done, and the obstacles to be overcome were immense. Though subjugated and forced upon reservations, the Apaches were still primitive savages, averse to civilized ways. The nature of the Apache was unchanged. He hated work and restraint. He was and always had been a nomad and marauder. The virtues that he inherited were the power and the will to steal and to kill. He had not lost his bitterness and distrust toward the white man. As long as he could, he had held out against cold, fatigue, starvation, and the bullets of his determined foe; and, though conquered, he was not reconciled, believing deep in his heart that he had been falsely and cruelly dealt with, brought as he was into bondage through a coercion beyond his power to understand or resist.

In fact, contrary to the common belief, Apache warfare did not close with the surrender of the great body of hostiles at Camp Verde. In a rare document entitled:

Chronological List
of
Actions with Indians
in
Arizona and New Mexico
Jan. 1866 to Jan. 1891 [1]

[1] There are only two known *copies* of the original document—one is in the A.G.O., War Department, Old Records Section, and the other in the A.G.O., War Department, Officers' Records Section. The transcript in my possession was made by Charles Morgan Wood.

upwards of thirty-five encounters are reported between the Army and the Apaches between April 6, 1873, and the time that Crook was relieved in March, 1875. In these fights more than two hundred and forty Indians were killed by the troops, about as many were captured, and a very large number were wounded. Not a few soldiers and Indian scouts were killed or wounded, also.

In considering progress toward permanent peace and security, account must be taken, also, of the temper and character of the whites into whose hands the Apache was delivered and the quality and intelligence of the Government that ruled over Indian, soldier, and civilian alike. In this respect the prospect was anything but reassuring. Bad white men were more numerous than good ones in the Southwest at that time. Outlaws; adventurers; rough, gambling, hard-drinking soldiers; shrewd, overreaching merchants and ranchers; greedy, nonresident contractors with political pull; unconscionable Indian traders; grafting officeholders; and inefficient, inexperienced Indian agents—all these, with the exception of Army officers in general and a fair share of able and honorable Indian agents, were imbued with hatred and contempt for the Apache, and many of them were eager to bring about his extermination. It was in the face of such a set-up as this that the Apache described above had to make his climb to salvation and civilization. Surely no honest, humane citizen of America can fail to blush with shame when he contemplates the attitude and the acts of our national Government in its dealings with the Apaches during this crisis in their history and in the history of the citizens of the Southwest. Indifference, incompetency, delay, vacillation, disregard of solemn understandings entered into through its Army officers and official representatives from Washington—this was the sort of bulwark that the United States Government threw up for the encouragement and protection of such Apaches as did seek the straight and narrow way of righteousness, and such citizens and soldiers as did with intelligence and right motives seek firm and sure ways to humane understanding and enduring peace.

Crook remained in command of the Department of Arizona up to March, 1875. His plan for the control and future welfare of the conquered Apaches was wise and honorable. He insisted that they should be looked upon as human beings, to be handled with firmness, yet with consideration and utter fairness. He believed they should be put to work and permitted to enjoy the profits of their own labor; that, as soon as possible, they should be required to support themselves, should raise crops, supply wood, hay, and other articles to the posts and agencies, and for such supplies should be paid the regular market price. He believed that control and discipline should be placed in the hands of a select body of scouts drawn from their own number and paid by the Government at the same rate as enlisted soldiers. With the money they earned, he advised them to buy horses, cattle, and sheep. It was his hope that in this way they would have aroused in them the love of property and the sense of pride and independence that comes from personal ownership; for he believed that as a result they would be led to give up their roaming habits, would become attached to their stock and crops, and gradually find pleasure in a settled life. Not all could be influenced to give up their wild, nomadic life, he very well knew; he advised, therefore, that they be allowed considerable freedom of movement within the limits of their own reservations, so that they might gratify the habits of centuries in the gathering and cooking of mescal, the collecting of their favorite seeds and grasses, and even, with proper supervision, the hunting of deer and antelope. It was made clear to the Indians that each one must have an identification tag so that he could be accounted for at any time, and so prove in case of need or suspicion that he had not left the reservation. The Army officers appointed by Crook to oversee and control the Apaches on their reservations were in sympathy with his views and tactful in their attempts to carry out his plans for the welfare and advancement of these Indians.

Says John G. Bourke: "The transformation effected was marvellous. Here were six thousand of the worst Indians in America sloughing off the old skin and taking on a new life. Detachments of the scouts were retained in service to maintain order; and also because money would in that way be distributed among the tribes. Some few at first spent their pay foolishly, but the majority clubbed together and sent to California for ponies and sheep. Trials by juries of their own people were introduced among them for the punishment of minor offences, the cutting off of women's noses was declared a crime, the manufacture of the intoxicant tizwin was broken up by every possible means, and the future of these Indians looked most promising, when a gang of politicians and contractors, remembered in the Territory as the 'Tucson Ring,' exerted an influence in Washington, and had the Apaches ordered down to the desolate sand waste of the San Carlos. . . .

"There is no brighter page in our Indian history than that which records the progress of the subjugated Apaches at Camp Apache and Camp Verde, nor is there a fouler blot than that which conceals the knavery which secured their removal to the junction of the San Carlos and Gila." [2]

Other powerful forces were at work to sow the seeds of discontent and to keep alive the fires of hatred. As pointed out in a previous paragraph, there were still many bold and recalcitrant outlaws who held out in their remote mountain retreats and vowed that they would never yield, and for years constant

---

[2] Bourke, John G. "General Crook in the Indian Country." In *The Century Magazine*, March, 1891.

scouts were conducted against them by the troops. Among these renegades were two or three minor chiefs of notoriously bad reputation. Occasionally they made secret visits to their relatives in the various agencies and stirred up discontent and unrest. Very serious was the departure of seven bands of Indians, nine hundred people in all, from the San Carlos reservation on January 4, 1874. Fear and misunderstanding of the purposes of the white men was the cause of their flight, it seems. They sought safety in their old mountain haunts; but within three or four days were rounded up and brought back to the reservation. They were located on the south side of the Gila and, as the weather was very cold, were allowed to erect huts there. Soon a flood came and the river rose so high that the agency was cut off from communication with them. During this time, several of the worst of the outlaw minor chiefs, who had been skulking in the canyons, came in and mingled freely with those in the encampment. While the stream was still impassable, a wagon train bound for Camp Apache with supplies halted on the south side of the river near the camping place of the Apaches. Some of the teamsters sold much bad whisky to the visiting renegade chiefs, and on the night of January 31, 1874, some of them got very drunk. When the white men refused to sell them any more liquor, the Apaches killed them. The outlaws then at once fled into the mountains, and all the other Indians, without grievance, but frightened and confused, went with them.

February 3 the outlaws attacked white settlers at Old Camp Grant, and two men, a woman, and two children were killed. General Crook came to San Carlos and announced to the leading chiefs of the reservation that they must find and deliver up the guilty outlaw chiefs or he would be compelled to lead his troops against the Indians who had left the reservation. With this stern warning he returned to his headquarters. Spies were

sent out by the chiefs to locate the outlaws. They were found;
refused to surrender; and were killed in the fight that ensued.
The bodies could not well be carried back as evidence that the
General's orders had been fulfilled, so the heads were cut off,
put in a sack, carried back to San Carlos, and dumped on the
parade ground in front of the tent of the commanding officer.
The women and children who had witlessly fled with the
renegades suffered greatly. Pitifully they pleaded to be allowed
to come in; but Crook's orders were inflexible, and until the
leading Indians on the reservation had proved their good faith
by the punishment of the murderers, both guilty and innocent
were compelled to face cold, starvation, and death in the wintry
mountains. It is pleasant to relate that the Army officers in
command of the scouts did their best to relieve the sufferings
of several bands of men, women, and children who would have
perished but for their aid and kindheartedness.

August 8, 1874, John P. Clum, not quite twenty-three years
of age, became Indian agent at San Carlos. During the eighteen
months previous to Clum's arrival there had been five different
agents—three civilians and two Army officers. Just at this
time a sharp controversy was going on between the Indian
Bureau and the Department of War as to the administration
of the Indian agencies. Of necessity troops had to be kept at
or near the agencies to control and punish unruly savages. On
the other hand, all administrative affairs were left in charge of
the agent. It was not strange under these circumstances that
clashes of authority should sometimes arise, very injurious to
Government efficiency and most perplexing to the Indians.

In a somewhat bumptious manner young Clum, when he
took charge at San Carlos, made it clear that he intended to assume full control of all affairs relating to the Indian service. He
was convinced that the mixed civil and military rule was detri-
mental to the Indians, and he wanted them to understand at

once that there was to be but one administrator. Major J. B. Babcock, in command of the troops at San Carlos, on September 3, 1874, very affably yielded to the new agent entire charge of affairs, and the officers who followed him worked amicably with the agent. There were at this time not quite one thousand Indians on the reservation. They were Pinals, Arivaipas, and Tontos. These Indians seemed peaceable and well disposed. After the customary friendly and formal smoke, during the course of which Clum made known to them his plans, agent and Indians were at once on very good terms. He explained that he wanted them to help him in local government, and assured them that if they would cooperate with him and do right it would not be long before they could get along without the presence of soldiers on the reservation. All this was very pleasing to them. He was fortunate in having as interpreter a famous individual—half Mexican, half Apache—Marijildo Grijalba; and very early in his administration he was so lucky as to secure as his chief clerk M. A. Sweeney, a sergeant of cavalry who had just given up Army life after fifteen years of service, but was enamored of life in Arizona and glad to get a job at the Indian agency. "Honest, industrious, good-natured, and fearless," well versed in the character and ways of the Apaches, yet sympathetic in his dealings with them, he proved invaluable to Clum, and Clum's success was largely due to the ability and devotion of this fine Irishman.

Clum's first step in his plan of self-government for these Apaches was the selection of four of their leaders as policemen. He also created an Apache Court, made up of four or five chiefs and himself as presiding judge, before which offenders arrested by the police were brought for trial and sentence. This, too, appealed very much to the Apache sense of fair dealing, and the whole system of self-government that he inaugurated worked out well in practice. Indian law was applied with severity rather than leniency; and though Clum early had occasion to put the policemen and his court to a very trying test, he found then and ever afterwards that he could trust them fully. His Indian police became famous in Arizona. Thoroughly drilled by Sweeney, and properly uniformed, they were the pride of the Agency, and time and again were called upon to meet trying emergencies during the next three years.

Though the Indians who surrendered at Camp Verde had been promised that this was to be their permanent home, before two years had passed the Government, on the plea of economy, moved these fifteen hundred Indians to the San Carlos Agency. Some of the bands were at enmity with tribes already residing there. The transfer was made against their will; and they submitted only because they believed military force would be used if they did not do so. The action was taken against the earnest advice of General Crook. In his official report these words occur: "There are now on the Verde reservation about fifteen hundred Indians; they have been among the worst in Arizona; but if the Government keeps its promise to them, that it shall be their home for all time, there will be no difficulty in keeping them at peace and engaged in peaceful pursuits."

En route to San Carlos there was a fight between two factions and several Indians were killed. A few slipped away into "Hell" and "Rattlesnake" Canyons and again took up their predatory life. Later, in bloody conflicts, they were again subdued by Captain Charles King, Lieutenant W. S. Schuyler, and Al Sieber, Chief of Scouts. Fourteen hundred were duly delivered to Clum. The San Carlos Indians from the first had been denied the use of firearms; and when the Verdes were brought to the reservation, Clum demanded that they give up their arms. They refused to do this at first; but Clum was firm and had good and persuasive reasons to offer. Moreover, the San Carlos Indians, some of whom had been hostile toward the newcomers in the past, stood squarely by him. So, after reconsidering the matter, the weapons were yielded up without bloodshed.

April 15, 1875, in accordance with an order from the Commissioner of Indian Affairs, Clum took control of the Camp Apache agency. There were about eighteen hundred Indians on this reservation. The previous month, the civil agent at Camp Apache, J. E. Roberts, had been removed by force of arms (so Clum asserts) [3] and Captain Ogilby, the commanding officer at Camp Apache, had assumed control. Young Clum went berserk when he arrived upon the scene. The military authorities were notified that he had come to Camp Apache with instructions to take over the agency and that he was now in full charge. April 19, he counted all the men at the agency. But hardly had the roll been completed when some of the Indians came to him in great anxiety and told him that Captain Ogilby had ordered them all to be at the post next morning to be counted there. "This order," Clum writes, "was given without regard to my plans, wishes, or instructions, even without my knowledge, and came directly in conflict with orders I had already given. I rode over to the post, saw Captain Ogilby, and requested him to withdraw the order. His reply was that he would carry it out if it took every man under his command, and he had four companies and forty Indian scouts. . . . I . . . instructed the Indians to come to the agency the next morning and I would suffer with them if there was any trouble." [4] Very careless playing with matches, and with plenty of explosive material about! Captain Ogilby had the good judgment to give up the attempt to make a separate enumeration and so the matter closed.

Orders were soon issued from Washington to transfer the

[3] Annual Report of the Commissioner of Indian Affairs, 1874, p. 216.
[4] Clum, Woodworth. *Apache Agent*, p. 157. Boston, Houghton Mifflin, 1936.

Indians of the Camp Apache agency to the San Carlos Reservation. In July Clum set about complying with his instructions. One reason given for the change was economy in expense of administration; another, the fact that "it would avert the trade with these Indians from New Mexico to Arizona, where it properly belongs." The wishes of the Indians were not taken into consideration, though some of them seemed willing to go. Eventually all except Petone and Diablo, who were scouts and could not be removed from the post, and the band of Penal, a petty chief, consented to go peaceably. About six hundred, mostly women, were allowed to stay behind to gather the corn crop; three or four hundred, including the Indian scouts and their families, remained until the scouts should have finished the period for which they had enlisted. The rest, consisting of fifteen White Mountain chiefs with their bands, between July 26 and 31, made the trek to San Carlos and from that time were rationed there. Clum in person led seven bands over the mountain trail, and the other eight were conducted by the post trader, Mr. George S. Stevens, by the wagon road. These were the only two white men in the company. The Army was much opposed to the transfer. Clum writes: "I met with vigorous and bitter opposition in my efforts to remove these Indians." Thus, before he had been agent at San Carlos a full year, he was in control of about forty-two hundred Indians. He was not yet twenty-four, and his salary was still sixteen hundred dollars as it had been when he had fewer than one thousand in charge.

With the arrival of these large groups from Verde and Camp Apache Clum increased his police force. Eight men had been added after the Camp Verde Indians arrived; and now with the accession of the White Mountain Apaches the number was increased to twenty-five, and Clay Beauford was placed in command of the entire company. Clum has this to say of his police organization: "They were carefully chosen from the various tribes and bands, armed with needle guns and fixed ammunition, and placed under the command of Mr. Clay Beauford, who has been guide and scout in this country for several years. . . . The duties of this force are to patrol the Indian camps, to quell disturbances, to arrest offenders, to report any signs of disorder or mutiny, to scour the entire reservation and arrest Indians who are absent from the agency without a pass, also to arrest whites who trespass contrary to the rules of the reservation." [5]

Just before Christmas, 1875, after the troops had been moved from the agency at Clum's request, Disalin, Chief of the Tontos, created a tragic situation. He was very jealous of one of his wives; and used to beat her and torture her in various ways. She complained to Clum. Young and chivalric, Clum took Disalin to task. This rebuke was not the sort of thing that an Apache husband—much less an Apache chief—submitted to. His wife was his to do with as he pleased. Clum's breach of Apache etiquette was very deeply resented. Disalin brooded over the insult. An hour after leaving the agent's office he returned. Over his shoulder he wore a blanket, which was unusual and should have aroused Clum's suspicion. Walking across the room and opening the door of the adjoining office (that of Sweeney, the clerk) to assure himself that they were alone, he turned and faced Clum. His eyes now opened, Clum spoke to Disalin sharply. The Indian scowled; but just then the Negro janitor entered with an armload of wood, and just behind him Chapin, the doctor at the agency. With some casual remark Disalin now walked into Sweeney's office and closed the door. Immediately there was the sound of a shot. Clum seized his revolver and started toward Sweeney's office. Another shot rang out and Sweeney came running into the room, yelling, "Disalin!" By the time Clum had reached the connecting door,

<hr>

[5] Official report.

the Indian had made his exit. Then there was a third shot. As soon as Clum got outside he saw Disalin with a smoking pistol in his hand running toward the guardhouse. It had evidently been the villain's purpose to kill Clum, Sweeney, and Beauford, captain of police. But the sudden chance entrance of the janitor and Dr. Chapin had upset his plans. He had shot at Sweeney and missed him, and now he was on his way to get Beauford.

Chased by Clum and Sweeney, Disalin dodged round the corner of the guardhouse and at that instant another shot was fired; then another, and in a moment a fusillade. Disalin had been killed by a shot from the loyal policeman, Tauelclyee, his own brother. During the very brief time that he was covering the two hundred yards to the guardhouse, two of the Apache police had become aware of what was happening; and two bullets struck him before he rounded the corner of the guardhouse. Though wounded he kept on running. Beauford, hearing the shouting, had come to the door of the guardhouse, and before he knew what was happening, Disalin shot at him twice. Beauford drew a careful bead; but before he could pull his trigger, Tauelclyee, with rifle steadied against the wall of the corral, fired and dropped the miscreant dead.

The Indian Bureau gave Clum and his policemen plenty to do. May 3, 1876, the Commissioner of Indian Affairs instructed Clum by telegraph to go to Apache Pass, take over the Chiricahua Agency, and remove the Indians of that reservation to San Carlos. From the time of the peace pact entered into between President Grant's representative, General O. O. Howard, and the great chief Cochise, and the establishment at that time of the Chiricahua reservation, Cochise and his people had remained true to their agreement and had not molested the Americans; though there seems to be no doubt that the young men of the tribe did now and then make raids into Mexico. In June, 1874, Cochise died, and Taza, his oldest son, succeeded him as chief. The Commissioner of Indian Affairs notified Jeffords in February, 1876, that no more beef could be furnished his agency during that fiscal year. As little beef remained on hand, Jeffords told the Indians that for the next four months, they would have to eke out their meat supply by hunting in the mountains. A part of Cochise's tribe thereupon moved over to the Dragoon Mountains, about thirteen miles from the Overland Mail Station at Sulphur Spring. A quarrel arose among these Indians, and two men and a grandchild of Cochise were killed. The band now separated into two factions, Taza with most of the Indians returned to the neighborhood of the Agency; while Skinya, the principal troublemaker, with about twelve adherents and their families remained in the Dragoons. Four of this party, together with three Coyotero Indians who had become dissatisfied at San Carlos, made a raid into Sonora and returned with about one hundred dollars' worth of gold dust and silver. Though Jeffords had warned Rogers, station keeper at Sulphur Spring, that he would be prosecuted and removed from the reservation if he sold whisky to the Indians, Rogers made known to these turbulent raiders that he could supply them with liquor in exchange for their gold and silver. On April 6 he did sell whisky of a very vile quality to Pionsenay. The next day this Indian returned and bought more; and in the afternoon returned with his nephew and demanded still more. But this time Rogers refused to sell it to him. Drunk with the rotten stuff he had already consumed, he killed Rogers, and also Spence the cook, who was the only other white man at the station. Stealing more whisky and some horses and ammunition, the Indians went back to their camp in the Dragoons.

The next morning, April 8, a few of the outlaws, who were still drunk, killed a man named Lewis, on the San Pedro, and stole four horses. When Jeffords, in the early morning of April 8, heard of the murder of Rogers and Spence, he set out with a troop of cavalry from Fort Bowie for the *rancherías* of Taza and his followers. These loyal Indians had taken to the mountaintops in great excitement. Jeffords sent the cavalry on to Sulphur Spring, while he went to the frightened Indians on the mountain and told them to return to the Agency and await him there, at the same time assuring them that they should not be harmed. He caught up with the cavalry at Sulphur Spring. After burying Rogers and Spence, Jeffords and the troops followed the trail of the murderers and, April 10, discovered Skinya's band on an all but inaccessible peak in the Dragoon Mountains. Some shots were exchanged, but to have attempted to dislodge and capture the band would have been too costly in American lives, so the cavalry marched back to Fort Bowie.

When Jeffords got back to the agency, he told Taza and his Indians that they must neither camp nor hunt west of the Chiricahuas. Thus all Apaches found west of the Chiricahuas would be known as hostiles, and Jeffords so informed the military officers. Scouting parties from Fort Bowie and Fort Grant were sent out, but they did not succeed in capturing any of Skinya's renegades.

June 4 Skinya and his party entered Taza's camp and tried to persuade his band to leave the reservation and go on the warpath. When they refused to do this, a fight ensued in which Skinya and six other men were killed and two wounded. Nachez, the younger son of Cochise, fired the shot that killed Skinya, while Taza himself wounded Pionsenay, Skinya's brother, with a shot through the shoulder. Taza, with his band, now camped near the Agency. Meantime, doughty agent John P. Clum had not been idle. Ably supported by General A. V. Kautz, commander of the Department of Arizona, with all available troops in the Territory, in addition to two hundred Indian scouts enlisted on the San Carlos Reservation and a picked bodyguard of fifty-four San Carlos Agency policemen, Clum proceeded to Apache Pass, which he reached the day after Taza's fight with Skinya. In a talk with Clum on the sixth of June, Taza consented to go peaceably with Clum to the San Carlos Reservation with all that were left of Cochise's own band—three hundred and twenty-five men, women, and children. June 8 a messenger came from Pionsenay with the request that he might come in to die. Twenty scouts were sent out and he was brought in a prisoner. There came with Pionsenay, also, the women and children of Skinya's party, the men who had not been killed having already made their escape into Mexico. About four hundred of the most turbulent Chiricahuas, led by Juh, Geronimo, and Nolgee, had previously fled to Sonora to carry on their depredations there and in New Mexico. Between the abandonment of the Chiricahua Agency and October, 1876, according to Jeffords' official report, these renegades had killed more than twenty people and stolen one hundred and seventy head of stock. But they were stout fellows whenever it became a matter of adherence to Uncle Sam's bread line. They never willingly allowed their names to get off the roll. About one hundred and forty other unsubdued Indians who had been permitted on the Chiricahua reservation, but who were really Hot Spring, New Mexico, Indians, went back to New Mexico under their chief, Gordo.

June 12 Clum left Apache Pass with three hundred and twenty-five Indians, besides Pionsenay, whom he kept strongly guarded. He proceeded toward Tucson to meet the sheriff of Pima County who was coming out to take the murderer into custody. About two P.M., June 13, he turned Pionsenay over to the civil officers and seven hours later the wily villain gave the sheriff the slip and escaped. On the eighteenth of June, Clum located the Chiricahuas on the San Carlos Reservation. There were only sixty warriors in this party. The removal of the Chiricahua Apaches from their reservation was the crowning folly of the Indian Bureau. Not only did the Chiricahuas dislike the region of San Carlos; not only was it already overpopulous with tribes averse, or even hostile to each other, held there against their will; but the Chiricahuas were keenly aware of the fact that their own reservation had been taken away from them, not because of the disloyalty of the Chiricahuas as a people but as a result of the misdeeds of a small, violent faction arising directly from the wicked greed of a white man placed in their midst.

In Jeffords' report to the Commissioner of Indian Affairs, dated October 3, 1876, he writes: "In conclusion, I have the honor to state that the killing of Messrs. Rogers, Spence, and Lewis was not an outbreak of the Indians of the agency; it was the result of selling whisky to Indians already outlawed from their tribe and who were anxious to have other Indians join them to make their number sufficiently strong to enable them to become hostile. When at the Sulphur Spring ranch, Lieutenant Henely and myself found a keg of whiskey that contained a quantity of tobacco and other materials to give strength to the liquor; and among civilized communities murders by men crazed from spirits are of frequent occurrence. The breaking of their treaty and attempted removal of nine hundred Indians for the criminality of three of their number has been the cause of the numerous murders and robberies that have been committed since the 12th of June."

Late in February, 1877, it was discovered that Geronimo and his band of murderers were in New Mexico trying to dispose of stolen stock to the Mexican and American ranchers. The headquarters of the marauders was at Ojo Caliente; and these hardened outlaws were drawing rations and blankets from the Hot Spring Government Agency whenever it pleased their fancy to round up there. March 20 Clum received this telegram from the Indian Commissioner at Washington: "If practicable take your Indian police and arrest renegade Indians at Ojo Caliente, New Mexico. . . . Remove renegades to San Carlos and hold them in confinement for murder and robbery. Call on military for aid, if needed."

Clum wired Clay Beauford, now in command of a company of Arizona Apache militia, to march at once to Silver City, New Mexico, and await his arrival there. He wired General Hatch, also, at Santa Fe, in command of troops in New Mexico, of his plans and requested his cooperation. Hatch replied that he had ordered troops of the Ninth Cavalry into the field and also that Major Wade, with three troops of cavalry, would meet Clum and the Apache police at dawn, April 21, at Ojo Caliente. Then, on foot, Clum began his four-hundred-mile march to Silver City.

Among the leaders in Clum's company of police at this time were Eskiminzin, Nachez, Tauelclyee, Goodah, and Sneezer— names of note in Apache history. Clum and his police met Beauford and his militia at Silver City as planned; and by the morning of April 20 they were all within forty miles of Ojo Caliente, which Clum reached late that afternoon. A trusty scout had been sent to the agency several days in advance, and he now reported that Geronimo, with one hundred followers, was camped three miles from the agency and that he had visited the agency that very day for rations. Unfortunately Clum found awaiting him a telegram from Wade informing him that the troops would be delayed one day. Clum was in a quandary. Since he was operating now conjointly with the troops, he doubted whether he would be justified in acting further without consultation with Major Wade; yet he was aware that, when the renegades found out that he was there with his San Carlos police, almost any untoward thing might happen. Since they had come all this four hundred miles for the purpose of capturing the renegade leaders, he determined to make a bold and prompt move.

Clum had pushed forward to Ojo Caliente on horseback with only twenty-two of his police. He at once sent a courier to Beauford to bring in the additional police and his militia at four the next morning and secretly take station in the commissary building with loaded guns and thirty rounds of ammunition. At daylight a message was sent to Geronimo and the renegade chiefs with him to come in for a talk. They came at once in war paint and armed. On the porch of the agency building, facing the parade ground, Clum took his seat, flanked by six Apache police. The rest of the twenty-two men were deployed to advantage. Beauford stationed himself between the commissary building and Clum. The police had been instructed to be ready for instant action, but not to shoot unless so ordered by Clum or Beauford, or unless one or the other of these two opened fire, or unless the Indians began shooting. The sullen outlaws, just at sunrise, gathered in a compact group in front of Clum—Geronimo, Gordo, Ponce, and Francisco in advance, about ten feet from the porch. It was a very fierce and threatening array.

Clum began by accusing Geronimo of robbing and murdering. He charged him, too, with having broken his promise at the time of the removal of the Chiricahuas, when he agreed with Clum that he would go with him to San Carlos to live there. "Now," he said, "we have come to take you back with us. We do not want to have any trouble and if you and your followers will come quietly, no harm will come to you."[6] Geronimo made a defiant and boastful reply. The moment of action was at hand and the situation was very tense. Clum raised his left hand and touched the brim of his sombrero, the prearranged signal for the militia to appear. Instantly the commissary doors flew open and an Apache sergeant popped out and raced along the south end of the parade ground, followed by his men in single file. Each scout had his thumb on the hammer of his ready rifle, but there was no sound except the patter of swift-running moccasined feet.

Clum watched Geronimo and saw his thumb creep slowly toward the hammer of his rifle. His own hand had rested on his hip very near the butt of his Colt revolver. When he read Geronimo's intention, he moved his hand over until it touched his weapon. This was the second preconcerted signal that had been rehearsed with Beauford and the twenty-two policemen. Beauford and the policemen instantly covered Geronimo and his companions with their guns. Geronimo hesitated for a moment but almost immediately realized that he was trapped and said very coolly he was now ready "to have big smoke and big talk." Clum turned and handed his rifle and revolver to Sneezer. Then he said to Geronimo, "Tell all your men to lay their guns on the ground, out here in the open, where my police can gather them up and keep them for you." [7]

Geronimo made no move to comply. The moment was ominous in the extreme. From his position on the porch about ten feet from Geronimo and Ponce, Clum beckoned to Beauford slightly with his head, and the latter moved forward slowly with his rifle aimed straight at Geronimo. Stepping down, Clum walked up to the renegade and said; "I'll take your gun myself." There was no reply, nor did Geronimo move a muscle, except that he half closed the lids of his sullen eyes. Clum lifted the rifle from his unresisting left arm.

"I have seen many looks of hate in my long life," Clum wrote in his very old age, "but never one so vicious, so vengeful. Geronimo's mouth had a natural droop on the right side, so that even in repose he seemed to sneer. But when I took his

[7] *Ibid.*

rifle from him, his lips tightened and the sneer was accentuated. The old scar on his right cheek was livid." [8] The remainder of the band were quietly disarmed. As there was no guard-house at Ojo Caliente, Geronimo and six other leaders were shut into the corral under the vigilant guard of ten policemen, and ankle irons were riveted upon them.

The next morning when all the renegades were assembled before Clum and he was about to tell them his plans concerning them, Victorio, who had succeeded Mangas Coloradas as chief of the Warm Spring Apaches, came into the Agency. Up to this time Victorio had been inclined toward peace, and had sometimes taken Geronimo to task for his raids. He was now much surprised at the state of affairs before him. Clum abruptly addressed him explaining the situation and offering to take him and his followers with him to San Carlos if they cared to go, but making it clear that they must first all be counted. Just before sunset both the renegades with Geronimo and Victorio's band appeared to be counted. Victorio's motley following were counted first. They numbered three hundred and forty-three. The total of the Chiricahuas was one hundred and ten. After a week of preparation, with a daily count of the Indians, May 1, the four hundred and fifty-three Apaches started for San Carlos, under guard of twenty-five Indian police and a military rear guard of twelve, commanded by Lieutenant Hugo. On May 20 these Chiricahua outlaws and Warm Spring Apaches with Victorio, their chief, were settled on the San Carlos Reservation. Four new policemen were appointed from the new-comers and Victorio was added to the council of judges. Clum's very rosy and self-gratulatory account of the transfer of the Warm Spring tribe differs decidedly from the account given by John G. Bourke. He writes: "The Warm Spring Apaches

<hr>

[8] Clum, Woodworth. *Op. cit.* I have followed Clum's own story of the capture of Geronimo somewhat closely.

were peremptorily deprived of their little fields and driven away from their crops, half-ripened, and ordered to tramp to the San Carlos; when the band reached there, the fighting men had disappeared, and only decrepit warriors, little boys and girls, and old women remained." [9] In the following chapter we shall learn how brief was Victorio's stay upon the reservation.

Clum sent word to the civil authorities in Tucson that Geronimo and the other criminal chiefs were in irons and that he was prepared, not only to deliver them at the jail in Tucson "for trial, conviction, and execution," but to testify personally against them. But Geronimo, the most voluble liar and bloody murderer in the Apache tribe, was released and new blankets and provisions were issued to him and his families. Very poor teamwork, this! If Geronimo had been executed then, as he richly deserved to be, hundreds of worthy lives would have been saved and infinite misery to both whites and Indians avoided.

At the request of the Commissioner of Indian Affairs officers of the Army had recently been detailed to inspect supplies furnished by the contractors to the various reservations. When the officer detailed to perform this work at the San Carlos Agency arrived, Clum was highly incensed and refused to permit the military inspector to perform this duty. Indeed, he told the Commissioner that he would resign rather than submit to such an inspection. According to the annual report of General August V. Kautz to the War Department under date of August 15, 1877, Clum did offer his resignation, with the request that it be accepted by July 1, 1877. As it had not been accepted by the Commissioner by that date, he abandoned his agency, on the ground that he was disgusted with the vacillating and dishonorable policies of the Indian Bureau. That the

[9] Bourke, John G. *On the Border with Crook*, p. 444. New York, Scribner, 1896.

actions of the Bureau of Indian Affairs had been vacillating and dishonorable there can be no doubt. However, Clum's sudden and headstrong action seems to have been due chiefly to his hostility toward the Army and Army officers. His attitude toward the military was often discourteous and denunciatory. The fact is, able, honest, and courageous as Clum undoubtedly was in his administration of the San Carlos Agency, his reputation and achievements suffer greatly from the egotism and bombast displayed throughout the account of his life as written in the book *Apache Agent*. The impression one gets from reading this book is that the daring and capable young man pictured there was fully convinced that he could make a perfect job of taking care of the whole Apache tribe without the aid of either the Department of War or the Department of the Interior.

BIBLIOGRAPHY

Annual Report of the Commissioner of Indian Affairs, 1874.

BOURKE, JOHN G. "General Crook in the Indian Country." In *The Century Magazine*, March, 1891.

BOURKE, JOHN G. *On the Border with Crook.* New York, Scribner, 1896.

Chronological List of Actions with Indians in Arizona and New Mexico, Jan. 1866 to Jan. 1891. A.G.O., War Department. Old Records Section.

CLUM, WOODWORTH. *Apache Agent.* Boston, Houghton Mifflin, 1936.

CHAPTER XII

Reaping the Whirlwind

FOR several years the Indian Bureau had been sowing the wind; now it was harvest time and it was to reap the whirlwind. In his annual reports Agent John P. Clum smugly implies that the transfers, one after another, of Indians from Camp Verde, Camp Apache, the Chiricahua Reservation, and Ojo Caliente, and their concentration on the San Carlos Reservation were successful and satisfactory. It was in reality far otherwise. In every instance the removal of the Indians was a breach of good faith on the part of the Government, was contrary to the best judgment of Army officers in command, and was in opposition to the desire of the Indians. Nor was the transfer in any case completely effected. Many members of the various bands refused to come along, and always it was the best fighting men who slipped away.

The failure of these attempts was shown clearly in the abortive transfer of the Chiricahua and Warm Spring band. In his annual report of August 15, 1877, General August V. Kautz, Commander of the Department of Arizona, calls attention to the conflicting reports of the Bureau of Indian Affairs for the years 1875 and 1876. Quoting the figures as set down for these two years, he says: "The two agencies, Warm Spring and Chiricahua, contained in 1875, before they were broken up, according to the report of that year, 965 and 2,100; total, 3,065. The number removed were 325 and 454; total, 779.

There are therefore 2,286 Indians unaccounted for since 1875. It is unnecessary to comment on these discrepancies."[1] Add to this statement of Kautz the comment of General John Pope (whose Department included New Mexico) in his report of September 22, 1880, and we begin to see the true state of affairs: "This outbreak of Victorio and the severe campaign against him . . . were due to the determined purpose of the Interior Department to effect the removal of the band to the San Carlos Agency in Arizona. . . . Victorio and his band have always bitterly objected to being placed there, one of the reasons given by him being the hostility of many of the Indians of the Agency. He always asserted his willingness to live peacefully with his people at the Warm Springs (Ojo Caliente) Agency and, so far as I am informed, gave no trouble to anyone whilst there. I do not know the reasons of the Interior Department for insisting upon the removal to San Carlos Agency, but certainly they should be cogent to justify the great trouble and severe losses occasioned by the attempt to coerce the removal. The present is the fourth time within five years that Victorio's band has broken out. Three times they have been brought in and turned over by the Military to the Indian Bureau authorities. Both Victorio and his band are resolved to die rather than go to the San Carlos Agency."[2]

In order to present the tragic story of Victorio—next to Cochise and Mangas Coloradas the greatest warrior in Apache history—we must begin with the year 1871. At that time some twelve hundred Mimbres, Gila, and Mogollon Apaches, referred to usually as the Southern Apaches, were brought together in the Cañada Alamosa Valley, a fertile and beautiful region which had been their favorite rendezvous for generations and was claimed by them as their own. Previous to this

[1] Kautz, August V. Report of the Secretary of War, 1877, p. 144.
[2] Pope, John. Report of the Secretary of War, Vol. I, 1880, p. 88.

time these bands had been assigned to no reservation. The scanty rations issued to them weekly were not half sufficient to sustain them, so they roamed about existing as best they could—chiefly, of course, by thievery. On August 29, 1871, Mr. Vincent Colyer set apart for these Indians the valley of the Tulerosa, some distance northwest of Ojo Caliente. They did not like this location. Only about four hundred and fifty could be induced to go there. Most of them took to the mountains, a good many joining their kindred, the Chiricahuas, in Arizona. Those who were removed to Tulerosa were unhappy and hard to manage. Many of them would leave the the reservation for months at a time. In the autumn of 1874 a change was made—the Warm Spring Reservation was set aside for them, not far from Cañada Alamosa, and the wanderers now gathered in the region they loved. From time to time other bands came in and joined them. A small body of soldiers was stationed at the Agency. In general there was quiet and satisfaction, though the Indians showed no interest in education and agriculture, and at times bands of the Warm Spring Indians left the agency to visit the Chiricahuas, for the purpose, no doubt, of joining these enterprising neighbors in their raids into Mexico.

Mention has been made of the fact that many of the Chiricahua Apaches had taken refuge with their Warm Spring friends and relatives when the Chiricahua reservation was abolished in 1876 and that a still larger number then became renegades in the mountains of Mexico. In March, 1877, it became evident that Indians from the Warm Spring Agency were in collusion with the Arizona outlaws, taking part in their raids, and harboring them when storm-tossed or in dire need of provisions. As a result, four hundred and fifty-three Southern Apaches, Victorio among them, were removed to San Carlos in May, 1877, and the Warm Spring Reservation was restored to the public domain. September 2, 1877, Victorio with three hundred Warm Spring and Chiricahua followers left the reservation and began marauding. They were promptly pursued and overhauled, but only thirty were recaptured. The main body attacked a settlement in New Mexico. They killed eight settlers and stole some horses. All available troops in New Mexico were now sent out against them. For about a month the renegades held out and continued their depredations; but, as the mountains now swarmed with soldiers and Indian scouts, early in October one hundred and ninety surrendered at Fort Wingate. Later, others gave themselves up. In all, two hundred and sixty were retaken and turned over to the War Department at Warm Spring. Upon recommendation of the Indian Bureau they were returned to San Carlos by a detail of troops in October, 1877. But before the start was made, eighty again escaped and took to the mountains, and the rest objected bitterly to being returned.

Near the close of the year 1877 sixty-three of the eighty who had escaped presented themselves at the Mescalero Agency in an almost starving condition and asked to be allowed to live there. In February, 1878, Victorio and twenty-two of his band who had been spending these months in Old Mexico approached the commanding officer at Ojo Caliente and expressed a desire to surrender, provided that Nana's band, who were among those who had sought refuge at the Mescalero Agency, be permitted to join them at Ojo Caliente. This request was granted, and messengers were sent to confer with the agent at Mescalero and with Nana and his people. It seems that only seventeen Warm Spring Indians cared to return. Victorio had remained quietly at Ojo Caliente awaiting the outcome; and now, February 16, these thirty-nine Southern Apaches surrendered as prisoners of war, but at the same time protested that they would resist to the death any effort to take them back to San Carlos.

It was then decided that they should be taken to the Mescalero Agency, but they were bitterly opposed to this also; and April 15, 1878, they all escaped and took to the mountains again. June 30 Victorio with a small party came to the agent at Mescalero who promised to treat them well if they would come there and *stay*. Twenty-eight agreed to do this and were entered on the roll with the other Southern Apaches then at this agency. So genuine seemed the desire of these harried renegades to settle down quietly at last that their earnest request to have their wives and children brought back to them from San Carlos was also granted.

July, 1879, a belated indictment was brought against Victorio in the civil court in Grant County, New Mexico, for horse stealing and murder. No steps were taken to arrest him, it would seem, but the Indians were aware of the danger that was hanging over their heads; and when, a little later, a hunting party rode through the reservation, among whom Victorio recognized a judge and a prosecuting attorney, alarm seized them, for they believed the expedition was a preliminary to the arrest of the chief and perhaps the whole band. In September, taking with them all the other Southern Apaches on the Mescalero Reservation, Victorio and his band escaped, rode westward into the wilds, and again took up their bloody occupation.

The career of this supremely daring and capable Apache chief was nearing its end. Such strategy and endurance, such command over a handful of desperate warriors, such defiance of interminable mountains and arid desert, and such victory over superior numbers of white foes armed and equipped with the best that a civilized nation could provide or invent has rarely been equaled in the records of savage warfare—perhaps never surpassed. To follow the fights and the retreats, the ambushes and the flights, the pillage, the wounds, the torture, and the slaughter through which this flaming savage rode as on a red whirlwind would require a volume. Already both writer and reader are weary of the frightful details of the insane and savage warfare so long waged between the white man and the Apache. As briefly as possible, then, let us complete the story of Victorio's outlawry.

Before Victorio had gone ten miles from the reservation, he began his depredations. With sixty warriors, September 4, he suddenly descended upon the horse guard of Company E, Ninth Cavalry, at Ojo Caliente, killing or wounding eight of the men and capturing about forty-six horses. Major Morrow, in command in Southern New Mexico, at once pursued the marauders with all the troops at his disposal. The chase was carried on with tireless energy and persistence; there were several spirited engagements; but just as often as the Indians were hard-pressed, they would scatter into small parties and make their escape into the mountains northwest of Ojo Caliente. There were Mexican sheepherders all through this region. Many of these were killed, and the Indians were able to subsist upon the stolen sheep. Major Morrow was never able to force the renegades to stand and fight, and the skirmishes were always indecisive. Finally, his horses nearly all dead or broken down from casualties, exposure, or lack of forage, and his troops exhausted and in tatters, Morrow was compelled to return to his post to refit.

In January, 1880, General Edward Hatch, Commander of the District of New Mexico, a brave and energetic officer, ordered his entire regiment to southern New Mexico and took personal command of operations in the field. March 16 he was reenforced by troops and Indian scouts from the Department of Arizona under Lieutenants Gatewood and Mills, numbering one hundred and twenty-eight men in all. A little later Captain McLellan of the Sixth Cavalry arrived with an additional troop and took command of the entire Arizona force.

VICTORIO, WARM SPRING CHIEF

THOMAS CRUSE, BRIG. GEN., U. S. ARMY, RET.

During the late winter and early spring of 1880 Victorio and his band, together with one hundred renegades from Old Mexico, were in the mountains within forty miles of the Mescalero Agency and were in frequent communication with their friends on the reservation. He had been so uniformly successful in his frequent fights and skirmishes that he was able to induce many of the Mescaleros to take the warpath with him. April 12, after a hard fight in the San Andreas Mountains, Colonel Hatch with a strong body of troops, supported by Colonel Grierson of the Tenth Cavalry from Texas with an equally strong force, surrounded the Mescalero Agency where the agent had brought together as many of the Indians as he could persuade to come in, and took their horses and arms from them. It was too late. Two hundred had left the reservation by April 1 to join Victorio in the mountains, fifty of them being effective fighting men.

Victorio's raids continued, frequent and furious; the hearts of the settlers in New Mexico, Arizona, and Chihuahua were filled with terror and they made little effort to resist the savages. Victorio rarely, if ever, had more than two hundred and fifty fighting men, and there were more than one thousand troops in the field against him, yet he nearly always got the best of it. The pursuit by the troops was unremitting and their number was constantly increasing. Though almost completely hemmed in by two thousand cavalrymen and several hundred Indian scouts at the last, about June 1, 1880, Victorio made his escape into Mexico; for the Mexican Government refused to let our troops cross the line. During the raids and skirmishes described above, it is estimated that at least two hundred settlers and soldiers had been killed in New Mexico and an equal number in Old Mexico. Not less than one hundred Indians had been slain—Victorio's son among others.

Given no respite, driven from pillar to post, hard beset by

both United States and Mexican troops, Victorio, now wounded and an old man, had about reached the end of his rope. Many of his warriors had been killed, many were suffering from wounds, and his band was divided. In October, 1880, a large force of Mexican troops under General Terrazas encountered Victorio with one hundred warriors and four hundred women and children at Tres Castillos. The Indians were trapped in a box canyon. A fight began in the evening and lasted all night. By morning the Apaches had run out of ammunition. Still, terribly as they had suffered and hopeless as their case seemed, not until Victorio, who had already been wounded more than once during the battle, fell dead on the field would they yield.

The accounts of Victorio's death vary in a perplexing way, and unfortunately, none of the writers who describe this last battle refer to official records or eyewitnesses. Twitchell [3] says that the Mexican troops, while on a march through Chihuahua, discovered Victorio encamped near a lake in the vicinity of Tres Castillos and in an all-night battle killed the chief and many of his followers and compelled the survivors to surrender. Paul I. Wellman, in *Death in the Desert,* [4] states that Colonel Joaquin Terrazas with a large body of irregular troops trapped Victorio and his band in the Tres Castillos Mountains; that in locating Victorio, Terrazas was joined by several fighting organizations from the United States, including a body of sixty-eight Chiricahua Apache scouts under Captain Charles Parker; that when, with this combined force, Terrazas had trailed Victorio to Tres Castillos, he dismissed his allies on the ground that he could not trust the Chiricahua scouts, and then took all the glory of the exploit to himself. Wellman says that Terrazas had with him Tarahumari Indian scouts, one of whom, Mauricio, a famous rifleman, caught sight of Victorio directing the battle

---

[3] Twitchell, Ralph E. *The Leading Facts of New Mexican History,* Vol. II. Torch Press Cedar Rapids, 1911.
[4] Wellman, Paul I. *Death in the Desert,* pp. 190–192. New York, Macmillan, 1935.

and with careful aim shot him down; and that the Governor of Sonora was so pleased with Mauricio's feat that he had the State present him with a beautiful nickle-plated rifle.

Lieutenant Thomas Cruse, who was in command of Company A Indian Scouts during an expedition led by General Carr into Mexico to cooperate with the Mexican Government in its attempt to destroy Victorio and his renegades, says that in the month of September, 1880, with his scouts he was far beyond the Mexican border. He gives this account of Victorio's end: "Victorio and his band stayed in the mountains for a month or so, but finally ventured into the vicinity of Santa Rosalia to buy ammunition and supplies if possible. They seemed to have plenty of money and a keen desire to be peaceful, all of which was taken at face value, but the Mexicans sent a courier to Chihuahua for some *rurales* to come to Santa Rosalia quietly. They then had a big fiesta to which all the Indians were invited and came. When it was over Victorio and his band had been exterminated summarily, except Nana and three others who had been sent into the mountains a few days before to get money *cached* by them on the road when retreating." [5]

In spite of their leader's death these desperate renegades remained irreconcilable. Nana, seventy years old, stepped into the breach. In the Sierra Madre he was able to bring together about fifteen members of the scattered survivors of Victorio. Twenty-five Mescaleros reenforced him, and a few renegade Chiricahuas joined him. With this last remnant of hardened and cruel outlaws, Nana, between July, 1881, and April, 1882, almost outdid the flaming deeds of Victorio at their best—or worst—crossing the Rio Grande and making his way into New Mexico on two whirlwind campaigns during which he butchered

[5] Cruse, Thomas. Unpublished *Autobiography* in the author's possession. Cruse is still living, a brigadier-general, retired. He is a man of eminent honor and ability, and since, both as to time and place, he was near the event, his statement must be respected.

mercilessly herders, prospectors, and all others who came in his path, plundered the country, and set the whole American Army in the Southwest in violent motion.

In June, 1881, Nock-ay-del-Klinne, a White Mountain medicine man, began a series of religious dances in the region about Fort Apache that continued for weeks, increasing constantly in fervor to the degree, at times, almost of frenzy. The meetings reached their climax late in the summer at Cibicu, about forty-five miles west of Fort Apache, though they had been held at various camps in the northern part of the reservation. They were instrumental in arousing to the highest degree the primitive and racial emotions of the people. They affected the Apaches very much as the exciting religious revivals carried on by Peter Cartwright and others did the frontier white people who gathered for camp meetings in the primeval forests a hundred years ago. The agent at San Carlos and the Army officers at Fort Apache were aware that these dances and incantations were going on and were not a little disturbed, as the summer advanced, by the tremendous excitement created and the ever-widening influence of the medicine man. They had even been present at one or two of the meetings held near the Fort.

"What particularly amazed me," wrote Lieutenant Thomas Cruse, "was the unusual mixture of his audience, which included Apaches who had been proscribed as murderers, horse-thieves, women-stealers; all there mingling with the best elements of the tribes who only a short time before had been trying to locate and exterminate these same renegades."[6] All seemed to be under the influence of some strange superstition that lifted them out of themselves and the affairs of this world. Nock-ay-del-Klinne, it seems, spoke of raising from the dead certain of their great chiefs; but this could not be accomplished, he said, until the white man had left the country, which would not be before

[6] *Ibid.*

the time of the corn harvest. He seemed to exercise some hypnotic power over the Indians, and long afterwards an Apache told Cruse that he had been one of three who went with Nock-ay-del-Klinne to a high mesa—a sort of Mount of Transfiguration—where, after many hours of silent prayer and fervent appeals to the dead to return, three of their former chiefs did actually rise part way out of the ground and address them, asking why they were disturbed, saying they did not wish to come back, as the hunting was poor, the buffalo gone, and the white people all over the land; exhorting them to let them rest and to remain at peace with the whites. Then they slowly faded from view.

Cruse and others believed that the medicine man was sincere and had the best interests of his people at heart, that he was the victim of his own belief and strange power, that he lost control of the tremendous forces of tribal enthusiasm and superstition that he had let loose, and that the bad men of the tribe, taking advantage of the situation created by his prophecies and incantations, determined to wipe out or drive out the white men from the hunting grounds of their fathers. Steeped in the legends of his tribe, reflective and introspective from boyhood, Nock-ay-del-Klinne naturally became a medicine man. In 1871, when he was twenty-six years of age, he was chosen as one of the delegates to go to Washington to meet President Grant. With the other representatives of the Indians who met the President of the United States at that time, he was presented with a silver medal as a souvenir of the trip and this he wore about his neck at the time he was killed. As a young man he went to Santa Fe, attended school there for a while, and became imbued, crudely, with some of the Christian doctrines. The account of the Resurrection, in particular, seemed to make a deep impression upon him. After he returned to the reservation he spent much time in seclusion and meditation in the mountains, but was always kind and attentive to the sick and disposed toward all good works. At the time of the events now to be narrated, he was about thirty-six, a slender, light-skinned, ascetic-looking man, about one hundred and twenty-five pounds in weight and less than five feet and a half in height.

By early August both Colonel E. A. Carr, in command at Fort Apache, and Tiffany, Indian agent at San Carlos, became alarmed as the strange excitement created by the medicine man's prophecies grew more intense and ominous. August 6 Carr telegraphed General Willcox, in command of the Department of Arizona, that he was informed by his interpreter that Nock-ay-del-Klinne was telling the Indians their dead chiefs would not return "because of the presence of the white people; that when the white people left, the dead would return, and the whites would be out of the country when the corn was ripe." August 11 Tiffany telegraphed Willcox that he was sure some medicine man of influence was moving on the San Carlos and White Mountain Indians for some evil purpose. He also requested additional arms. August 13 Carr received the following telegram from Willcox: "The commanding general desires that you arrest the Indian doctor whom you report as stirring up hostilities as soon as possible"; and August 14 a formal request came to Carr from Tiffany to arrest Nock-ay-del-Klinne or kill him or both. Bitter disputes later arose as a result of the killing of the medicine man and the battle of Cibicu now to be related. Both General Willcox and Tiffany were disposed to evade responsibility and to throw blame upon Colonel Carr.

In his telegram to headquarters from Fort Apache, after the tragic events at Cibicu, Carr said: "I first hoped to arrest him when he came to hold his dances and incantations here, but he did not keep his appointment. I then sent two Indian scouts with message that I wanted to see him on Sunday, August 28.

I received an evasive reply from him, and next day marched with troops D, E, Sixth Cavalry, and Company A, Indian Scouts, the command numbering 6 officers, 79 soldiers, and 23 Indian scouts. I reached his village on the 30th, and arrested the medicine man. He professed entire willingness to come with me, said he would not try to escape, and there would be no attempt at rescue; but as we were making camp, our own scouts and many other Indians opened fire upon us, killed Captain Hentig the first fire, and ran off the animals already turned out to graze. The medicine man was killed as soon as they commenced firing, and we drove them off after a severe fight in which we lost Captain Hentig, shot in the back by our own Indian scouts as he turned to get his gun; four privates killed, one sergeant and three privates wounded, two mortally." [7]

Second Lieutenant Thomas Cruse, in command of Company A, Indian Scouts, in his story of his life adds graphic details to this terse report concerning the battle at Cibicu. For some time past both Cruse and Carr had feared that the scouts, however good their intention, could not remain loyal in view of the religious frenzy that was taking possession of the whole tribe. Some of them had grown sullen and truculent. For a time their arms were called in. Cruse suggested that he be ordered to Fort Huachuca with his Company and that Company C scouts under Lieutenant Mills, a mixed organization made up of Mohave-Apaches, Yuma-Apaches, and some Chiricahuas, be brought to replace them. It was so ordered, but before the reply could be sent from headquarters, the telegraph line went down; and when authorization for the transfer came, August 30, both Carr and Cruse were fighting desperately for their lives at Cibicu.

Nock-ay-del-Klinne was in camp about three miles above the point where the expedition struck Cibicu Creek. As they started

[7] Report of Secretary of War, 1881, Vol. I.

up the valley toward his *rancheria,* they met armed and painted Indians everywhere. Nock-ay-del-Klinne was reclining on a pile of Navajo blankets. He greeted the officers gravely and courteously, and after the General had explained the situation to him, he was promptly arrested. About twenty Indians were gathered about him, but at that time they showed no hostile intent. Nock-ay-del-Klinne said that he could not leave at once but would return to the post in a few days. Carr replied that he must go with the command at once. So tense was the situation at this instant that Cruse thought the clash was coming. He felt a thrill run through the crowd—Indians and white men alike.

Two scouts took charge of the medicine man and Carr sent for McDonald, an army sergeant, and made him personally responsible for Nock-ay-del-Klinne. He was to see that no harm came to him unless he tried to escape or his friends fired on the troops. In such an event the Sergeant was ordered to shoot Nock-ay-del-Klinne instantly. Cruse, with the scouts and Lieutenant Stanton, brought up the rear, as the command started down the stream to look for a suitable camping place. The medicine man gave orders to bring in his pony and to gather up some of his belongings, which caused some delay. Meantime he had seated himself on the ground. Finally McDonald was ordered by Stanton to lift him to his feet, and the march began. All this time more and more Indians were flocking down the side canyons. In about twenty minutes Stanton and Cruse, with the prisoner, reached the spot selected for the night's camp. Cruse remarked to General Carr:

"Things looked pretty 'scaley' as we marched along."

"What do you mean by 'scaley'?" Carr asked somewhat sharply.

Cruse replied: "The Indians, armed and painted for fight, have kept pouring into the valley from the side canyons, and it looked to Stanton and me as if we might be attacked any minute."

He looked surprised and exclaimed: "Where are those Indians now?"

"There are some of them crossing at the ford right now," replied Cruse.

He looked, and turning to Adjutant Carter, said: "Those Indians must not be allowed to come into camp; direct the troop commanders to keep them out."

The medicine man was now brought up and Cruse turned to lead him and his guards to the place he was to camp. Then, in the words of Cruse, "Hell broke loose." A mounted Indian among those who were crossing the creek waved his Winchester and told the Indians to fire. Three or four nearest him raised their guns and shot; then there was a volley from a hundred rifles. "Dandy Jim," one of the scouts, shot Captain Hentig in the back and killed him instantly. At the sound of the first rifle, McDonald shot the medicine man and almost at the same moment he himself fell with a bullet through his leg. Both General Carr and his officers and men showed magnificent self-possession and courage. The Indians were constantly firing at the General from a distance of only fifty feet, at first, but he was as "calm and unruffled as if in his own parlor," Cruse writes. By his orders and the cool, steady firing of the officers, soldiers, and packers, the plateau where the troops had encamped was soon cleared, and the hostiles were pressed back across the ford.

The battle opened about five o'clock, and though the first bloody onslaught of the Indians was quickly repulsed, they kept up an almost incessant fusillade until nearly nightfall, from a distance of three or four hundred yards. By that time the number of Indians engaged was thought to be at least six hundred. As soon as possible the dead were buried and the wounded cared for. Then supper was prepared for the weary and hungry command. It was eaten in heaviness and sorrow. Carr next called his officers into consultation. As there was nothing to be gained by remaining where they were, and as they felt sure that the Indians, aware of the depleted condition of Fort Apache, would attack it next day, the decision was to retreat under cover of night, perilous as the march would be over the dim trail and through the rough, deep canyons. By ten o'clock the command was in perfect order to begin the return march. They determined to push through to Fort Apache without stopping. Cruse, with Mose, first sergeant of Indian scouts, who had remained faithful, led the van. It was a night of desperate danger and suffering. With rare good fortune they slipped by the Apaches who had been sent to ambush and annihilate them on their retreat. The three wounded men had to be carried on horseback. One was in a dying condition, and did die just at dawn, after the surgeon and Cruse had walked for many hours at the side of his horse, supporting him in his mortal agony.

The command reached Fort Apache at two-thirty, August 31. Runners had been sent by the Apaches to Fort Apache and San Carlos during the night to announce to their friends that Carr and nearly all his command had been wiped out, that the few who survived were to be killed the next day, and that Fort Apache was then to be attacked and destroyed. This word was covertly passed in to the post trader as early as two o'clock on the morning of the thirty-first, and the same report was brought to San Carlos twelve hours later. September 1 the papers throughout the country heralded the massacre of Carr's entire force. There was great grief and anxiety at Fort Apache that morning, for added to the awful news of the disaster was the certainty that the Fort was to be attacked. Major Cochran who had been left in command and the officers and men to the number of about forty, who were all that remained to defend the post, took prompt measures for a desperate struggle.

"While we were marching in," Cruse writes, "occurred one of those deeds of heroic daring that appeal to the heart of every American. Stationed at the post at that time, was a young sergeant of the Signal Corps, Will C. Barnes. . . . As the morning of the 31st wore slowly along, the suspense regarding our fate became almost unbearable, and Major Cochran . . . became almost frantic. Barnes noticed this, and about eleven o'clock volunteered to cross the river and climb to the top of a steep mesa about a mile and a half away, that gave a view of the Cibicu trail for four or five miles. The commanding officer knew that the mesa and every foot between it and the post was under observation by hidden hostiles, so he demurred at first but . . . finally yielded to Barnes' entreaties and let him go, armed with a good pair of field glasses and a small red signal flag and a revolver. . . . He finally gained the top of the mesa and nothing was seen or heard of him for an hour or so, and the Indians started a party up the other side to find out what he was doing and then kill him, when suddenly he appeared on the edge next to the post waving his signal flag frantically. The message read that we were on the trail, and seemingly all there, anyway he was sure the General was. . . . Later on Barnes was awarded the Medal of Honor, which he fully deserved." [8]

During the night of the thirtieth scores, even hundreds, of the Apaches who had taken part in the engagement at Cibicu were scurrying back, in small bands and large, afoot and horseback, to their own encampments—some to escape the punishment they feared, many to capture Fort Apache and continue the work of slaughter throughout the reservation. On that very morning of August thirty-first a party was killing and burning four Mormon travelers at the top of Seven Mile Hill, and the same party before night killed the sergeant and his repairmen who were

[8] This was the Congressional Medal of Honor. The author knows Barnes intimately and has heard him relate the details of the incident. There is a vivid account of the Cibicu and Fort Apache fights in Barnes' unpublished Autobiography.

out mending the telegraph line between Forts Apache and Thomas.

About three hundred of the most actively hostile had awaited the dawn of August 31, with full expectation that they would then complete the slaughter of Carr's troops. How great was their surprise to find the encampment deserted! They hastened back toward Fort Apache, supposing that at Carizo Canyon, where an ambush had been prepared for any soldiers who might escape the attack of the morning as they retreated toward Fort Apache, they would find the troops. But here again they were disappointed. There was no evidence that the command had suffered disaster. Then they marched on hurriedly to the Fort. They were coming in all that afternoon and the following morning, making threatening demonstrations in parties of fifty or more, and firing a few shots from long range, for they did not dare to come out into the open. No reply was made to their scattered fire. About two o'clock, September 1, they opened from rather close range with several heavy volleys and kept up desultory firing from several points, winding up finally with a crashing fusillade from across the river. No one in the Fort was killed and only two or three wounded. The following morning no Indians were to be seen in any direction.

So prompt and overpowering had been the concentration of troops by General Willcox at or near Fort Apache that the Indians were overawed; and a great many, realizing that their punishment would be the greater the longer they held out, surrendered at Fort Apache and San Carlos. September 21 was fixed by the Indian agent as the date when all who had failed to surrender unconditionally to the military officers would be hunted down as hostiles. September 20 five of the leading mutineers among the scouts gave themselves up, and during the coming week sixty who had taken an active part in the uprising did likewise. Six of the scouts had been killed in battle, several had been arrested and brought in by the Indian police, and a few were still at large as irreconcilable outlaws. In November, 1881, the five scouts considered most guilty—"Dead Shot," a sergeant, "Dandy Jim," a corporal, "Skippy," a private, and two other privates—were tried by court martial as regularly enlisted soldiers, charged with mutiny in the face of the enemy. "Dead Shot," "Dandy Jim," and "Skippy" were executed at Fort Grant, March 3, 1882. The other two were sentenced to dishonorable discharge and were given long sentences on Alcatraz Island.

September 30, just a month after the battle of Cibicu, seventy-four of the Chiricahuas, after killing Sterling, chief of Indian police, left the reservation and fled with all speed toward Mexico. These renegades belonged to the party under Juh and Geronimo that in January, 1880, had been persuaded by Captain Haskell and Jeffords, their former agent, to come in and settle down on the reservation. The leaders in the present outbreak were Juh and Nachez. Tiffany, the Indian agent at San Carlos, gives the following account of the circumstances that led up to the flight. About September 20 the Chiricahuas came to him to ask why there were so many troops about the Agency. He explained and told them to have no fear, that none of the Indians who had been peaceful would be harmed. They wanted to know whether the movements of the troops had anything to do with their former acts when on the warpath in Mexico. Tiffany assured them that it had not, and they went away, apparently happy and satisfied. But meantime an untoward incident occurred. After the Cibicu affair George and Benito, White Mountain subchiefs, had surrendered to General Willcox at Fort Thomas, and he had paroled and sent them back to the subagency. September 30 Colonel Biddle was sent to bring them and their bands back to Fort Thomas. It was the day that rations were being issued and there were many Indians at the subagency. George and Benito said they would go back with the troops as soon as they had received their issue of beef. Later in the day they sent word to Biddle that he need not wait for them, that they would follow with Hoag, the Agency clerk who was issuing the beef. Biddle replied that they must go at once and started toward their camp with his detachment. George and Benito "fled to the Chiricahuas and so alarmed them that during the night 74 Chiricahuas, including women and children, fled from the reserve."

The reasons assigned by General Willcox for this sudden and violent outbreak were: first, "that the reservation authorities did not help them take out a water ditch," and second, their fear of being disarmed. Very likely we shall have to go much deeper for a real explanation than any of the reasons here given. By reading the blistering indictment brought against Tiffany by the Federal Grand Jury of Arizona a year later, we shall probably get at the root of the matter. Passages from that report are here quoted:

"How any official possessing the slightest manhood could keep eleven men in confinement for fourteen months without charges or any attempt to accuse them, knowing them to be innocent, is a mystery which can only be solved by an Indian agent of the Tiffany stamp. The investigations of the Grand Jury have brought to light a course of procedure at the San Carlos Reservation, under the government of Agent Tiffany, which is a disgrace to the civilization of the age and a foul blot upon the national escutcheon. While many of the details connected with these matters are outside of our jurisdiction, we nevertheless feel it our duty, as honest American citizens, to express our bitter abhorrence of the conduct of Agent Tiffany. . . .

"We have made diligent inquiry into the various charges presented in regard to Indian goods and the traffic at San Carlos and elsewhere, and have acquired a vast amount of information which we think will be of benefit. For several years the people of this Territory have been gradually arriving at the conclusion that the management of the Indian reservations in Arizona was a fraud upon the Government; that the constantly recurring outbreaks among the Indians and their consequent devastations were due to the criminal neglect or apathy of the Indian agent at San Carlos; but never until the present investigations of the Grand Jury have laid bare the infamy of Agent Tiffany could a proper idea be formed of the fraud and villainy which are constantly practised in open violation of law and in defiance of public justice. Fraud, peculation, conspiracy, larceny, plots and counterplots, seem to be the rule of action upon this reservation.

"With the immense power wielded by the Indian agent almost any crime is possible. There seems to be no check upon his conduct. In collusion with the chief clerk and storekeeper, rations can be issued *ad libitum* for which the Government must pay, while the proceeds pass into the capacious pockets of the agent. Indians are sent to work on the coal-fields, superintended by white men; all the workmen and superintendents are fed and frequently paid from the agency stores, and no return of the same is made. Government tools and wagons are used in transporting goods and working the coal-mines, in the interest of this close corporation and with the same result. All surplus supplies are used in the interest of the agent and no return made thereof. Government contractors, in collusion with Agent Tiffany, get receipts for large amounts of supplies never furnished, and the profit is divided mutually. . . . In the meantime, the Indians are neglected, half-fed, discontented, and turbulent, until at last, with the vigilant eye peculiar to the savage, the Indians observe the manner in which the Government, through its agent, complies with its sacred obligations.

"This was the united testimony of the Grand Jury, corroborated by white witnesses, and to these and kindred causes may be attributed the desolation and bloodshed which have dotted our plains with the graves of murdered victims." [9]

We must now return to the fleeing Chiricahuas. They took the shortest route to Mexico—right through their old reservation, to the west of Mount Graham, through the Sulphur Spring Valley, along the east side and south end of the Dragoon Mountains, and so across the border to their old familiar raiding ground and their haunts in the Sierra Madre. October 2, near Cedar Springs they attacked a wagon train; but troops were near at hand and immediately gave chase. There was a determined running fight that lasted until nine o'clock at night. Two troops of the First Cavalry, commanded by Captain Reuben F. Bernard, and Companies A and F of the Sixth Cavalry under Lieutenants G. E. Overton and J. N. Glass bore the brunt of the engagement. A sergeant was killed and three privates wounded. The Indians were forced back into the hills; but about eight o'clock at night they made a desperate attempt to drive the soldiers off—firing seven volleys and at times coming within ten feet of the men. The troops held their own until it grew too dark to carry on the battle. The object of this long and stubborn stand (contrary to the Apache custom) was to get the women and children and cattle well on the way. No further fight was made after this had been accomplished. They made their escape into Mexico, pursued, as usual, gallantly but ineffectually, all the way by the cavalry.

Loco, chief of the Warm Spring band, who with a good many of the Chiricahuas, had remained quietly on the reservation, was warned about the middle of January, 1882, by messengers from Juh and Nachez, that they were coming up on a raid in about forty days and would expect him and his people to join them and return with them to the Sierra Madres. They de-

[9] *Arizona Star,* Tucson, October 24, 1882.

Munitions Bldg., Wash.

LOCO, WARM SPRING CHIEF

Munitions Bldg., Wash.

NACHEZ AND GERONIMO IN CUSTODY

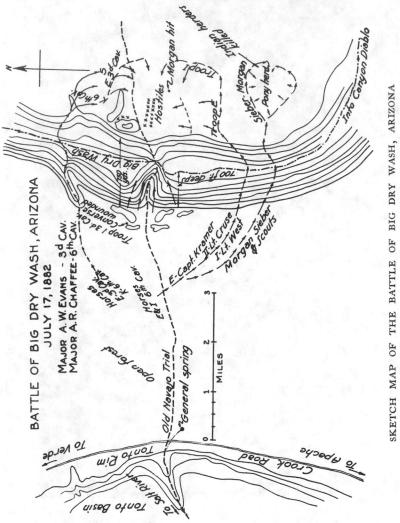

BATTLE OF BIG DRY WASH, ARIZONA
JULY 17, 1882

MAJOR A. W. EVANS - 3d CAV.
MAJOR A. R. CHAFFEE - 6th CAV.

SKETCH MAP OF THE BATTLE OF BIG DRY WASH, ARIZONA

Drawn by General Thomas Cruse from memory, in 1937, fifty-five years after the event.

clared that they would kill all who refused to go with them. By February 15 this information was in the hands of General Willcox, and every precaution was taken by him to ward off the threatened incursion. Two troops of cavalry were sent to posts very near the border and all posts and commanding officers instructed to be more than ever on the alert. April 19, the hostiles, led by Nachez and Chatto, made their appearance near the sub-agency at Fort Goodwin and at the point of the rifle compelled Loco and his band and the remaining Chiricahuas on the reservation to take the war trail with them back to Mexico. After killing Sterling and one of his Indian policemen, they all broke from the reservation, going by way of Eagle Creek and the San Francisco River, and then down Stein's Peak range, headed for Chihùahua or Sonora. There were about seventy-five warriors and three times that many women and children. Troop after troop of cavalry were immediately in the field attempting to halt the fleeing Indians. It was the usual story of hot but futile pursuit. There was, however, one real battle in which Loco suffered the loss of a good many men in killed and wounded, yet in the end came off best, for he was able to hold off for some hours four times his number of fighters and so achieve his main object—the escape of his women and children into Mexico. This engagement occurred at Horse Shoe Canyon in the Stein's Peak Mountains. The Apaches were here brought to bay by the redoubtable Colonel Forsyth, of the Fourth Cavalry, who was in command at Fort Cummings, New Mexico. He attacked vigorously with four troops. Loco had chosen well his position when he saw that he must make a stand in order to give the noncombatants time to get away. The canyon is very steep and rocky. Loco stationed his warriors among the rocks in impregnable redoubts. As the hours wore on, the Indians were compelled to retire slowly up the canyon, and when night came they were beyond the reach of the troopers. Passing over the high range, Loco descended the western slope into the San Simon Valley and made for the Chiricahua Mountains to the westward. Cavalry was converging on him from every point, but doing their best, troopers and scouts were unable to catch him; so, stealing and murdering as they fled, the whole body crossed into Mexico, having suffered comparatively little loss.

But their heaviest punishment came to the renegades after they had crossed the border. Two days after they had entered Mexico, Colonel García in command of a body of Mexican Infantry, numbering about two hundred and fifty, while on the march changing from one post to another, saw a great cloud of dust approaching from the northward. He suspected at once that it was caused by Apache renegades returning from a raid in Arizona. Concealing his soldiers where the fleeing Apaches were sure to pass, he opened fire upon them with terrible effect before they knew what threatened them. However, García made a serious mistake in attacking the van of the column, which was made up of old men, women, and children, instead of waiting until the fighting men came up and ambushing them; for while many of the noncombatants were slain, the chiefs and warriors were warned in time. Loco, Chatto, and Nachez came swiftly to the scene of slaughter and with the fury of fiends fought their way past the ambuscade and, following the surviving women and children, who had scurried for cover among the rocks and in the brush, slowly retreated, firing as they went. It was a terrible blow for the Apaches. They lost seventy-eight, mostly women and children. The Mexican loss was two officers and nineteen men killed and about as many wounded.

Rumors drifted into Fort Apache during the early summer of 1882 that the renegades who had gone into hiding after the Cibicu revolt—including some of the guilty scouts—had united under the leadership of Na-ti-o-tish, a Tonto. The band was supposed to number about seventy-five men. Attempts were being made by the Indian police to find them and bring them in. Early in July they were located some eight miles from the agency and the police went out to arrest them; but, having been forewarned by their friends, they lay in wait and killed Colvig, Indian Chief of Police, and seven of his men. Then, pursuing the surviving policemen back to the agency, they got together as much ammunition as they could and started for the Tonto Basin. On the way they attacked the mining camp at McMillenville. The first news of the outbreak came from the telegraph operator at Globe.

General Willcox immediately ordered a concentration of troops in the Tonto Basin: from Fort Thomas, Captain Drew with two troops of the Third Cavalry was ordered to strike McMillenville and follow the trail of the renegades from there; Colonel Evans, from Fort Apache, with four troops, two of the Third Cavalry and two of the Sixth, was to march down the north side of the Salt River for Cherry Creek; and Captain Adrian B. Chaffee with his white-horse Troop I of the Sixth Cavalry, from Fort McDowell, and Major Mason from Whipple Barracks, with a troop of the Third Cavalry, were instructed to come together on the Wild Rye branch of Tonto Creek. The movements of these scattered commands were perfectly coordinated. The Indians, after passing to the east of Globe, turned northwest and crossed the Salt River at the mouth of Tonto Creek, the present site of Roosevelt Dam. They stole some stock and killed ten citizens in all, but the various rapidly advancing commands forced them steadily northward and eastward. Evans left Fort Apache early on the morning of July 14, and a little before dark bivouacked on Cibicu Creek. Resuming his march early next morning, he reached the mouth of Tonto Creek that day. Here he found fresh signs of an Indian encampment. He halted for the night and sent out scouts to ascertain what route the renegades had taken.

It was found that their trail led toward the Navajo reservation. Next morning, July 16, as Evans was ascending the canyon wall, moving northward, he saw Drew's column painfully descending the other side, after an all-night march.

The farther Evans advanced, the fresher grew the trail; so all day he proceeded with great caution. At dark scouts reported that a large detachment of cavalry had cut the trail, just ahead. Camp was made, with horses lariated and mules closely herded and an officer's patrol was sent forward to find out the lay of the ground. They very soon came upon Chaffee and his troop. With him was a small company of Apache scouts under the famous Al Sieber. Like Evans, Chaffee had bivouacked beside the trail. Before long he came riding back to report to Evans that the hostiles were only a few miles ahead. Sieber said he thought they would make a stand at General's Spring at the foot of a lofty cliff where the trail climbs up from the Tonto Basin and joins the Crook Military Road along the rim of the Mogollons.

Na-ti-o-tish had other plans. Early in the afternoon he had spotted Chaffee's troop, had counted the men, and had watched their progress until dark. He did not know that there were two white-horse troops; indeed he had not seen Evans' troops at all. Confident in his knowledge that he outnumbered Chaffee, he decided to ambush him and cut his troop to pieces the following day. Next morning his scouts brought back word that the white-horse troop was unsupported. At dawn Chaffee ascended to the rim of the plateau without opposition. Evans had instructed him to proceed independently, adding that he would move his command at daybreak and that Converse, with white-horse Troop I of the Third Cavalry, would lead the column. The two white-horse troops could thus easily unite in case the Indians stopped to make a fight, and Evans would dispose of the rest of his force to the best advantage as circumstances might indicate.

As Evans and his men moved out cautiously at sun-up, July 17, Chaffee was seen slowly climbing the trail toward the rim of the plateau. At General's Spring there was every evidence that the hostiles had camped there the previous night. Evans had marched only about a mile beyond the Spring when a courier from Chaffee rode up; and then off galloped Converse with his troop. The word was that the renegades had taken their stand about three miles ahead on the north side of Chevelon's Fork (Big Dry Wash), an appalling crack in the earth's surface. Directly above the trail, just under the brink of the canyon, behind improvised redoubts, they waited invitingly for Chaffee to enter their parlor. But the sharp eyes of Sieber and his scouts soon saw them there, and as Evans trotted rapidly to the front, he could hear the opening shots of the battle. Chaffee's men had dismounted and a few had been sent forward to the edge of the canyon. The renegades at once opened fire on them. By this time Converse had galloped up, probably unseen by the Indians in their ambuscade. He dismounted his men, sent the horses to the rear, and advanced in skirmish line along the edge of the chasm, as if intending to descend the trail and cross to the other side. Cruse etches the setting of the battle with masterly effect:

"The scene of the action was in a heavy pine forest, thickly set with large pine trees, parklike, with no underbrush or shrubbery whatever; on a high mesa at the summit of the Mogollon Range. Across this mesa from east to west ran a gigantic slash in the face of the earth, a volcanic crack, some seven hundred yards across and about one thousand feet deep, with almost perpendicular walls for miles on either side of the very steep trail which led to the Navajo country, and this crossing point was held by the hostiles and their fire covered every foot of the trail, descending and ascending."

When Evans came up with his three additional troops, Chaffee reported to him, briefly explained the situation, and outlined a plan of battle; Evans, though Chaffee's senior and the ranking officer in the field, magnanimously told him to make such disposition of the troops as he thought best. He said to Chaffee, "You have located the Indians and it is your fight." Captain Kramer and Lieutenant Cruse with Troop E, Sixth Cavalry, and Chaffee's own Troop I led by West, with some of the Indian scouts under Sieber, were ordered to proceed with great caution about a mile to the east, cross the canyon there, and then form for attack and press westward toward the central position of the renegades. Troop K of the Sixth Cavalry, led by Captain Abbot, and a troop of the Third Cavalry, together with the rest of the scouts under Lieutenant Morgan, were instructed to cross the canyon in like manner to the west of the trail and then push eastward to complete the enveloping maneuver. Meantime, Converse was to keep up a heavy fire across the gorge. These coordinated movements started about three o'clock. As the men looked up from the bottom of the canyon, though the sun was shining in full splendor, above them they saw the sky studded with stars.

The descent into the canyon and the climb out of it were made by Kramer, Cruse, Sieber, and West with great difficulty. As they began to move in toward the hostiles, they heard volleys from the westward and knew that those who had crossed there were already in action. Almost immediately Sieber and West ran into the pony herd of the Indians. The guard was quickly routed and the ponies sent to the rear. Meantime, Abbot and his scouts, before they emerged from the gorge, suddenly met a party of the enemy coming from a side canyon for the purpose of getting in the rear of Converse and his men who had kept up a steady fire from the south rim. These Indians were hurrying forward incautiously, in entire ignorance of the fact that they were both confronted and surrounded by a large force. Abbot opened fire, to their utter astonishment. Several

of them were killed or wounded and the rest beat a speedy retreat and ran into their fleeing companions who had been driven
or dislodged from their concealed positions under the brink
of the canyon by the advance of West and Kramer. None of
them could figure out what was wrong. From their main position some of the Apaches came running through the pines
toward the troops, advancing from the east. Cruse and Sieber
thought at first that they were making an attack in order to recapture their pony herd. The fact is they knew nothing about
soldiers approaching from that direction until they were met
point-blank by a volley from them. By this time West had
crossed the trail to their rear, cutting off their only line of retreat. Cruse and Sieber now closed in on their main camp and
forced them up to the edge of the canyon. In command of the
left flank of Troop E, at the end of the line nearest the canyon,
Cruse about five o'clock, with Al Sieber at his side, found himself within two hundred yards of what had been the camp of the
renegades, now marked only by a clutter of blankets, skillets,
buckets, and kettles. As the line pressed in closer and closer, the
Indians in desperation poured a furious volley into the troopers,
several of whom fell dead or wounded. As Cruse and Sieber
advanced, Cruse saw the scout, within a few minutes, shoot
three Indians who were creeping toward the edge of the canyon.
Not until they were shot and plunged forward into the canyon
was Cruse able to see them. "There he goes," Sieber would
say. Then crack went his rifle and the poor wretch would plunge
headfirst into the chasm.

At five-thirty the evening shadows were growing deep in the
forest. About two hundred feet ahead of Cruse, separating him
from the Indians' camp, was a ravine about seven feet deep.
He knew that, unless the surviving Indians were captured soon,
they would make their escape in the darkness. He said to Sieber:

"I am going over there."

"Don't you do it, Lieutenant, don't you do it! There are lots of Indians over there and they will get you sure," Sieber protested.

Cruse replied, "Why, Al, you have killed everyone of them," and with that, he ordered his men to rush forward to the ravine, take cover there, and when the word came to advance, to run toward the camp with guns loaded and extra cartridges in their hands. Thanks to the fact that Captain Kramer's troopers and Al Sieber kept the Indians blanketed by a well-directed fire, this was done without casualties. Sieber was right: lots of Indians were there, and Cruse and his men had their hands full. Everything was going all right, though, as he had with him eight or ten seasoned Army men, when all at once, only six feet away, an Apache rose up and confronted him with rifle aimed point-blank at him. Cruse braced himself for the impact of the bullet, raising his own gun at the same time. A little nervous, the Indian pulled the trigger with a jerk, barely missing Cruse, but hitting McClellan, just behind him on his left. Cruse shot and threw himself upon the ground. Sieber and Kramer thought Cruse had been hit. But, when there was a brief cessation in the firing, Cruse got to his feet and dragged the unconscious McClellan back to the protecting slope of the ravine, and after a little rest, with the help of Sergeant Horan, to the bottom. As darkness fell, Kramer's men rushed into the camp, and all was over. McClellan died within an hour. He was the only soldier killed, though a good many were wounded—some of them seriously. Among the wounded were Lieutenants George L. Converse and George H. Morgan.

Twenty-two Indians were found dead within a quarter of a mile of their main camp, and many others were known to have perished. There were, perhaps, seventy-five warriors in the band. Not more than fifteen of them were known to have escaped. The dead bodies of Na-ti-o-tish and two of Cruse's former scouts were picked up on the field. None of the survivors of this rebellious crew were ever again known to be in arms against the Government.[10] In the hands of a Cochise or a Victorio, this band probably would have cut a wide swath of death in the white settlements of Arizona and have ravaged the country for months. Their disaster was due as much to inefficient leadership as it was to the masterly strategy of General Willcox and Captain Chaffee, and the extraordinary dash and bravery in action of Evans, Kramer, Converse, Cruse, West, Abbot, Sieber, and their companions in arms, both rank and file. There has been no finer coordination and concentration of troops from widely separated posts for a given end in the long war against the Apaches. Cruse was awarded the Congressional Medal of Honor for the gallant part he bore in this engagement.

BIBLIOGRAPHY

Arizona Daily Star, April, May, October, 1882.

BOURKE, JOHN G. *An Apache Campaign in the Sierra Madre*. New York, 1886.

BOURKE, JOHN G. *The Medicine Men of the Apaches*. Annual Report of the Bureau of Ethnology, 1887–1888.

CARTER, WILLIAM H. *The Life of Lieutenant General Chaffee*. Chicago, 1917.

CRUSE, THOMAS. Unpublished Autobiography.

LUMMIS, CHARLES F. *The Land of Poco Tiempo*. New York, 1893.

Reports of War Department, 1877–1882.

RUSSELL, DON. *One Hundred and Three Fights and Scrimmages, The Story of General Reuben F. Bernard*. Washington, 1936.

TWITCHELL, RALPH E. *The Leading Facts of New Mexican History*, Vol. II.

WELLMAN, PAUL I. *Death in the Desert*. New York, Macmillan, 1935.

[10] In the above account, I have followed closely the autobiographic manuscript of Thomas Cruse. It is the only full and accurate account of the battle written by one who participated in it.

CHAPTER XIII

Crook Again in the Saddle

EARLY in the summer of 1882 Crook was reassigned to the command of the Department of Arizona. He took up his duties at Whipple Barracks, Prescott, September 4. During the years of his absence all the good work he had accomplished in Arizona at the cost of so much blood and toil had been torn down. Conditions could scarcely be worse than he found them. The Chiricahuas were all in the Sierra Madre on the warpath; many of the Indians on the reservation were hostile—ready to break out in case of the slightest exciting disturbance; all were miserable, sullen, distrustful.

Within a week after reaching his headquarters, Crook was once more in the saddle, steering his stout mule eastward toward the deep and gloomy canyons and forests around Fort Apache. In these remote places he met and talked both with those openly hostile and those still firmly loyal in spite of their distrust and discontent. He knew all these Indians personally, and the Indians of all conditions and tempers knew him—knew him and trusted him. What Crook wanted now was to get exactly and fully the point of view of the Apaches themselves; to reassure them as to his good and just intentions toward them; and to give stern warning to those among them who were determined to make trouble that he intended to handle them with a glove of steel. On this tour Crook took with him only Captain John G. Bourke and C. E. Cooley as interpreter, Al Sieber the scout, and Surgeon J. O. Skinner. He met everywhere influential bands and leaders, hostile as well as friendly, in conferences where all that was said was taken down in formal fashion and put on paper. He had private talks, also, with scores of the Indians at Fort Apache, San Carlos, and other places. He found that the Indians were much more timid and cautious in what they said in council when what they uttered was set down on paper than in private conversations. He found out that the words and actions of the various Government officials placed over them were so contradictory that the Indians were in doubt about everything and did not know what to believe. They were constantly being told by one person or another that they were to be disarmed, were to be attacked by troops, were to be sent away from their own country, etc., etc.; and as a result many of them had decided that they had better die fighting like men than be crushed under foot or driven out.

There were both pathos and humor in the remarks of some of Crook's old-time friends now in all but open rebellion. Said Alchise: "The officers you had here were all taken away, and new ones came in—a different kind. . . . We couldn't make out what they wanted; one day they seemed to want one thing, the next day something else. . . . The agent at the San Carlos never gave us any rations, but we did not mind that, as we were taking care of ourselves. One day the agent at the San Carlos sent up and said that we must give up our own country and our corn patches and go down there to live, and he sent Indian soldiers to seize our women and children and drive us all down to that hot land. 'Uc'lenni' and I were doing all we could to help the whites, when we were both put in the guard-house. All that I have ever done has been true and honest. I have always been true and obeyed orders. I made campaigns against Apache-Yumas, Apache-Tontos, Pinaleños, and all kinds of people, and even went against my own people. When the Indians broke out at the San Carlos, when Major Randall was here, I helped him to go fight them; I have been in all the campaigns. When Major Randall was here we were all happy. . . . Where has he gone? Why don't he come back? . . . Oh, where is my friend, the captain with the big mustache which he always pulled? Why don't he come back? He was my brother and I think of him all the time." [1]

After his many and extended conferences with the Indians Crook was satisfied that, in all manner of ways, they had been treated unjustly and outrageously by dishonest agents and scheming citizens. In his report to the Department of War, he writes: "The simple story of their wrongs, as told by various representatives of their bands, under circumstances that convinced me they were speaking the truth, satisfied me that the Apaches had not only the best of reasons for complaining, but had displayed remarkable forbearance in remaining at peace." Five different times the limits of the reservation had been cut down. The copper camps of Globe and McMillenville on the west and Clifton on the east had encroached upon the territory allotted to the Indians. Coal mines and a silver mine had been discovered near the south extremity of the reservation, and speculators, in connivance with the agent, were doing their best to get control of these properties for their own enrichment. "The agent had approached a circle of twenty of the chiefs and head men assembled at the San Carlos and offered each of them a small bag containing one hundred dollars—Mexican—and told them that they must agree to sign a paper, giving up all the southern part of the reservation, or troops would be sent to kill them." [2] At the north limit of the reservation Mormon settlers had encroached on fields already planted by the Apaches at Forestdale. In these greedy attempts of white men to grab

---

[1] Bourke, John G. *On the Border with Crook*, p. 436.
[2] *Ibid.*, p. 441.

territory that did not belong to them the interest of the Indians was never taken into account. All this, and much more of like damnable import, Crook brought to light in his preliminary inquiries.

When Crook returned to Arizona, the civil agent at San Carlos was P. P. Willcox. However, full control of the Indians on the reservation was placed in Crook's hands. The sole duty of the agent was the rationing of the Indians. There were at that time five thousand Apaches on the reservation. Four thousand were settled near the agency at San Carlos, and one thousand White Mountain Apaches had been allowed to remain in the neighborhood of Fort Apache. Both Willcox and Colonel Beaumont, his clerk, a former Civil War officer, an able and honorable gentleman, cooperated harmoniously with Crook and his representatives.

The General now set about his program of reconstruction. He drove off all squatters and miners who could not show clear right and title to be on the reservation, boldly and strenuously resisted further efforts to cut down the limits of the reservation, and squelched the disturbing talk about removing the Apaches to the Indian Territory. He caused a complete census to be taken of every Indian able to bear arms, and made it obligatory for each one to have constantly on his person a metal tag whereon should be written his number and a letter to indicate his band. On the census roll, opposite each name, a description must be written to correspond with the tag. It was required that, for the present, the Indians be counted at frequent intervals. He made it clear to them that all this was done for their own protection, as in this way they could prove at any time, if ill-disposed white men accused them of committing depredations off of the reservation, that they were not guilty. Crook told them that as soon as they had convinced him that they could be trusted, the roll call would be infrequent, and promised them that the different bands, under the direction of the Army officer placed over them, could go where they pleased on the reservation to select for themselves the places to plant the crops they would be expected to raise for their own support. He notified them sternly that a stop would be put to the making of tizwin. In the spring of 1883, when new scouts were enlisted, they were placed on a different basis from the one used in the past. When not engaged in scouting expeditions on the war trail, they were to be assigned to duty among their respective bands to direct and advise their people and to keep the military officers informed concerning their progress and behavior. Crook's dictum, in brief, was that they should "live among their own people and control them just as we control ours."

October 5, as soon as Crook returned from his intimate survey of conditions on the reservation, he issued a general order in which he said, "Officers and soldiers serving in this department are reminded that one of the fundamental principles of the military character is justice to all—Indians as well as white men—and that disregard of this principle is likely to bring about hostilities and cause the death of the very persons whom they are sent here to protect.

"In all their dealings with the Indians, officers must be careful not only to observe the strictest fidelity, but to make no promises not in their power to carry out; all grievances, arising within their jurisdiction, should be redressed, so that an accumulation of them may not cause an outbreak. Grievances, however petty, if permitted to accumulate, will be like embers that smoulder and eventually break into flame.

"When officers are applied to for the employment of force against Indians, they should thoroughly satisfy themselves of the necessity for the application, and of the legality of compliance therewith, in order that they may not, through the inexperience of others, or through their own hastiness, allow the troops under them to become the instruments of oppression.

"There must be no division of responsibility in this matter; each officer will be held to a strict accountability that his actions have been fully authorized by law and justice, and that Indians evincing a desire to enter upon a career of peace shall have no cause for complaint through hasty or injudicious acts of the military."

October 15, at San Carlos, and again, November 2, Crook called into council the chief representatives of the various bands on the reservation and made known to them in terse and simple language his plans for them and the rules by which they were to conduct themselves in future. The Indian Agent was present at the conference of November 2, and the following officers reported to him there: Captain Emmet Crawford, Lieutenant Charles B. Gatewood, and Lieutenant Britton Davis. To Crawford was committed full military control of the reservation, with headquarters at San Carlos; Gatewood was stationed at Fort Apache and given particular supervision of the White Mountain Apache; and Davis was assigned to duty at San Carlos as assistant to Crawford and commander of the Apache scouts there. They were listed as on detached service and were to report directly to Crook. No braver, more honorable, more competent soldiers ever had dealings with American Indians than General Crook and these three young officers into whose hands he now committed the affairs of the reservation. All four of them have achieved lasting fame in the history of the Army and the literature of the Southwest for their resolute and just, yet gentle and humane, dealings with these fierce, misguided, mistreated Apaches.

Crook's plans worked out well. One hundred and seventy-nine families in the spring of 1883 moved from the hot, flat San Carlos region to the cool mountain valleys around Fort

Apache, Cibicu, and Carizo. They were encouraged to farm and raise stock. They produced crops ten times as large as those of the previous year, and cut and sold to the quartermaster four hundred tons of hay and three hundred cords of wood, for all of which they received good pay. They behaved themselves well. There were no more cases of evil-doing and consequent punishment than among the same number of civilized people. Said Crawford in his annual report: "These Indians will require nothing from the Government after they gather their crops"; and Crook wrote in his report: "From the date of my arrival in this Territory until the latter part of March, there was not a single outrage or depredation committed on Arizona soil, either by reservation Indians or renegades."

It was, after all, the outlaw Chiricahua and Warm Spring Indians, some five hundred strong, in the wild, high mountains of northern Mexico that gave Crook and everybody else in Arizona the greatest anxiety. The General was convinced, from information he had been able to pick up on the reservation, that these turbulent absentees would cross the border before long to make trouble in Arizona. He lost no time in taking what precautions were possible. Even before mid-October, with two staff officers, an interpreter, and half a dozen Apache scouts, he rode to the extreme southeastern corner of the Territory and sent out his scouts into the mountain ranges to try to get some news of them. But no trace could be found of them. He was, however, none the less confident that sooner or later they would make a raid into Arizona; so he began at once to get his pack trains into tiptop order. In the art of the pack train he was now, as ever, supreme; and in the pursuit of hostile Apaches the only hope of success and salvation resided in the pack train.

For the strenuous work ahead of him Crook enlisted five companies of Indian scouts. Usually a company of scouts con-

LIEUTENANT CHARLES B. GATEWOOD
Courtesy, Col. Chas. B. Gatewood, Ret.

CAPTAIN EMMET CRAWFORD
Courtesy, Col. Chas. B. Gatewood, Ret.

ARRIVAL OF A COURIER

Drawing by Frederick Remington, in the Century Magazine. Used by permission of D. Appleton—Century Company, Inc.

sisted of twenty-six privates, two sergeants, and two corporals, but in the expectation of a campaign in Mexico, the companies now enlisted were much larger. Sergeants and corporals were chosen from the chiefs and other leading men of the tribe; and so far as possible the personnel of a particular company was drawn from the same band. Seven scouts were selected to serve as a secret-service force—very dangerous duty assigned only to the most discreet and trustworthy Indians on the reservation. Two of the seven were women. They had no part in military expeditions; their duty was to note and report secretly to Crawford and Gatewood any sign of mutiny, hostility, or unrest. Al Sieber was made chief of scouts and Sam Bowman and Archie MacIntosh served with him as assistants and masters of the pack trains. The ill-starred Mickey Free (adopted son of the Irishman, John Ward) was attached to the organization as interpreter with the rank of a first sergeant. A chapter might well be devoted to extended characterizations of these four remarkable men, each of whom bore a significant part in Apache affairs during the seventies and eighties. As soon as the enlistment and organization of the scouts had been completed, the five pack trains in the department were ordered to San Carlos to be reorganized and equipped. Each train consisted of forty pack mules, and to each unit was assigned a chief packer and ten assistants. When these five pack trains had been whipped into shape under Crook's own vigilant eye, it goes without saying they represented the very top notch of what pack trains should be.

By late October all was in readiness for active campaigning. Small garrisons had been called in from scattered positions and located at strategic central points where they could be used to the greatest advantage in case of emergency. Crawford, with three companies of Indian scouts, had been ordered to take station in the neighborhood of Cloverdale, New Mexico, and from that point to patrol the border westward. He sent his spies far south into Mexico in search of some trace of the renegades, but none was found. All remained quiet in Arizona up to late March, 1883. Then came the anticipated irruption. Two raiding parties left their remote strongholds in the Sierra Madre—one under Geronimo with about fifty warriors to harry Sonora and steal stock; a band of twenty-six under Chatto to secure ammunition in Arizona.

Chatto's raid was cyclonic in swiftness and destructiveness. His party crossed the border southwest of Fort Huachuca, March 21. That evening they killed four men at a charcoal camp. The next evening three men near the Total Wreck mine, west of the Whetstone Mountains, suffered a like fate. That night the party crossed the San Pedro River and the Southern Pacific railroad near Benson. Two men were killed at Point of Mountain on the twenty-third. The raiders now broke up into small parties. A main trail led across the Pinaleño Range into the San Simon Valley, thence northward to the Gila Valley, and near Ash Springs, crossed into New Mexico—not later than March 27. March 28 Judge McComas and his family were killed on the road between Silver City and Lordsburg and their small son was carried away. Chatto was in Arizona not more than six days. During that time he traveled about four hundred miles. Nothing that alert and experienced generalship, supported by the prompt and indefatigable efforts of brave veteran soldiers, could do was left undone in the attempt to catch and punish the raiders; but not a soldier got a glimpse of a single hostile during the six-day raid, and Chatto rode triumphantly back into the mountains of Mexico. He returned, however, without any additional supply of ammunition.

On March 24 Crook had telegraphed Britton Davis, temporarily in command at San Carlos, notifying him that a band of renegades had crossed the border and cautioning him to be on the alert for them. When the news of the raid was made known to the Indians who daily frequented the agency, they instantly betook themselves to their respective villages, brought out arms and ammunition that the officers had no knowledge they possessed, and prepared to fight the hostiles in case they should appear. Some of the Tontos volunteered to do outpost duty in the mountains. It was supposed that the object of the raiders was to persuade disaffected Indians on the reservation to join them and, in particular, to replenish their supply of ammunition. On the night of March 28 Davis received a telegram informing him of the McComas tragedy. He was in constant suspense and for days had been able to get little rest. At midnight, March 30, he had barely dropped to sleep when he was awakened by the slight creaking of his door to find confronting him an armed Indian. He reached instantly for his revolver; but the intruder was no enemy; he was a secret-service man. He informed Davis in an excited whisper that the Chiricahuas had come. Word had reached this scout that they were in the village of some White Mountain Apaches who lived about fourteen miles from San Carlos. Davis called in the scouts near the agency, and in the starlight led the way to within half a mile of the White Mountain Camp and waited for day to break. He advanced cautiously upon the camp at dawn. None of the people were in sight, but the Indian first sergeant called out to them. A man's voice replied from one of the wickiups. It was that of Tzoe—a member of the raiding band, but not a willing one. He was not a Chiricahua but a White Mountain Apache married to a Chiricahua. He had been forced to go with the Chiricahuas when last they fled into Mexico, and he was here now trying to get news about his mother and his family. Because he had a certain rosiness of complexion, the soldiers always called this Indian "Peaches." He seemed glad to give himself up. From him and from others of the party captured later, Davis learned the details of the raid. He said that with Chatto was the subchief Benito; that during the six days they were in Arizona they traveled about four hundred miles; that they were armed with the latest Winchesters; that they repeatedly changed their mounts from horses stolen at ranches along the way; and that Chatto got no sleep during the raid except what he could snatch on horseback, since he stood guard whenever the party stopped to rest.

Even before Chatto's raid, Crook had been pushing preparations for a strong expedition into the Sierra Madre. March 31 he received orders from the General of the Army to pursue the raiders without regard to Army Department or national boundary lines. Crook telegraphed to Davis to ask if "Peaches" could be induced to lead the expedition into the mountain haunts of the hostiles. Tzoe willingly agreed to assume this most dangerous task.[3]

As a preliminary to his campaign in Mexican territory, Crook journeyed by rail to both Sonora and Chihuahua in order to have a clear understanding with the civil and military officers of these states. He was received kindly and hospitably and was promised full cooperation in his determined attempt to subjugate the Chiricahuas. May 1 Crook left San Barnardino Springs on the international border with one hundred and ninety-three Apache scouts, forty-five cavalrymen, and two pack trains. The other officers in the expedition were Captains Crawford, Chaffee, and Bourke, and Lieutenants Gatewood, West, MacKay, Fieberger, and W. W. Forsyth. Dr. George Andrews went as surgeon, J. B. Sweeney as hospital steward,

---

[3] I met and interviewed Tzoe in the summer of 1933 at his home on Cibicu Creek. His hut, a sort of combination ramada and shack, was located on the site of the Battle of Cibicu fought in August, 1881. "Peaches" was then a very old man and was ill. He died about a year later. He was able to give interesting details concerning his part in the events here narrated.

Munitions Bldg., Wash.

CHATTO, APACHE CHIEF

Munitions Bldg., Wash.

TONTO APACHE SCOUTS

Sieber as chief of scouts, MacIntosh as his assistant, and Mickey Free and Severiano as interpreters. Every pack animal in the Department was used. Provisions were carried sufficient to last for sixty days, and every man was provided with one hundred and fifty rounds of ammunition. The officers messed with the packers, and clothing and bedding were reduced to the minimum.

The command moved southwestward for three days without seeing a human being. The whole region through which they marched had been ravaged by the Apaches. Moving now only at night, May 8, they entered the Sierra Madre. Here were found fresh and abundant signs of the hostiles—abandoned camps that gave evidence they had recently been occupied by families of from fifteen to forty, and cattle and horses both living and dead all along the route. No rougher terrain could be imagined, "hopeless for any kind of campaigning other than with Indians afoot." It was a paradise, however, for those who could reach it and inhabit it. Says Crook: "We found at all times an abundance of the purest water and plenty of fuel, the mountains being covered with forests of pine and oak. We made our way cautiously, and with considerable difficulty farther and farther into the recesses of the Sierra Madre, the trail becoming very precipitous. A number of mules were lost by slipping over precipices, but in each case the contents of their packs, when not too much damaged, were saved with much trouble.

"On the 12th, the guide 'Peaches' conducted us to the stronghold of the enemy, a formidable place, impregnable to attack, had such been dreamed of. To be explicit, the whole Sierra Madre is a natural fortress, and to drive the Chiricahuas from which, by any other method than those we employed, would have cost hundreds of lives. The enemy was not to be found in this particular fortress. The nature of the Apache impels them to change their camps every few days, and thus avoid as much as possible anything like a surprise."

On May 15 the scouts, led by Gatewood, found the camp of Chatto and Benito. These two chiefs were absent at the time. The camp was located halfway up the front of a very steep mountain, cut by ravines and arroyos. The attack by Crook's scouts came as a complete surprise. A fight ensued that lasted seven hours. The Indians were defeated and the camp was captured. Nine renegades were killed and five half-grown children captured. About forty mules and horses were taken and other property, all of which had been stolen from Mexicans or Americans. When the attack was made, some of the women had fled into the thick undergrowth taking with them a captive white boy whom Crook believed to be Charlie McComas. He was not recovered and his fate has never been known. The oldest of the girls who had been captured by the scouts said that only a few days before two messengers had been sent to San Carlos to find out whether the renegades would be allowed to return to the reservation. She said she knew her people wanted to make peace and that, if permitted to do so, she would find a delegation of them and bring them in. She was given permission to go. The next day a signal smoke went up which heralded the approach of six women. Crook declined to talk with them. He said that if the hostiles wanted to surrender their chief men must come to him for a talk.

May 18 Chihuahua, one of the ablest and most intelligent leaders among the renegades, made his appearance. He said that hitherto they had thought these strongholds to be unapproachable; that never before had either Mexican or American soldiers been able to come beyond the foothills; that several of the chiefs were now out on raids into Sonora and Chihuahua, but that he was sure most of the Chiricahuas were very tired of constant war and would gladly settle down and be at peace.

Soon after this the scattered renegades began to come in—among them Loco, Nachez, Chatto, Geronimo, Benito, and Ka-ya-ten-nae, a very capable and popular young chief who had never been on a reservation but had always remained in the Sierra Madre. All of them wanted to surrender and go on the reservation. Geronimo, with thirty-six warriors, had been on a long raid in western Chihuahua. They had stolen hundreds of cattle and had been killing Mexicans all along the route. May 9 five Mexican women and a child had been captured. They had suffered cruel treatment for two weeks but had been abandoned to their fate and had found their way into the American camp. They said it had been Geronimo's intention to exchange them for Apache women and children captured by the Mexicans; but that when he and his band found out that a large force of Apache scouts had penetrated into the Sierra Madre they were so alarmed that they released them and also abandoned three hundred head of cattle they had rounded up during their raid.

When these leading chiefs came before him and made known their desire to go back to the reservation, Crook sternly charged them with their bloody and innumerable crimes, and told them he had not gone to the trouble of coming there with this expedition merely to capture them, but to wipe them out. He told them that they were bad Indians and deserved to be exterminated; that if they wanted to fight he was able and ready to fight them at any time; that the Mexican troops, also, were approaching from every side; and that, if they thought they could do it, the best thing for them was to fight their way out. Several days passed before he would give his consent to their surrender. At the last the chiefs fairly besought him to take them back to San Carlos. He replied that he had no authority to place them on the reservation again; that both Army and civilians were demanding their utter destruction; and that the

Mexicans, also, demanded satisfaction for the outrages committed against them. Geronimo and the others then said they would give themselves up and he could do as he pleased with them. They begged him to stay a few days until they could gather up all their people, so widely scattered and in places so difficult to reach that they could not be brought in at once. Crook could not do this as his rations were running so low that he feared, with the additional demands made upon him by the many Chiricahuas he was already feeding, his command might suffer before he could get back to his supply camp at the border.

It was finally agreed that the General should proceed toward the border, by short marches, with Nana, Loco, and Benito, and about fifty other men and two hundred and seventy-three women and children ready to start at once; and that runners should be sent out to get word to those who had not come in that they should come on and overtake Crook at San Bernardino or, failing in this, come on along the mountain ridges to San Carlos at their own risk. Crook reached his supply camp June 10, and the Chiricahuas were sent on to San Carlos in charge of Captain Crawford and the scouts, where they arrived June 23, 1883. It was supposed that it would be about "two moons" before the remaining chiefs and their one hundred and fifty followers would arrive at the border. In his report of July 23, 1883, Crook wrote: "The fact that the Indians left behind have not come in is a matter of no significance. Indians have no idea of the value of time. The members of Loco's band who came into San Carlos in May last were sixty-six days in making the journey, though they had 40 or 50 miles less distance to travel than those whom I left in the Sierra Madre." By way of comment on these words of the General, it is perhaps only fair to say that Geronimo's tardiness in making his appearance was extremely significant as a mark of his despicable

GENERAL GEORGE CROOK

Munitions Bldg., Wash.

LIEUTENANT BRITTON DAVIS

Courtesy, Col. Chas. B. Gatewood, Ret.

Munitions Bldg., Wash.

'TZOE—CALLED "PEACHES" BY CROOK'S SOLDIERS

Munitions Bldg., Wash.

BENITO, SUBCHIEF

character, for he was taking his time in order to add to his large herd of stolen stock which he fondly hoped to trade to good advantage to reservation Indians when once more in their midst. The Indians who came in with the General were nearly all of the Warm Spring band. Most of the Chiricahuas were still behind, with their leaders Nachez, Mangus, Geronimo, Chatto, and Zele.

The months rolled by; October arrived; and still nothing was heard from the loitering Chiricahuas. Meantime, the newspapers of Arizona lost no opportunity to abuse Crook for bringing back these hostiles. "The telegraph wires were loaded with false reports of outrages, attacks, and massacres which had never occurred; these reports were scattered broadcast with the intention and in the hope that they might do him injury. Crook made no reply to these scurrilous attempts at defamation. . . . But he did order the most complete investigation to be made of each and every report, and in each and every case the utter recklessness of the authors of these lies was made manifest." [4]

Britton Davis was now ordered to take station on the border with a company of Indian scouts to try to send word to the tardy chiefs to hurry up and protect them, also, on their march from the border to San Carlos. At San Bernardino he waited for weeks but was unable to get word from the delayed bands. Finally, there rode into camp Nachez and Zele with about twelve warriors and twenty-five women and children. They were all in prime condition and were riding Mexican ponies. Davis gave them swift and safe conduct to San Carlos. Then he returned to his camp, and after a wait of several more weeks Chatto and Mangus arrived with about sixty followers and a hundred stolen horses. Riding from thirty to forty miles a

[4] Bourke, J. G. *Op. cit.*, p. 454. See following pages for a fuller account of these attempts of Crook's detractors.

day, Davis delivered them at the agency without interference on the part of the whites.

No news had been received concerning Geronimo. So back to the border with his scouts rode Lieutenant Davis to await his coming. Six weeks passed and still there was no sign of him. Disgusted at the long delay, Davis was about to leave the border with his scouts, when one day in April, 1884, to the southward a great cloud of dust was seen approaching, and within a few hours Geronimo appeared, mounted on a white horse, accompanied by some fifteen men and seventy women and children, and behind him a herd of three hundred and fifty Mexican cattle. With his usual insolence he rode up to Davis, and wanted to know why he was to go into San Carlos under military guard. He insisted that they move very slowly so that his cattle could feed and rest along the way. At Sulphur Spring, in the ugliest of moods, he demanded that a three-day halt be made so that the cattle could rest and graze. With great difficulty Davis compromised on a halt of one day. But now something serious happened. The Collector of Customs from the port of entry at Nogales and the United States Marshal for the Southern District of Arizona made their appearance and demanded the arrest of Geronimo and his men for the murder of Arizona citizens, and the confiscation of the stock they had smuggled in from Mexico. Davis said he could not allow such action to be taken without a direct order from General Crook. The Marshal had no such order; but then and there he wrote out a subpoena and served it on Davis as a citizen of the United States, and ordered him to effect the arrest of the Indians. Davis was thus placed in an almost incredibly difficult situation—as between the domineering attitude of the fierce and faithless Geronimo and the demand of these reckless and stupid officers of the Federal Government. He was equal to the situation, however. At Fort Bowie was a young officer, J. Y. F. Blake, who had been Davis' chum at West Point. Davis had written to him, naming the day he would be at Sulphur Spring and inviting him to ride over for a talk. To Davis' delight Blake rode into camp at this moment of direst need; and like a flash there came to the mind of the·perplexed officer a solution to his problem. He explained his predicament to Blake, reminded him that he was his senior in rank, besought him to take command, order him, Davis, to remain at Sulphur Spring subject to the orders of the United States Marshal, and, as soon as the civil officers and the cowboys were all asleep, to pull out with the pack train, the Apaches, and their stock, and make a rapid night march toward the reservation. Blake fell in with the plan at once. He and Davis spent a convivial evening with the Marshal and the Collector, in the course of which these patriots drank freely of Blake's Scotch whisky. The seriousness and urgency of the situation was at once made known to Geronimo and he consented to slip away in the night. The officers slept long and deep; and when they awoke after sunrise, Geronimo with his entire outfit had been gone for many hours. Davis was on hand, but was unable to inform them of the direction taken by his superior officer and the Indians. The Marshal climbed to the roof of the house and surveyed the horizon in every direction, but there was no sign of a marching body within twenty miles. The chagrin of the two officers can better be imagined than described, when they discovered how adroitly they had been outwitted. Geronimo's success in stealing his large herd of cattle and getting them to San Carlos availed him little; for he was forced to turn them over to the agency for beef, the Mexican owners in due time receiving pay for them from our Government.

When the five hundred and twelve hostile Chiricahuas were all back on the reservation, it was a problem how and what to do with them. They were feared and hated by the other

Indians on the reservation—Geronimo in particular was dreaded and cordially disliked. It became a matter of controversy between the Interior and the War Departments what disposition should be made of them. Crook was called to Washington for consultation with the Secretary of War and the Secretary of the Interior. Careful consideration was given to the problem, and, July 7, 1883, the result was made public over the signatures of Robert E. Lincoln, Secretary of War, and H. M. Teller, Secretary of the Interior. The Chiricahuas captured by General Crook, and all others who later should surrender to him, were to "be kept under the control of the War Department at such points on the San Carlos Reservation as may be determined by the War Department (but not at the agency without the consent of the Indian agent), to be fed and cared for by the War Department until further orders." Entire police control of all Indians on the reservation was to be in the hands of Crook and the duties of the Indian agent were to be limited, as before, to the ordinary routine of a civilian agent.

July 24, 1883, Crook issued an order placing entire police control of the reservation under charge of Captain Emmet Crawford. His duties were: to keep the peace, administer justice, punish refractory Indians, and prevent them from leaving the reservation except when properly authorized to do so. He was placed in control of all the Apache prisoners recently captured by General Crook, and all others who might later surrender, and he was to care for them and feed them. Further, he was to "protect the Indian agent in the discharge of his legitimate duties on the reservation."

Geronimo did not reach the reservation until April, 1884. In May the five hundred and twelve Chiricahuas were allowed to select a location on the reservation wherever they might desire. They chose to settle on Turkey Creek, about seventeen miles southwest of Fort Apache. They were turned over to

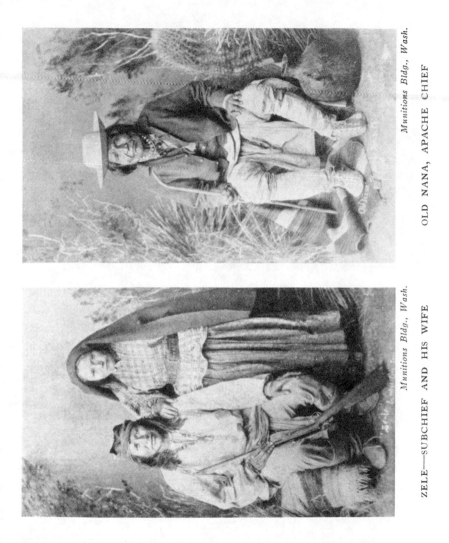

Munitions Bldg., Wash.

ZELE—SUBCHIEF AND HIS WIFE

Munitions Bldg., Wash.

OLD NANA, APACHE CHIEF

Munitions Bldg., Wash.

MANGUS, SON OF MANGAS
COLORADAS

Munitions Bldg., Wash.

CHIHUAHUA, APACHE SUBCHIEF

the immediate care and control of Lieutenant Britton Davis. For eleven months he supervised these turbulent Indians with rare courage and discretion. He was the only white man in their midst. Mickey Free and Sam Bowman, both half-breed Indians, served respectively as interpreter and cook. None too eagerly, the Chiricahuas went to work cultivating their small crops. Chatto was now a sergeant of scouts—and ever afterwards he proved a most efficient and trustworthy one. He and Geronimo were the best farmers, though that is not saying much. Only one serious situation arose during Davis' long and lonely months of vigil with these Indians. For a dramatic account of this thrilling incident the reader is referred to Lieutenant Davis' own report.[5] I quote here from Captain Crawford's condensed annual report made to General Crook in 1884: "These Indians have been extremely tractable, with one exception, that of Ke-e-te-na, chief of the Chiricahua and Warm Spring Indians, who on the night of the twenty-first of June, undertook at a dance to recall to his tribe their success in the fights in which he had led them, and at the same time hinted of future engagements in which they might hope to be equally fortunate. For such expressions Ke-e-te-na was, by the order of Lieutenant Davis, promptly arrested by the Indian scouts of his own tribe, and sent here under guard, where he was tried by an Indian jury, and sentenced by me to three years' confinement (in irons) at Alcatras Island, to which place he has been sent." Ka-e-te-na was released after eighteen months. He became a changed man—learned to read, and write, and to desire peace. He became the warm friend of Crook, and was later of great service to him.

But the storm clouds were again gathering over the San Carlos Reservation. Discord had again arisen between the

[5] Davis, Britton. *The Truth about Geronimo*, ch. 8. New Haven, Yale University Press, 1929.

Indian Agent and the Army officers; between the Department
of the Interior and the Department of War. Scarcely had Crook
started westward from his conference in Washington, July,
1883, before letters were exchanged between the Secretary
of the Interior and Agent Willcox which showed that neither
of these officials was in accord with Crook's views regarding
the management of the Apaches; that they considered the
present agreement a makeshift; and that the Secretary of the
Interior was open to the presentation of other views from the
Bureau of Indian Affairs. By September 12 the agent at
San Carlos was complaining to the Department of the Interior
that his authority and influence were being interfered with and
requesting that the plan of control be changed. By December
the Secretary of the Interior was arguing that the police authority on the reservation was to be exercised only "under
the direction and with the approval" of the Indian Agent.
December, 1884, Willcox resigned, and Mr. Ford was appointed in his place. Ford was ignorant of the Apache and his
ways, but was strong for exercising all the authority of an
Indian agent. He revived the Agency chief of police and appointed a head farmer who opposed Crawford and his assistants. Men whom Crawford wanted to arrest were shielded
by the chief of police, and the farmer and the Agent stopped
work on an irrigation ditch that was being constructed by the
military officers. When on January 17, 1885, Ford took away
the picks and shovels from the Indians, Crook wrote to his
Division Commander, General John Pope, requesting that he
either be supported in his administration or relieved from the
responsibilities involved. General Pope forwarded this letter
to the Adjutant General, forcefully pointing out the dangers of
divided control on the reservation and recommending that
Crook's powers be enlarged rather than abridged. The result
was a reply from the War Department, February 14, 1885,

instructing Crook, pending an attempt to remove the discord between the Departments of the Interior and of War, "not to interfere with farming operations of Indians who are not considered as prisoners of war," and also informing him that his request to be relieved must remain undecided temporarily in the public interest. In reply to the Adjutant-General Crook wrote the following, February 19:

"General: . . . I have the honor to say that the agreement of July 7, 1883, by which 'the War Department was intrusted with the entire police control of all the Indians on the San Carlos Reservation,' was entered into upon my own expressed willingness to be personally responsible for the good conduct of all the Indians there congregated. My understanding then was, and still is, that I should put them to work and set them to raising corn instead of scalps.

"This right I have exercised for two years without a word of complaint from any source. During all this time, not a single depredation of any kind has been committed. The whole country has looked to me individually for the preservation of order among the Apaches, and the prevention of outrages from which the southwest frontier has suffered for so many years.

"In pursuance of this understanding, the Chiricahuas, although nominally prisoners, have been to a great extent scattered over the reservation and placed upon farms, the object being to quietly and gradually effect a tribal disintegration and lead them out from a life of vagabondage to one of peace and self-maintenance. . . .

"As this right of control has now been withdrawn from me, I must respectfully decline to be any longer held responsible for the behavior of any of the Indians on that reservation. . . .

"Further, I regret being compelled to say that in refusing to relieve me from this responsibility (as requested in my letter of January 20) and at the same time taking from me the power by which these dangerous Indians have been controlled and managed, and compelled to engage in industrial pursuits, the War Department destroys my influence and does an injustice to me and to the service which I represent."

In forwarding Crook's protest to the Adjutant-General, February 24, 1885, Major General John Pope, commanding the Division of the Pacific, commented in the following language: "If General Crook's authority over the Indians at San Carlos be curtailed or modified in any way, there are certain to follow very serious results, if not a renewal of Indian wars and depredations in Arizona. It is impossible to understand why anyone having the interests of the Government and the people at heart should object to measures which have secured peace to Arizona for the past two years, and have in addition, done so much to improve the condition of the Indians; or to the control of the officer who has inaugurated these measures and brought them to so satisfactory an issue."

As sensitive as he was brave and humane, Crawford felt that his honor had been impugned, and requested that his actions be looked into by a court of inquiry made up of his military superiors. His desire was granted; and in the decision rendered he was sustained in every particular. Nevertheless, realizing how hopeless the situation was, he asked to be relieved and assigned to his troop then in Texas. With unqualified praise for the rare ability and tact that he had displayed in his thankless and dangerous task, Crook consented to Crawford's release; and, on April 11, 1885, in his letter endorsing Captain Crawford's report, he reiterated the dangers of divided control and again asked "that, if divided authority is to obtain on the Apache Reservation, the entire control and management be relegated to the Interior Department," and that he be freed from future responsibility. By this time the Government at Washington was beginning to realize the folly of its actions. The Secretary of

War in a communication to the Secretary of the Interior, April 18, raised the question "whether the public interests would not be best safe-guarded if the entire control of these Indians be placed under the charge of General Crook, with full authority to prescribe and enforce such regulations for their management as in his judgment may be proper." This proposal was at last acted upon; Ford, the civil agent, was removed; control of the Agency was placed in the hands of Captain F. E. Pierce, First Infantry, and he was formally appointed Indian Agent by the President.

The action came too late to save the situation. The disintegrating forces had already done their work; and the bad men among the Chiricahuas did the rest. Throughout the reservation, the spirit of dissension between the Indian Bureau and the War Department had been working like poison. Its effects had become apparent at Turkey Creek and Fort Apache. On the night of May 17, 1885, a hundred and forty-four Chiricahuas—forty-three fighting men and one hundred and one women and children—broke away from the reservation once more. The revolt was led by Chihuahua, Mangus, Geronimo, Nachez, and old Nana. It was difficult for the Army officers to explain exactly what caused the outbreak. It had its roots, of course, in the attempts of the Indian Bureau, the grafting politicians, and the newspapers to discredit Crawford and Crook. Crook wrote: "In the management of such Indians as the Apaches, a power once exercised can never be withdrawn from the person in charge without loss of respect and influence. These Indians are politicians of the first class, and rival their white brothers in worshipping the rising sun and excel them in contempt for those from whom authority has been withdrawn."

The immediate cause of the irruption was a tixwin drunk led by Chihuahua, Geronimo, and Mangus. Indeed, in order to shield the movers in the spree and make it as difficult as possible for Lieutenant Davis to deal with, all the prominent chiefs drank this liquor and went to Davis and defiantly admitted it. Davis told them that the issue was one of such importance that he would have to report it to Crook and act according to his instructions. On May 15 Davis did report the situation to the General by telegram, through Captain Pierce at San Carlos, his superior officer. Pierce did not see fit to relay the telegram; so Crook did not know until months afterwards that it had been sent. Crook states in his annual report that he was sure he could have settled the trouble and prevented the outbreak if he had received the telegram. "Lieutenant Davis wrote the telegram in the presence of the Indians, and told them what he had written, and said that he should act in accordance with my personal instructions, and that he would notify them when my orders were received. . . . The Indians waited until dark, and again assembled the next day, but receiving no reply became alarmed, and doubtless concluded that I was making preparations to seize the whole of them and punish them as I had Ka-e-te-na." [6]

The making and drinking of tizwin was not the only offense of which these Chiricahuas had been guilty of late. They had shown an ugly and defiant spirit in various ways. Crook had not only sternly prohibited the making of tizwin; he had insisted, also, that the brutal custom of cutting off the noses of unfaithful wives must positively cease. Not only had the bad men under Davis' charge begun to make and drink tizwin again; they belligerently asserted that they had never signed away their right to make tizwin, to cut off the nose of an unfaithful wife, or to beat and punish their women at any time and in any way they pleased. For some time before the outbreak, Davis had found Chihuahua, Mangus, Nana, and others in open and

---

[6] Crook, George. Report of War Department, Vol. I. 1886–1887, p. 147.

scornful rebellion against these prohibitions. Indeed, such hostile demonstrations had been made on May 15, the day that Davis wired to Crook through Captain Pierce. At the council held that morning, Chihuahua was drunk and in a very ugly humor, and old Nana got up and left the meeting, saying to the interpreter: "Tell the stout chief [Davis] that he can't advise me how to treat my women. He is only a boy. I *killed* men before he was born." [7]

The guilty chiefs by persuasion and threats induced as many as they could to leave the reservation; but three-fourths of the band refused to go—among them Chatto, Loco, Benito, and Zele. A little later Nachez and Chihuahua threatened to kill Geronimo and Mangus on the ground that they had lied to them, asserting that Chatto had been killed and that the troops were coming to arrest all the Chiricahua and Warm Spring Indians and send them away. There followed, as usual, a gallant, grilling, unsuccessful pursuit. It was led by Captain Allen Smith with two troops of the Fourth Cavalry, and Lieutenants Gatewood and Davis with their Indian scouts. Crook set all other available troops in motion; the commanding officer in New Mexico was notified of the irruption of the Indians and the movement of Arizona troops; and settlers in the danger belt were warned. But the runaways traveled one hundred and twenty miles without making camp or stopping for food, and made their escape into Mexico, so far as could be discovered, without the loss of an individual. Owing to the quarrel among the chiefs caused by Geronimo's lying to them at the start, the band broke up into several parties. Mangus with a small following made straight for Mexico, and never again united with the main body of the renegades; Chihuahua, unable at once to make up his mind whether to return to the reservation or to flee to his old haunts in the Sierra Madre,

Ibid., pp. 145–147.

halted northeast of Morenci some days, and later barely escaped capture and the annihilation of his party.

June 11 Captain Crawford, with a troop of cavalry and additional Indian scouts under Sieber, joined Britton Davis; and Crawford was placed in command of the combined force of ninety-two scouts and Troop A, Sixth Cavalry, that continued the pursuit of the hostiles into the Sierra Madre. Crook took up his headquarters at Fort Bowie and proceeded to enlist two hundred new scouts at San Carlos and Fort Apache. With one hundred of these recruits Lieutenant Gatewood made an extended scout through the Mogollon and Black Range Mountains, but found none of the renegades lingering on American soil. June 23 Crawford's scouts, led by Chatto, found and attacked Chihuahua's party, northeast of Oputo in the Bavispe Mountains, but it was impossible to surround the camp, so the renegades got away; though fifteen women and children were captured, a good many horses, and not a little plunder. Captain Wirt Davis, who, with a troop of the Fourth Cavalry and one hundred Indian scouts and their supporting pack trains, had been ordered into Mexico, July 13, surprised a camp of Geronimo's near Nacori, killed three noncombatants and captured fifteen.

Though Crawford and Wirt Davis continued their indescribably difficult scouts through the Sierra Madre until late in September they were unable to find and fight the enemy. On September 22 Captain Davis did bring twenty of them to bay in the Torres Mountains, and suffered the loss of one scout as a result. The hostiles were driven out of Mexico into the United States through Guadalupe Cañon, on September 28. Davis and Crawford were in close pursuit. Taking the roughest trails over the Chiricahua Mountains, followed steadily by Crawford's scouts, the hostiles crossed the Sulphur Spring Valley at night, passed into the Dragoon Mountains, then back again south-

Confluence of East + North Forks of
White River, Ft. Apache, A.T.
Sept. 1.ˢᵗ '95.

FORT APACHE, ON THE WHITE RIVER, 1895

Munitions Bldg., Wash.

Munitions Bldg., Wash.

RENEGADE APACHE HOME

ward across the Valley toward the Mule Mountains, sharp to the east again into the Chiricahuas, with Crawford's scouts constantly at their heels. Though they had repeatedly stolen fresh horses along the route, their mounts were by this time completely played out. By a circumstance maddening to the soldiers, they succeeded at this last gasp in capturing thirty of the best horses in Arizona, and galloped back into Mexico. It was no credit to the ranchmen of southwestern Arizona that the Indians got away with these mounts. At White Tail Cañon the cattlemen of the San Simon Valley had met for their fall round-up. Only the night before, they had been warned that these dismounted Indians were in the vicinity; yet they went to sleep at a ranch house around which was lariated their thirty crack cow ponies. The next morning the horses were gone; and, better mounted than ever, the Apaches were beyond pursuit.

There was now a short breathing spell while new scouts were enlisted and the worn-out pack trains refitted. But the renegades struck again like lightning. Early in November a band of eleven made a raid across the border; and in a period of less than four weeks, in the course of which they traveled fully twelve hundred miles and wore out two hundred and fifty head of stock, they murdered thirty-eight people; and though twice dismounted during this time, were able to recross the border with the loss of only one man during the entire raid.

On the night of January 10, 1886, Captain Crawford attacked the Indians sixty miles below Nacori near the Aros River. All the stock and supplies of the outlaws were captured. Convinced now that Crook would pursue them relentlessly to the end, the renegades sent word to Crawford asking for a talk the next morning concerning terms of surrender. No doubt they would have yielded at the proposed conference had it not been for a most untoward and tragic incident, for no one except Crook knew them so thoroughly as Crawford and possessed so completely their confidence and respect. Just at daylight, January 11, while the scouts were still asleep, they were attacked at close range by a Mexican force of about one hundred and fifty. At the first volley three scouts were wounded. At the time of the attack, Captain Crawford and Lieutenants Marion P. Maus and W. E. Shipp were lying by their campfire. Maus and Shipp were already awake, but Crawford was still asleep. Maus and Tom Horn, chief of scouts and Spanish interpreter, at once ran forward and tried to stop the firing, explaining to the Mexican officers in Spanish that they were all United States soldiers and scouts in pursuit of the hostile Apaches. The scouts at once took shelter among the rocks. Some of them ran forward, unarmed, to see what was the matter. Only a few of them fired back at the Mexicans, and they in self-defense. Captain Crawford at once ordered all firing stopped; and within about fifteen minutes, with the aid of Horn, Maus, and Shipp, succeeded in halting the battle.

Some Mexican officers now came forward and in American Army uniforms Crawford and Maus went toward them. When they were not more than ten yards apart Crawford and Maus told the Mexicans in Spanish that they were officers in the United States Army and called attention to their uniforms as evidence of this. The Mexicans began backing away, saying, "Do not fire! Do not fire!" and Maus replied that they would not. Crawford now directed Maus to go back and make sure there should be no more firing. Crawford himself mounted a rock where he stood in full view of the Mexicans and continued his efforts to quiet both sides. But at this instant, without warning, the Mexicans fired at the officers. Crawford fell, mortally wounded, and Horn was shot through the arm. As the Mexicans were not a hundred feet away, it is hardly possible that they could have mistaken Horn and the three officers for

SIERRA MADRE MOUNTAINS, MEXICO

Arrow indicates the place of Captain Crawford's death

NEAR FORT BOWIE, NACHEZ, GERONIMO AND THEIR FELLOW
PRISONERS LEAVING FORT BOWIE FOR FLORIDA

Munitions Bldg., Wash.

KA-YA-TEN-NA

Munitions Bldg., Wash.

ALCHISE, WHITE MOUNTAIN CHIEF

Apaches. At the time the Mexicans thus renewed the attack, Horn was explaining to them in Spanish that this was an expedition from the United States in pursuit of hostile Apaches. He was dressed in civilian clothes, and standing near him was Lieutenant Shipp, unarmed, in blue trousers, brown canvas coat, and brown hat. Nor, at the time that Crawford was calling out from his exposed position on the boulder, and Maus, Horn, and Shipp were talking to the Mexicans, was there any demonstration on the part of the scouts. All the Americans present looked upon Crawford's death as an assassination, and it was reported as such by General Crook.

The battle now opened again on both sides and continued for about an hour. Crawford never regained consciousness after he was shot; but all the time Horn and the other two officers were doing their best to stop the fighting, shouting repeatedly to the Mexicans that they were friends, and at the same time doing their best to restrain the scouts. Realizing, finally, that they could not drive the scouts out of the rocks, the Mexicans retired to a hill about five hundred yards distant. Though wounded, Horn went unarmed into their camp, followed soon by Maus, and they both explained the situation in Spanish. The Mexicans were told about the fight with the hostile Apaches the day before, the capture of their stock, and their desire to talk about terms of surrender. The treachery and dishonesty of these Mexicans was revealed the next day when both Maus and Concepcion, his interpreter, were detained in their camp by force until the Apache scouts began to strip for action. Maus was then released so that he might control them.

Crawford all this time had remained unconscious; so the command devolved upon Maus. While the fight was in progress on the morning of January 11, the renegade Apaches gathered on the opposite bank of the river about a mile distant and had sent messengers again asking for a talk regarding

terms of surrender. Maus could do nothing more than promise
to secure for them a conference with Crook at some point near
the border. The renegades agreed to meet Crook at Cañon de
los Embudos, twenty-five miles south of San Bernardino, in
about "two moons," but with the proviso that the General was
to come unaccompanied by regular soldiers.

Crook met the renegades at the appointed spot, March 25,
1886. A Mr. Thomas Moore had been sent ahead with a pack
train. With him went the very friendly and intelligent Apache
intermediaries, Alchise and Ka-ya-ten-na, and also two Chiricahua women from among the prisoners at Fort Bowie, supplied
with the latest news items from the reservation front. These
four were sent forward as agents of peaceful penetration. Those
present at the historic and picturesque conference were, in addition to Crook, Geronimo, Nachez, Chihuahua, Nana (and
about a score of Chiricahua warriors, who came and went, or
hung about suspiciously, heavily armed), Bourke, Dr. Davis,
Mr. Moore, Mayor Strauss of Tucson; Lieutenants Maus,
Shipp, and Faison; Captain Roberts and his handsome ten-year-
old boy, Charlie; Fly, the Tombstone photographer and his
assistant, Chase; a small boy named Howell who had tagged
along from San Bernardino Ranch; packers Daily, Carlisle,
Shaw, and Foster; Alchise and Ka-ya-ten-na; Antonio Bessias,
Montoya, Concepcion, José Maria, and other interpreters. The
scene was photographed by the intrepid Fly; and Bourke has
preserved a picture of it in the following words: "The whole
ravine was romantically beautiful; shading the rippling water
were smooth, white-trunked, long, and slender sycamores, dark
gnarly ash, rough-barked cottonwoods, pliant willows, briery
buckthorn, and much of the more tropical vegetation already
enumerated." [8]

The Apaches had chosen their camp on a rocky hill com-

[8] *Op. cit.,* p. 474.

pletely surrounded by gulches and canyons, through which they could quickly make their escape to higher ridges and peaks in case they were attacked. They were in prime physical condition, heavily armed, and loaded down with ammunition. "The youngsters had on brand-new shirts, such as are made and sold in Mexico, of German cotton, and nearly all—young or old—wore new parti-colored blankets, of some manufacture, showing that since the destruction of the village by Crawford, in January, they had refitted themselves either by plunder or purchase." [9] Lieutenant Maus and the scouts were camped on lower ground, five or six hundred yards away, with a deep canyon separating them from the hostiles, who, both suspicious and self-reliant, would allow no nearer approach than this.

Crook was well aware that in consenting to meet them under these conditions he was placing his own life and the lives of those who accompanied him in great jeopardy, and that he might be killed as General Canby had been in the Modoc War. But he was not able to persuade them to meet him on American soil in the presence of United States soldiers, so he had either to take the risk or permit them to return to their strongholds in Mexico. At the conference on the first day they seemed determined to make no agreement that would not permit them to return to the reservation on the same status as of old. Crook positively refused to promise them such terms, and they returned to their camp. Alchise and Ka-ya-ten-na were sent into their stronghold that night for the purpose of impressing them with the hopelessness of the situation and the desirability of complete surrender, but the leaders excitedly refused even to hear any talk about surrender. Geronimo directed his people to keep their arms constantly in hand ready for instant action. Crook said in his report: "Even after they surrendered to me they did not cease their vigilance. They kept mounted men

[9] *Ibid.*, p. 476.

constantly on the watch; there were never more than from five to eight of their men in our camp at one time, and even after the march northward began, the hostiles did not keep together but scattered over the country in parties of two and three. At night they camped in the same way, and, had I desired, it would have been an absolute impossibility to have seized more than half a dozen of them. The remainder would have escaped, and one breach of faith would have prevented forever any possibility of any settlement with them."

Crook's third and last conference with the hostiles took place March 27, in the afternoon. Before daylight on the morning of the twenty-eighth the General was awakened by Alchise and Ka-ya-ten-na and informed that several of the renegade chiefs were drunk—Nachez so drunk he could not stand up and was lying flat on the ground. Geronimo and four other Chiricahua warriors—"all as drunk as lords"—made their appearance, all five mounted on two mules. However, before the morning was far advanced, Chihuahua came to Crook and told him that while many of them had been drunk the night before, all were ready now to move toward the border. The whisky had been sold to the Indians by a wretch named Tribollet, who had a ranch on the Mexican side of the line, and had for a long time been smuggling liquor to the Apaches whenever he had opportunity. Crook gave orders to guard the camp of the hostiles so closely that it would be impossible for Tribollet to sell them any more. Maus and his officers had destroyed fifteen gallons of the stuff—all that they could find; but plenty more was forthcoming in spite of their best efforts. A white man told Bourke that he had seen Tribollet take in thirty dollars from the Chiricahuas for mescal within less than an hour, and heard him boast that he could have sold ten gallons more that day at ten dollars a gallon.

As it was necessary for Crook to reach a telegraph station as

CONFERENCE OF CROOK WITH NACHEZ AND GERONIMO

NACHEZ AND GERONIMO, MOUNTED

Photograph by Fly

soon as possible, he started for Fort Bowie at once, when Chihuahua brought word that all the Chiricahuas were ready to follow. He left Alchise, Ka-ya-ten-na, and his interpreter to assist Maus and his scouts in conducting the renegades to Fort Bowie. The second day after leaving Cañon de los Embudos, Maus camped with his Indians at the Smugglers' Springs near the border. As a result of Tribollet's whisky and the alarming lies that he and his ranchmen told the Indians, that night Geronimo, Nachez, twenty warriors, two young boys, and fourteen women stampeded and fled again to the Sierra Madre. Two of the men after they had had time for sober reflection returned. Maus reached Fort Bowie with the rest of the renegades April 2. There were fifteen warriors, thirty-three women, and twenty-nine children in this company.

From Fort Bowie, March 30, Crook telegraphed Lieutenant-General P. H. Sheridan the news that Geronimo and Nachez had fled taking with them a small band of their followers. Telegrams came back from Sheridan in reply, on March 31 and April 1, in effect censuring Crook, throwing doubt on the trustworthiness of the Apache scouts, and asking Crook what course of action he contemplated for the future. Crook's reply was calm and dignified, and was lucid with respect to the situation and the course he thought it wise to pursue. In concluding his telegram, April 1, 1886, he said: "I believe that the plan upon which I have conducted operations is the one most likely to prove successful in the end. It may be, however, that I am too much wedded to my own views in this matter, and as I have spent nearly eight years of the hardest work of my life in this department, I respectfully request that I may be now relieved from its command."

Crook had accepted the surrender of the hostiles on the terms that their lives were to be spared; that they were to be imprisoned in the East for two years, and were then to be allowed to return to the reservation. President Cleveland and General Sheridan repudiated these terms, demanding that Crook should require their unconditional surrender, with no promise except that their lives would be spared. Crook, as a man of honor, had no choice but to resign. He "was unable to see how he could allow Indians, or anybody else, to enter his camp under assurances of personal safety, and at the same time 'take every precaution against escape.' Unless he treacherously murdered them in cold blood, he was unable to see a way out of the dilemma; and Crook was not a man to lie to any one or deal treacherously with him. If there was one point in his character which shone more resplendent than any other, it was his absolute integrity in his dealings with representatives of inferior races." [10]

Crook was relieved from command of the Department of Arizona April 2; and Brigadier General Nelson A. Miles was that day appointed to succeed him. By instructions of the Secretary of War the Chiricahua prisoners at Fort Bowie, numbering seventy-seven—fifteen men, thirty-three women, and twenty-nine children—were entrained on April 7 for Fort Marion, Florida, in charge of First Lieutenant J. R. Richards, Jr., under an escort of the Eighth Infantry.

BIBLIOGRAPHY

BOURKE, JOHN G. *On the Border with Crook.* New York, Scribner, 1896.

CROOK, GEORGE. *Résumé of Operations against Apache Indians from 1882 to 1886.*

DAVIS, BRITTON. *The Truth about Geronimo.* New Haven, Yale University Press, 1929.

Reports of the Commissioner of Indian Affairs, 1883–1886.

Reports of the War Department, 1883–1886.

Senate Executive Document No. 117, 49th Congress, 2nd Session.

[10] Bourke. *Ibid.,* p. 483.

CHAPTER XIV

Victory with Dishonor

WHEN General Nelson A. Miles relieved Crook, April 12, 1886, there were still at large thirty-six Chiricahua hostiles—seventeen men, including Geronimo and Nachez, and nineteen women and children. In addition to this murderous band, led by Geronimo and Nachez, Mangus was still somewhere in the Sierra Madre with a party of eleven men, women, and children.[1] He had, however, cut himself off from all contact with the other renegades in August, 1885; and, so far as was known, had committed no depredations since that time. On the other hand, of the five hundred and twelve Chiricahua and Warm Spring Apaches whom Crook had brought back and placed on the reservation, three-fourths had remained loyal and were still living at or near Fort Apache.

The orders issued to Miles by Lieutenant-General P. H. Sheridan at the time he was placed in command were more drastic than those under which Crook had operated. Crook's instructions were "to secure the surrender of the hostiles without conditions, if possible; with conditions, if necessary." Miles was ordered to carry on ceaselessly "the most vigorous operations looking to the destruction or capture of the hostiles." He was never able either to capture or to destroy the renegades; and the fact that he failed to carry out the exact orders of President

[1] October 18, 1886, Mangus, two other warriors, three women, and seven children were captured in the White Mountains by Captain Charles L. Cooper of the Fourth Cavalry, and sent to Florida.

291

Cleveland and General Sheridan at the time he accepted Geronimo's surrender led later to almost endless dispute and his own discomfiture as a result of criticisms aimed at him by his superiors, President Cleveland and General Sheridan. He had been ordered to capture these Indians, without any promise of mercy whatsoever, or to kill them.

Sheridan specifically urged upon Miles "the necessity of making active and prominent use of the regular troops" under his command. This order concerning the "active and prominent use of regular troops," together with other implied criticisms of Crook's military methods, was deeply resented by Crook and the other able officers who with him had borne the stress of the long war with the Apaches. In December, 1886, after Nachez and Geronimo and their followers had been finally disposed of, Crook wrote a letter to the Adjutant-General of the Army, entitled "Résumé of Operations against Apache Indians, 1882–1886," in which he vindicates his course of action in dealing with Geronimo and the other hostiles and ably defends his methods of Indian warfare. At this point in my narrative it seems desirable to introduce passages from this strong and illuminating document, for it deals vitally with Miles' military policies and operations as dictated to him by Sheridan.

Crook writes: "The policy pursued by me in the operations mentioned above has been criticised as one 'of operating almost exclusively with Indian Scouts.' I am unwilling that such a summary should be placed on official record without a protest, lest by my silence I should seem to acquiesce in the justice of a criticism which would seem to imply that the regular troops at my disposal were not used at all, or were used to little advantage.

"A further criticism is implied in the suggestion of the Lieutenant-General that the troops be used defensively for the protection of life and property. The hostiles were in Mexico; it was therefore necessary to secure this protection, to prevent, if possible, their recrossing the line. To attain this end, troops were stationed in detachments along the frontier. To each detachment was assigned five Indian scouts to watch the front and detect the approach of the hostiles. These troops were stationed at every point where it was thought possible for the hostiles to pass. Every trail, every water-hole, from the Patagonia Mountains to the Rio Grande was thus guarded. The troops were under the strictest orders, constantly to patrol this line, each detachment having a particular section of country assigned to its special charge.

"In addition to this, a second line was similarly established in rear of the first, both to act as a reserve and to prevent the passing of the hostiles who might elude the vigilance of the first line. Behind this again were stationed troops on the railroad who might be sent to any desired point on the whole front, forming thus a third line.

"The posts of Fort Thomas, Grant, and Bayard, with troops stationed at various points on the Gila, at Ash Springs, in the Mogollon Mountains, and other places, formed in reality a fourth line.

"The approach of the hostiles toward any point on the border was telegraphed to all threatened points and the citizens warned in advance. In no case did the hostiles succeed in passing the first line of troops without detection and pursuit. All troops, wherever stationed, had orders to pursue vigorously, and as long as possible, any hostiles who might come within striking distance. In spite, however, of all the efforts of the troops the hostiles did pass these lines, and the pursuits that ensued, though they were persistent, indefatigable, and untiring, and frequently successful in capturing the Indians' stock, resulted in no other loss to the enemy. Troops never worked harder or more deserved success, but during the entire sixteen months of these operations, not a single man, woman, or child of the hostiles was killed or captured by the troops of the regular Army." [2]

Crook had had under his command three thousand troops, and had considered this number all that could be used advantageously under the conditions. Miles was assigned two thousand additional men. The most noteworthy deviations in policy that Miles made from the methods employed by Crook were: first, the introduction of the heliostat for purposes of signaling; second, the stationing of troops at all ranches most in danger of attack; and third, the limitation of enlisted Apaches to service as scouts and trailers in cooperation with picked cavalry and infantry commands who were to pursue and fight the renegades wherever they might go. Much credit is due Miles for introducing and successfully operating the heliograph —a telegraphic device for communicating over great distances by means of long and short flashes of the sun's rays reflected from mirrors, in accordance with the code of the Morse telegraphic system. At Miles' request General William B. Hazen, Chief Signal Officer of the Army, sent a body of officers and men highly skilled in the use of this instrument to establish and operate the heliograph in the Department of Arizona. Twenty-seven intercommunicating stations were established on high mountain peaks in Arizona and New Mexico.[3] His mobile infantry, Miles used to search out the enemy's common resorts and lurking places in the nearer mountain ranges, to occupy strategic mountain passes, and to guard the supplies. The cavalry he proposed to use in light scouting parties, with a sufficient force always in readiness to make the most determined and effective pursuit.

[2] From a photostat copy made by Charles Morgan Wood.
[3] Miles, Nelson A. *Personal Recollections*, pp. 481–485. Chicago, Werner, 1896.

Munitions Bldg., Wash.

HELIOGRAPHIC STATION NEAR FORT BOWIE

THE RESCUE OF CORPORAL SCOTT

Drawing by Frederick Remington. An incident in the Geronimo campaign, 1886. Lieut. Powhatan Clark was awarded the Congressional Medal of Honor for this act. He was under heavy fire at the time of the rescue.

These cavalry commands, in reality, were to take the place of the Indian scouts as utilized by Crook. Commanding officers were ordered to continue the pursuit until the quarry was captured or until certain that a fresh command was on the trail. Miles selected Captain H. W. Lawton, Fourth Cavalry, to lead his crack cavalry pursuit column; and with Lawton went Acting Assistant Surgeon, young Leonard Wood. Lawton was chosen for this most crucial and difficult part in the campaign, not only because of his exceptional record during the Civil War and his general high qualities as an officer, but also because of his extraordinary strength and toughness of physique and his confident belief that the Apaches could be outmaneuvered, worn down, and subjugated by white soldiers. This attempt to make use of regular troops for pursuit of the Apaches in their wildest and most distant mountain fastnesses in Mexico was such a service as few white men could possibly endure, and such as should not have been required of regular troops. Lawton and Wood, however, were not the first officers to pit themselves against the savage Chiricahua on his own ground and in his own manner. An account has been given in the previous chapter of the almost superhuman hardships in this kind endured by Crawford, Gatewood, Wirt Davis, Britton Davis, Maus, Bourke, and Crook himself. But now, for the first time, an effort was made to engage in such a campaign with a whole command of white men; and the outcome was very disappointing. Lawton and Leonard Wood undertook thus to match the Apache in his own primitive way in his own wild habitat with a sort of grim, yet buoyant daring. They were out to show that white men were more than a match for savages, catch as catch can. Wood, like Lawton, was picked by Miles on account of his combined qualities of keen intelligence, physical endurance, and resoluteness of spirit. When it came to the supreme test in the campaign through June, July, and most of

August, 1886, during which they passed over one mountain range after another, nine and ten thousand feet above sea level, and through canyons where the July and August heat was of scorching intensity, Lawton and Wood alone of the white soldiers were able to endure to the end. The command, as organized at that time, consisted of one company of infantry, thirty-five picked cavalrymen, twenty select Indian scouts, one hundred pack mules, and thirty packers. This organization was to operate only in Mexico. Britton Davis writes: "Five days in the mountains of Northern Sonora finished the mounted cavalry. They were dismounted, the horses were discarded, and the men joined the infantry." [4]

Miles' order to the troops in the field, reiterating that of Cleveland and Sheridan, was brief and peremptory: "Capture or destroy." Lawton and Wood and other brave, vigilant officers and detachments, did all that mortal men could do to carry out this command; but the months of April, May, and June went by and still Miles' army of five thousand men had failed either to capture or to destroy Nachez, Geronimo, and their fellow demons. Lawton and Wood were the most enduring among those in active pursuit. Wood equaled Lawton as an heroic figure during these months of indescribable hardship.[5] Lawton wrote concerning him: "I found Wood the most remarkable man in the command on all occasions, doing the work of three men, surgeon, commander of infantry, and commander as well as personal leader of scouts and trailers." And in his official report at the end of the campaign he refers to Wood as "the only officer who has been with me through the whole campaign. His courage, energy, and loyal support during the whole time, his encouraging example to the command when work was the hardest and prospects the darkest . . . has placed

[4] *Ibid.*, p. 219.
[5] Hagedorn, Hermann. *Leonard Wood, A Biography*, Vol. I, p. 78. New York, Harper, 1931.

me under obligations so great that I cannot even express them." At the end of the summer Wood was garbed in nothing "but a pair of canton flannel drawers, and an old blue blouse, a pair of moccasins and a hat without a crown." Lawton, six feet five inches in stature, presented a more stately appearance, costumed "in a pair of over-alls, an undershirt, and the rim of a felt hat." [6]

Lawton, Wood, Captains T. C. Lebo and C. A. P. Hatfield, and Lieutenants Leighton Finley, R. D. Walsh, R. A. Brown, H. C. Benson, A. L. Smith, and other officers, as well as packers, scouts, and privates who had grimly continued the chase far into the wilds of Mexico, had done their work well; but to no one of these goes the credit of the final surrender of the hostiles. That distinction was reserved for First Lieutenant Charles B. Gatewood, though he was long denied the full meed of honor he deserved through Army jealousies and through the pettiness and vanity that marred the really great soldierly qualities of Miles. Gatewood, a very reticent and sensitive man, though indignant at the treatment accorded him, never entered into controversy over the matter nor related the full and intimate facts in the case even to his closest friends; for to have done so would have been to wound and embitter other officers who reaped an undue share of the glory of the event.

July 1, from a Chiricahua who had been with Nachez and Geronimo, but had recently made his way back to the reservation, Miles learned that the renegades could not hold out much longer and might consider terms of surrender. Acting upon this hint, on July 13, Miles ordered Gatewood to go into Sonora, taking with him two Chiricahuas then at Fort Apache, Kayitah and Martine, find the hostiles, demand their surrender, and make known to them the terms upon which it would be received. Though still a young man, Gatewood, for about nine years had served continuously in campaigns against the Apaches, usually as commander of Indian scouts in the field, though for a considerable time he acted as Indian agent, under Crook at Fort Apache. He knew nearly every warrior and scout personally and was known and trusted by all the Indians, hostile and friendly alike. He was an officer of the highest valor and discretion and was as humane and honorable as he was brave.

Gatewood hastened to Fort Bowie, with written orders from Miles to secure an escort of at least twenty-five men from the commanding officer at Fort Bowie. Indeed, his authority extended so far as to require these men from any commanding officer in the department. At Fort Bowie he picked up the necessary animals for the expedition and added to his party (so far consisting of only the two Indian guides) George Wratten as interpreter, and Frank Huston as packer. Later he hired a rancher, "Old Tex" Whaley, as courier. But the commanding officer at Fort Bowie was unwilling to detach from his small command twenty-five men to serve as an escort. Gatewood did not press his demand, as he was assured that Captain Stretch at Cloverdale would provide the necessary soldiers. But Captain Stretch had such a small force that it seemed to the courteous Gatewood improper to ask his old West Point instructor to turn over to him what would amount almost to his entire command. So he proceeded across the border and soon fell in with a small command of thirty or forty men under Lieutenant James Parker. As Parker's force was too small to divide, Parker accompanied Gatewood with his entire command in search of Captain Lawton and his troops. It was thought that of all the officers in the field, Lawton would be most likely to know the whereabouts of the hostiles. Lawton was located on the Arros River in the high Sierra Madre about a hundred and fifty miles south of the border. He had lost track of the renegades and was now seeking their trail to the southward; though the Indians at that time were more than a hundred miles northwest of him. Releasing Parker and his command, Gatewood voluntarily placed himself under Lawton; though with the understanding that at his discretion he should be free to pursue his mission independently. From first to last Gatewood was at the head of an independent expedition. Indeed, Gatewood was in some doubt, and wrote to Miles asking rather anxiously whether he was at fault in thus voluntarily subordinating himself to Lawton. The fact is, Lawton himself had only about twenty-five men.

News came now that the hostiles were more than one hundred miles away, not far from Frontéras. About the middle of August, with his own little party and six men supplied him by Lawton, Gatewood moved rapidly toward Frontéras. Marching eighty miles in one day, he camped near Frontéras. The next day he visited that town and learned that two Indian women from the company of the hostiles had recently been there and had hinted to the Mexicans that Geronimo wanted to make terms. While these women were in Frontéras, Lieutenant Wilder of our Army had talked with them about the surrender of their band.

Geronimo later told Gatewood that he had no intention of giving up to the Mexicans but purposely had the hint dropped that he was eager to surrender so that his party could get supplies, secure a little time for rest, and have a glorious drunk on the mescal they had secured. On his part, the Prefect of the district thought he saw a chance to lure the renegades into Frontéras, get them drunk, and then kill all the men and enslave all the women. He did his best to get rid of the American troops in Frontéras so that the Mexicans might have the glory of capturing the hostiles. The Prefect forbade Gatewood to follow the trail of the women who had visited the town. However, with two additional interpreters, Tom Horn and José Maria, whom Lieutenant Wilder allowed him to take, Gatewood set out as if to rejoin Lawton's command, which had

by this time come up within twenty miles of Frontéras. Then
as soon as he could do so without being discovered, he turned
northward again, picked up the trail of the Indian women
about six miles east of Frontéras, and cautiously followed it
over very rough country for three days, advancing always with
a white piece of flour sack attached to a stick as a flag of truce.
The third day Gatewood came to the place where the fresh
tracks of the Indian women joined the main trail made by the
renegades. From this point the way led down a narrow canyon
to the Bavispe River. So dangerous seemed the situation that
Martine and Kayitah, who were ahead, hesitated. However,
they soon moved on and the white men after them, and crossed
the Bavispe River in safety, where at the farthest point in its
northward course it makes a great bend to the eastward before
flowing south. Camp was made for the night in a canebrake,
a sentinel keeping watch on a near-by mound that commanded a
view of the entire surrounding country.

The next day the two Indians scouted ahead, with the
flour sack always conspicuously displayed. Martine returned
at nightfall with word that the hostiles had been located about
four miles in advance, high up in the rocks of the Torres
Mountains. Geronimo kept Kayitah in his camp, and sent
Martine back to say that he would talk with Gatewood, but with
no one else. Gatewood said later that he would hardly have
trusted himself in the hostile camp had not word come also
from Nachez, who was the real chief, telling Gatewood to come
on and assuring him that he would be safe unless trouble
should be started by his men. Nachez had more influence with
the renegades than had Geronimo or anyone else, so Gatewood
now felt that he might venture into their camp with some degree
of safety.

During the past three days Gatewood had kept Lawton informed through couriers of the state of affairs. Lawton's

thirty Indian scouts had already reached Gatewood's camp, and Lawton himself was reported to be not far away. On the morning of August 24 Gatewood moved out toward the hostile camp, with Lawton's thirty scouts under Command of Lieutenant R. A. Brown. When they had approached to within a mile of Geronimo's stronghold, an unarmed Chiricahua met them and repeated the reassuring message of the previous evening. Then came three armed members of the band with a request from Nachez for Gatewood to meet him and the other renegades in the river bend and for Brown, his scouts, and any soldiers who had come up, to return to Gatewood's camp and there remain. Shots and smoke signals were exchanged between Gatewood and the hostiles to give notice that the agreement was understood. Gatewood and his own little party went down to the bank of the river, where they were soon joined by members of the outlaw band. Geronimo was among the last to arrive. Depositing his rifle about twenty feet from Gatewood, he came forward to shake hands. Gatewood had brought an ample supply of tobacco in his pack saddles and soon the smoking began, with Geronimo seated so close to Gatewood that the latter could feel the revolver that Geronimo carried in his coat pocket pressing against his thigh. When a semicircle had been formed, Geronimo, always the voluble spokesman, said they were ready to listen to General Miles' message. Gatewood very tersely delivered it in these words:

"Surrender, and you will be sent with your families to Florida, there to await the decision of the President as to your future disposition. Accept these terms or fight it out to the bitter end." [7]

There was great silence and tension for a long time—as it

[7] "Lieutenant Charles B. Gatewood, 6th U. S. Cavalry, and the Surrender of Geronimo." Compiled by Major C. B. Gatewood, U.S.A., Retired. Edited by Brigadier General Edward S. Godfrey. Copyrighted 1929. Copy supplied by Charles Morgan Wood.

seemed to Gatewood. Geronimo asked for liquor, but Gatewood replied that they had brought no whisky with them. Then, in reply to the terms offered by Miles, Geronimo said they would continue to fight unless they were returned to their old status on the reservation and promised exemption from punishment. Gatewood answered that he could offer nothing more than the ultimatum already quoted from Miles; that, if he made promises he could not fulfill, it would only make matters worse; that most likely this was the last chance they would have to surrender; that if they continued on the warpath they would all be killed; or, if they surrendered later, would have to do so on more severe terms. This led to much talk, and finally to an hour's conference among themselves. After that, as it was now noon, everyone ate dinner. Then Geronimo said, with a savage glint in his eye as he looked straight in Gatewood's face:

"Take us to the reservation—or *fight!*"

Here Nachez spoke up and said that, whether or not hostilities continued, Gatewood and his companions should be safe so long as they made no trouble. As they had come in peace, they should depart in peace. Now for the first time Gatewood made known to them a crushing bit of news. He told them that all the Chiricahuas had already been removed from the Apache Reservation, the mother and daughter of Nachez among them, and had been sent to Florida. They well knew that all the remaining Apaches in Arizona were their enemies; so for them to return to the reservation would bring them no happiness. This was a grievous and unexpected blow and in view of this new aspect of the matter they again went apart for private conference. They conferred for an hour and then came back to Gatewood and talked on until sunset. Then Gatewood said he would return to this camp. But Geronimo wanted him to wait, as there was a request he desired to make;

and after further beating about the bush, he said to Gatewood:

"We want your advice. Consider yourself not a white man but one of us; remember all that has been said today and tell us what we should do."

Gatewood earnestly replied: "Trust General Miles and surrender to him." [8]

They were all very solemn at this. They said they would hold another council that night and make their final reply in the morning. Then after a friendly shaking of hands all around, Gatewood and his attendants went back to their own camp, where, meantime, Lawton had arrived. From the picket line next morning came a call for Gatewood. With his interpreters, he met Nachez, Geronimo, and several others of the band about a quarter of a mile from the camp. They had decided that they would all go to Miles and surrender. They stipulated, however, that Gatewood should accompany them continually and sleep in their camp; that they should retain their arms until they had finally surrendered to Miles; and that Lawton's troops should march near enough to their band to protect them from other troops as they proceeded toward the border. Both Gatewood and the Indians now entered Lawton's camp, explained the agreement to him, and obtained his approval. A courier was at once sent to Miles, notifying him of the situation and naming a time and place where they would meet him; and on that very day, August 25th, Gatewood and the Indians, thirty-eight in all—twenty-four men with fourteen women and children—started for the border.

Gatewood and Lawton, as they began their march toward the border, were faced by difficulties similar to those that Lieutenant Maus had to deal with after Crawford's death. The Chiricahuas were heavily armed and unsubdued. They were not

---

[8] *Ibid.*

prisoners. They refused to march with Lawton's troops and were always distant two miles or more from Lawton's flank. They invariably made camp for the night in places where it would have been impossible to take them by surprise. But there was this difference: the escort consisted of officers as grim and capable and seasoned as any in the field during that generation; and at the end, Miles had Crook's experience to profit by. On the first day's march, a very exciting incident occurred: just as Gatewood and the Indians were about to make camp, the Mexican commander from Frontéras, with two hundred Mexican infantry, made his appearance at no great distance. Now that the renegades seemed within their reach, the Mexicans demanded the right to effect their capture. While Lawton and his command disputed the matter with them, Gatewood fled northward about ten miles with the renegades, and then halted to see how Lawton would make out. A courier soon came up to say that the Mexicans demanded a conference with Geronimo in order to assure themselves that the renegades intended actually to surrender to General Miles. The Indians wanted nothing to do with the Mexicans; and it was very difficult to bring about the desired meeting. But it was at last agreed that the Mexican officer with an escort of seven men should meet the hostiles for a talk. Geronimo and his party met them—alert, suspicious, and fully armed.

Gatewood writes in his official report: "The Prefect asked Geronimo why he had not surrendered at Frontéras. 'Because I did not want to be murdered,' retorted the latter.

" 'Are you going to surrender to the Americans?'

" 'I am; for I can trust them not to murder me and my people.'

" 'Then I shall go along and see that you surrender.'

" 'No,' shouted Geronimo, '*You* are going *south,* and *I* am going *north.*' "

However, a Mexican soldier was sent along and later reported to the officer that the Chiricahuas had surrendered and had been sent by Miles to Florida.

During the march toward the border Miles himself was on the anxious seat. Much was expected of him. He had promised much. Yet for four months his army of five thousand men had been employed against these thirty-eight Chiricahuas. His troops had suffered serious fatalities and casualties, yet not a single renegade had been killed or captured. Now they were coming to surrender to him. Would they hold fast to their intention? And would they yield on terms that matched his promises to the public and that fulfilled the requirements laid upon him by the President and the commanding General of the Army?

To Gatewood, Lawton, and other officers who were bringing in the hostilities the uncertainty as to the outcome became agonizing, for Miles refused for several days to meet Gatewood, Lawton and the Indians for the conference that had been agreed upon. He ordered Lawton not to bring the Chiricahuas on American soil unless they delivered hostages into his hands. But Lawton had promised them safe conduct into Miles' presence. He was bound by the honor of an American officer! Miles would not stir. The Indians were growing very restive and suspicious. More than once they had urged Gatewood to run away with them through the mountains toward Fort Bowie so that they could get into direct contact with Miles; but knowing that Miles was not then at Fort Bowie and fearing that if he left them to go in search of the General, they might be attacked either by the Mexicans or by one of our own commands operating in that neighborhood, Gatewood refused their pleas. Lawton at last, in desperation, said to Lieutenant Abiel Smith, next in command, that he saw no way out but to let them go, give them a start of twenty-four hours in accordance with a promise made to them, and then go after them again. Smith's soldierly honor did not irk him to the degree Crook's did, or Gatewood's, or Lawton's. He said with a grim and knowing smile:

"I haven't promised them anything. You stay here [at the San Bernardino Ranch] and communicate with Miles and I'll take command." Days went by and still Miles refused to come to meet the Indians. Lawton wrote to his wife, September 2: "I am too anxious and worried to write you much. I cannot get the General to come out and see them and they are very uneasy about it. What will occur, no one can tell." [9] Lawton being temporarily absent, there was talk of attacking the Indians and killing Geronimo. The renegades got wind of this, and mounting their horses, took the back trail. But Gatewood followed them at once and was able to restore their confidence. Abiel Smith was rather strong for direct action. Geronimo asked Gatewood what he would do if the soldiers fired upon his people. Gatewood said he would try to stop it, but that, if he could not do so, he would run away with them. Nachez then said: "Better stay right with us lest some of our men believe you treacherous and kill you." Gatewood was in a very difficult situation, indeed. He was so sensitive to any mention of attacking the Indians that he asked to be transferred to some other command; but Lawton gave him to understand that, if necessary, he would use force to compel him to remain with his command. At last, at Skeleton Canyon on September 3, Geronimo's brother having been sent to Miles as a hostage, the General met Gatewood and Lawton for the promised parley with the renegades.

September 4 Miles met Geronimo and Nachez and agreed upon the terms of surrender. There was tremendous commotion in officialdom following Miles' report that the hostiles had surrendered. It developed into a "battle above the clouds,"

[9] For this quotation and many additional details, see Hagedorn, *op. cit.*, Vol. I, chap. 5.

PURSUING GERONIMO

Drawing by Frederick Remington, in Remington's "Frontier Sketches"
Courtesy of the Werner Publishing Company

Munitions Bldg., Wash.

CAPTAIN LAWTON AND LEONARD WOOD *en route* TO SAN ANTONIO WITH CHIRICAHUA RENEGADES

Lawton, second from left; Wood, reclining in front of him

and ended in a Senate investigation during which every order, report, telegram, and comment dealing with the event was introduced. The language of war is best adapted for the elucidation of the matter. It began with a machine-gun chatter of telegrams from such high officials as President Cleveland, Lieutenant-General Sheridan, the Secretary of War, and General O. O. Howard, Commander of the Division of the Pacific. This was replied to by a smoke screen of rhetoric on the part of General Miles: "their surrender as prisoners of war to the troops in the field," "the last hereditary chief of the hostile Apaches," "direct result of the intrepid zeal and indefatigable efforts of the troops in the field," "Skeleton Cañon, a favorite resort of the Indians in former years and well suited by name and tradition to witness the closing scenes of such an Indian war." Then came the camouflage that led the effete gentlemen of the East to suppose that Geronimo and his band had been *captured* or had *surrendered* without *conditions;* the disappearance of one telegram—"sunk without trace"—and the temporary suppression of another one at a very crucial moment by Miles' Adjutant-General—these are some of the colorful aspects of this battle of words.

Unfortunately, Cleveland, Sheridan, the Secretary of War, and Howard all interpreted Miles' account of the submission of the hostiles as meaning that they had been captured or had surrendered unconditionally. The news was immeasurably gratifying to Cleveland and Sheridan. As early as August 23 Cleveland had telegraphed to the War Department: "I hope nothing will be done with Geronimo which will prevent our treating him as a prisoner of war, if we cannot hang him, which I would much prefer." September 7 he telegraphed to the Secretary of War urging that "all the hostiles should be very safely kept as prisoners until they can be tried for their crimes or otherwise disposed of." The same day, September 7, Sheridan telegraphed Miles as follows: "As the disposition of Geronimo and his hostile band is yet to be decided by the President and as they are prisoners without conditions, you are hereby directed to hold them in close confinement at Fort Bowie until the decision of the President is communicated to you." This same day, September 7, Sheridan telegraphed Cleveland recommending "that Geronimo and all the adult males that have surrendered with him to General Miles be held as prisoners by the military at such point in the Department of Arizona as General Miles may determine, subject to such trial and punishment as may be awarded them by the civil authorities of the Territories of Arizona and New Mexico." In reply to the above telegram came one from Cleveland, September 8, saying: "I think Geronimo and the rest of the hostiles should be immediately sent to the nearest fort or prison where they can be securely confined. The most important thing now is to guard against all chances of escape."

Now what Miles had actually reported to his superior officers was this: "I informed [them] should they throw down their arms and place themselves entirely at our mercy we should certainly not kill them, but that they must surrender absolutely as prisoners of war to the Federal authorities, and rely upon the Government to treat them fairly and justly. I informed them that I was removing all the Chiricahuas and Warm Springs from Arizona, and that they would all be removed from this country at once and for all time." Did Cleveland and Sheridan misinterpret Miles' words because they lacked adequate training in logic and the correct use of the English language, or did Miles report an unconditional surrender and the conditions upon which the surrender was made in one and the same breath? It is for the reader to decide. What is plain is that Miles was handling a very hot potato and desired to pass it on just as soon as possible. In reality, on the morning of September 8, before he had read Sheridan's telegram of September 7, he had entrained the hostiles and started them for San Antonio in charge of Lawton, Wood, and a strong escort. Howard, Miles' immediate superior in command, charged Miles with starting the hostiles for Florida "in direct contravention of the Lieutenant-General and without waiting to hear the decision of the President or of the War Department." Miles denied this. But there are other ways of killing a cat than by choking it with butter. Hagedorn, basing his statement upon an entry in Leonard Wood's *Diary* for September 8, 1886, says: "The acting adjutant-general on Miles' staff [Captain William A. Thompson] . . . received the telegram as the troops were preparing to take the Indians to the railroad, read it, tucked it in his pocket. . . . Wood, arriving with Lawton and the balance of the hostiles, with orders to go with them as far as San Antonio, had time only to refresh his tattered wardrobe before the escort wagons drew up. . . . Captain Thompson, riding down to the railroad at Wood's side, very mellow and friendly, patted his pocket. 'I've got something here which would stop this movement, but I am not going to let the old man see it until you are gone.' " [10]

Miles must have drawn a long breath of relief the moment that the entrained Indians crossed the limits of his Department. September 10 the Secretary of War telegraphed to General D. S. Stanley at San Antonio, commanding the Department of Texas: "You will take charge of these Indians and securely confine them at San Antonio barracks and hold them until further orders." The same day Stanley replied by wire: "Geronimo and party have arrived and are quartered in quartermaster's depot under guard. There is no permanent or safe guardhouse and no place of security at the post proper, which is only

[10] *Ibid.,* pp. 102–103.

now in course of construction." Miles' disposition of the hostiles was playing hob with the plans of the President and the higher Army officials. Not until September 11 was Sheridan informed that the Indians had been stopped at San Antonio. September 13 he instructed Miles "to forward without delay a special report of the capture of Geronimo and the hostile Apaches." Evidently Miles did not report promptly. September 17 General Howard sent this telegram to the Adjutant-General at Washington: "The special field order of General Miles directing that Geronimo and his band be sent to Fort Marion, Florida, states it is issued in obedience to telegraphic instructions from the Acting Secretary of War, dated September 4. Will you please furnish me with a copy of these instructions?" September 18 the Acting Adjutant-General replied to Howard: "There is no record of a telegram of September 4, *or any other date, from the Acting Secretary of War to General Miles,* directing him to send Geronimo and band to Fort Marion, Florida. No such order has been given." September 23 the Acting Secretary of War sent the following telegram to Howard: "The President desires you, without delay, to send him by telegraph a full report of the capture of Geronimo and the Apaches who were with him." The same day Howard replied: "General Miles was ordered by telegraph on the 13th instant to forward without delay a special report of the capture of Geronimo and the Apaches who were with him. On the 18th instant he acknowledged the receipt of the telegram, and stated the report would be forwarded by mail." September 24 the President wired Howard that he would "be satisfied with a detailed account of the immediate circumstances attending the capture." That same day Howard replied in a dispatch of considerable length that concluded with this paragraph:

"I believed at first from official reports that the surrender was unconditional, except that the troops themselves would not

kill the hostiles. Now from General Miles' dispatches and from
his annual report . . . the conditions are plain: first, that the
lives of all the Indians should be spared; second, that they
should be sent to Fort Marion, Florida, where their tribe,
including their families, had already been ordered."

Howard's telegram was referred to Sheridan, and September 25 he returned it to the Secretary of War with this endorse-
ment: "It was my understanding that Geronimo and the hostiles
surrendered unconditionally, and it was on that account that
I recommended that they should be turned over to the civil
authorities of Arizona and New Mexico for trial and such
punishment as might be awarded them."

September 24 Miles made his belated special report. It
contained nothing that had not already been included in the
annual report summarized above by Howard. September 25
the Secretary of War wired Miles: "It would appear from dis-
dispatches received through division headquarters that Geronimo, instead of being captured, surrendered, and that the surrender, instead of being unconditional, was, contrary to expec-
tations here, accompanied with conditions and promises. That
the President may clearly understand the present status of
Geronimo and his band, he desires you to report by telegraph
direct the exact promises, if any, made to them at the time of
surrender." In reply, on the twenty-fifth, Miles telegraphed
to the President requesting that he might report to him in
person. The following day Cleveland wired denying this request on the ground that it was important for Miles to remain
with his command at that time. He also emphatically repeated
his request of the previous day. At last poor Miles telegraphed,
September 29: "On the 6th instant, I forwarded telegraphic
report of 153 words, and on 19th forwarded special report, together with report in full of Captain Lawton, also my annual
report. These give as full an account of facts, circumstances,

and conversations as language can express, and as this matter involves the lives of men, I beg that they may be carefully read before any further action is taken."

The President was a man slow to get impressions, but determined in his efforts to learn. So, September 29, the following telegram was sent by the Secretary of War to Stanley at San Antonio: "That there may be no misunderstanding here as to the status of Geronimo and the Indians who surrendered with him, the President desires you to ascertain, as fully and clearly as possible, the exact understanding of Geronimo and Nachez as to the conditions of the surrender and the immediate circumstances which led to it."

Stanley's report showed that Geronimo and Nachez had clearly understood all that Miles promised them—and quite a little more. "Both chiefs say they never thought of surrender until Lieutenant Gatewood, interpreter George Wratten, and the two scouts came to them and said the Great Father wanted them to surrender; that they believed this, but did not believe Crook, because he talked ugly to them, and that they thought he would put them under Chatto, and that when Geronimo met Miles at Skeleton Cañon, the latter said: 'Lay down your arms and come with me to Fort Bowie, and in five days you will see your families, now in Florida with Chihuahua, and no harm will be done.' "

October 11 the Secretary of War directed Stanley to supply by telegram the name, age, sex, and condition of health of each one of the hostile Apaches in his custody at San Antonio. Stanley replied the same day giving details concerning the fifteen men, eleven women, and six children in the band, and also the names of the two enlisted scouts who had gone with Gatewood into their camp to demand their surrender. October 19 the Secretary of War issued an order to Sheridan to send the fifteen adult male hostiles under proper guard to Fort

Pickens, Florida, to be kept there in close custody. The same order decreed that the eleven women, six children, and two scouts should be sent to Fort Marion, Florida, to be placed with the other Chiricahua and Warm Spring Indians who had been taken there in September.[11]

October 20 L. Q. C. Lamar, the Secretary of the Interior, gave his approval of the above order. The prisoners for both Fort Pickens and Fort Marion left San Antonio by special train, October 22. October 25 General Schofield telegraphed the Adjutant-General that the fifteen male hostiles had been delivered at Fort Pickens.

At the same time that Miles was pressing the campaign against the renegades in Mexico he was deeply employed in an attempt to remove forever from Arizona the Chiricahua and Warm Spring Indians located on the military reservation near Fort Apache. Men, women, and children, they numbered four hundred and forty. Their status was that of prisoners of war. They were kept under strict surveillance by the military, but had never been disarmed or dismounted. Among them were Chatto, Loco, Ka-ya-ten-na, and many other scouts who had served faithfully and efficiently under Crook in his campaigns against Nachez, Chihuahua, Mangus, and Geronimo in 1885, and in 1886. These four hundred and forty prisoners of war had been more or less industriously cultivating little farms near Fort Apache, accumulating cows, sheep, horses and mules, and cutting and selling hay and wood to the Government. The leaders seemed to be doing their best under the very difficult circumstances to live the life of the white man so earnestly pointed out to them by Crook. They were intensely hated and

---

[11] There is a discrepancy between this report and that of Lieutenant Gatewood. Stanley reports thirty-two Apaches in all. Gatewood states that thirty-eight surrendered. The contradiction is accounted for by the fact that the night before Lawton reached Fort Bowie with his prisoners, three men and three women slipped out of his camp and escaped into the mountains.

feared by the citizens of Arizona and heartily disliked by the White Mountain and other Apaches.

In July Miles went to Fort Apache for the purpose of working out some plan by which these Indians could be removed to a remote location in the East. He talked with the leading men, holding before them rosy pictures of what the Government might be persuaded to do for them in money and farms and stock if they would consent peaceably to leave their native mountains and mesas and give up their plots of ground for larger and more productive holdings in some new land. He was able to induce a delegation of ten or twelve of the principal men to go to Washington for the purpose of inquiring what the Government would be willing to do for them if they moved. It was an ill-advised step on the part of Miles; there was no good ground to believe that the Government would or could relocate them satisfactorily on an Eastern reservation. However, about the middle of July, the delegation journeyed to Washington in charge of Captain J. H. Dorst, with Mickey Free, Concepcion, and Sam Bowman as interpreters. Chatto was the leading man in the delegation.

The Indians met the Secretary of War and the Secretary of the Interior and were presented to President Cleveland. But no decision was reached concerning a new location, nor was anything important accomplished. Chatto was presented with a large silver medal, and Secretary Endicott of the War Department gave him a certificate to carry away. These gifts pleased Chatto and set his disturbed mind at rest, for he supposed, naturally, that they were marks of approval from the highest officers of the Government and carried with them the assurance that he and his people were not to be removed from the Apache reservation. He was soon disillusioned. While the delegation was still in Washington, Cleveland and Sheridan had made up their minds that all of the Chiricahuas, both the delegation in Washington and those at home on the reservation, should be sent to Fort Marion, Florida, and held there as prisoners. Sheridan telegraphed to Miles, July 31: "The President wishes me to ask what you think of the proposition to forcibly arrest all on the reservation and send them to Fort Marion, Florida, where they can be joined by the party now here." Miles replied by wire, August 2, giving his reactions, *pro* and *con*, to the President's proposal. On the whole, he favored it; but he pointed out this serious objection: "As the delegation went to Washington by authority of the Government with a view of making some permanent arrangement for their future, I fear it would be charged that the Government had taken advantage of them, and believe the Indians would consider it an act of bad faith. . . ." However, he protested against the return of the delegation to Arizona; for he had already taken steps for the forcible removal of the Chiricahuas in Arizona. Colonel Wade, in command at Fort Apache, had been directed to keep them completely under his control. Accordingly, Chatto and his party were delayed at Carlisle, Pennsylvania, for five days; and then, notwithstanding Miles' request that they be detained still longer, were again started on their way to Arizona. By the time they reached Kansas, the War Department, yielding to Miles' repeated request, ordered that they be stopped and taken to Fort Leavenworth; and there they were held, in fear and great anxiety of mind, until September 12. The Secretary of War then sent the following order to the Commanding General of the Division of the Missouri: "You will cause the Apache Indians now at Fort Leavenworth to be sent under charge of Captain Dorst, Fourth Cavalry, by the most direct and expeditious route to St. Augustine, Florida, and upon arrival to be turned over to the commanding officer at that post for confinement with other Indian prisoners now there." This disposition of the delegation met the approval of President Cleveland, Endicott, the Secretary of War, L. Q. C. Lamar, the Secretary of the Interior, and Lieutenant-General Sheridan.

During August and September, while the delegation was confined at Fort Leavenworth, Miles had made ample military preparation for the removal of the four hundred and twenty-eight Indians on the reservation. He had added to Colonel Wade's five troops stationed at Fort Apache a troop from San Carlos, two from Fort Thomas, and one from Alma, New Mexico. The Indian men were placed under guard and disarmed; and on September 7 the whole camp—men, women, and children—were started for Holbrook, one hundred miles away, where they were put on the Atlantic and Pacific Railway train and sent by way of Albuquerque, St. Louis, and Atlanta, to Fort Marion, Florida, which they reached on September 20, the same day that Chatto and his party arrived.

It has seemed to citizens of sensitive honor—particularly to men like Captain John G. Bourke, Lieutenants Charles B. Gatewood and Britton Davis, and General George Crook, humane and chivalrous soldiers—that these Chiricahua and Warm Spring Reservation Indians were dishonorably dealt with by the Government. In the closing pages of his excellent book, Britton Davis, with caustic force, arraigns the Government for its treatment of these Indians; and the valiant John G. Bourke, at the close of Chapter XXIX of his great book, *On the Border with Crook*, has this to say about Miles' campaign against the outlaw Chiricahuas and concerning the final disposition of the well-behaved Indians who had remained on the reservation:

"Not a single Chiricahua had been killed, captured, or wounded throughout the entire campaign—with two exceptions—unless by Chiricahua-Apache scouts who, like 'Chato,' had kept the pledges given to General Crook in the Sierra Madre in 1883. The exceptions were: one killed by the White Mountain Apaches near Fort Apache, and one killed by a white

CHIRICAHUA RENEGADES *en route* TO FLORIDA

Munitions Bldg., Wash.

Munitions Bldg., Wash.

CHIRICAHUA APACHE CHILDREN, PHOTOGRAPHED UPON THEIR AR-
RIVAL AT CARLISLE INDIAN SCHOOL, PENNSYLVANIA, IN 1888.

man in northern Mexico. Yet every one of those faithful scouts—especially the two 'Ki-e-ta' and 'Martinez,' who had at imminent personal peril gone into the Sierra Madre to hunt up 'Geronimo' and induce him to surrender, were transplanted to Florida and there subjected to the same punishment as had been meted out to 'Geronimo.' And with them were sent men like 'Goth-Kli' and 'Toklanni,' who were not Chiricahuas at all, but had only lately married wives of that band, who had never been on the war-path in any capacity except as soldiers of the Government, and had devoted years to its service. There is no more disgraceful page in the history of our relations with the American Indians than that which conceals the treachery visited upon the Chiricahuas who remained faithful in their allegiance to our people. An examination of the documents cited [on a preceding page] will show that I have used extremely mild language in alluding to this affair."

General Crook, in a report dated January 6, 1890, to the Secretary of War (who had asked him to assist in finding a suitable reservation for these Chiricahua Apaches after they had suffered four years of blighting confinement in Florida), with his usual gravity and calm clarity, shows just how callous and unjust was the action of Cleveland and the military authorities in their dealings with Chatto and his fellow scouts:

"In the operation against the hostiles, Chatto and others of his band were enlisted as scouts in the service of the United States and rendered invaluable services in that capacity. It is not too much to say that the surrender of Nachez, Chihuahua, Geronimo, and their bands could not have been effected except for the assistance of Chatto and his Chiricahua scouts.

"The final surrender of Geronimo and his small band to General Miles was brought about only through Chiricahuas who had remained friendly to the Government.

"When the services were no longer required Chatto received an honorable discharge and returned to his farm. He planted wheat and barley, raised sheep and owned horses and mules. Before his crops had ripened he was summoned to Washington. After an interview with the President he left the capital expecting to return to his farm at Camp Apache. On the way he was stopped at Fort Leavenworth, Kansas, and kept there for two months. At the end of this time he was taken to St. Augustine, and placed in confinement with the captive hostiles, whose surrender he had been so instrumental in securing. Ever since, he has been continued in confinement with them on the same terms, and with the yet more guilty band of Geronimo, which subsequently joined them. . . .

"During my interview with him at Mount Vernon Barracks, Chatto took from his breast a large medal that had been presented to him by President Cleveland and holding it out, asked, 'Why was I given that to wear in the guard-house? I thought that something good would come to me when they gave it to me, but I have been in confinement ever since I have had it.' I submit that this Indian has received but scant encouragement from the Government in his efforts to become a self-sustaining citizen.

"And Chatto is not alone in this experience. By far the greater part of the tribe remained true to the Government in the outbreak of 1885, and the most valuable and trustworthy of the Indian scouts were taken from among them. For their allegiance all have been rewarded alike—by captivity in a strange land." [12]

BIBLIOGRAPHY

BOURKE, JOHN G. *On the Border with Crook*. New York, Scribner, 1896.
CROOK, GEORGE. *Résumé of Operations against Apache Indians from 1882 to 1886*. Washington, 1886.

[12] Fifty-first Congress, First Session, Executive Document No. 83.

DAVIS, BRITTON. *The Truth about Geronimo*. New Haven, Yale University Press, 1929.

GATEWOOD, CHARLES B. *The Surrender of Geronimo*. Ed. by Brigadier General Edward S. Godfrey. 1929.

HAGEDORN, HERMANN. *Leonard Wood, A Biography*, Vol. I. New York, Harper, 1931.

MILES, NELSON A. *Personal Recollections*. Chicago, Werner, 1896.

Senate Executive Document No. 117, 49th Congress, 2d Session.

Senate Executive Document No. 83, 51st Congress, 1st Session.

War Department Reports, 1886–1887.

CHAPTER XV

Fifty Years of Peace

BY November 7, 1886, four hundred and ninety-eight Chiricahua Indians from Arizona had arrived in Florida as prisoners of war. Ninety-nine were men; three hundred and ninety-nine, women and children. Seventeen of the hostile warriors were confined at Fort Pickens, Pensacola, Florida, away from their families. Up to April, 1887, all the rest of the adults were kept in camp under guard at Fort Marion (the ancient Spanish fortress, San Marco), St. Augustine, Florida. The families of the prisoners at Fort Pickens were then sent to them there.[1] All the rest were taken to Mount Vernon Barracks, near Mobile. In May, 1888, all those at Fort Pickens were likewise removed to the camp at Mount Vernon Barracks. Previous to December, 1889, a hundred and twelve boys and girls had been sent to the Indian School at Carlisle, Pennsylvania. Thirty died there; twelve came back to their parents on account of sickness; and seventy were still at Carlisle in December, 1889.

On December 23, 1889, Lieutenant Guy Howard, Aide-de-Camp to the Commander of the Division of the Atlantic, who was in immediate charge of the Chiricahua prisoners in Florida, addressed a letter to the Adjutant-General of the Army ac-

---

[1] This was the result of a Report made by Herbert Welsh, corresponding Secretary of the Indian Rights Association. In the spring of 1887 he had been sent by the Executive Committee of the Association to get exact information concerning the dealings of the Government with these prisoners.

quainting him with the following facts: Eighty-nine of the Apaches held in captivity in Florida had died since their arrival three years before. Counting the children who had died at school, death had taken one hundred and nineteen of the Chiricahuas. At the time Howard made his report there were not more than thirty men among these prisoners who would have been capable of bearing arms. The remaining four hundred and thirty were old men, or cripples, and women and children. Yet they were all being held prisoners of war under conditions so wretched as to be almost positively inhuman. Howard pointed out that the normal death rate among civilized people was two per cent; while among these people it was more than three times as great. One fourth of these Apaches had died since they were brought to Florida a little more than three years before.

The Report of Herbert Welsh, previously referred to, and the above facts set forth by Lieutenant Howard convinced good and thoughtful citizens that the Government had dealt dishonorably with the Chiricahua Indians—particularly with Chatto and others who had long lived peaceably on the reservation. Humane people were greatly aroused and pressure was brought upon the Government authorities. As a result, January 13, 1890, the Secretary of War transmitted to President Benjamin Harrison the Report of Lieutenant Guy Howard and a Report of General George Crook, with endorsements by General Howard and General Schofield, recommending that the Chiricahua Apaches be removed to Fort Sill in the Indian Territory with a view to their permanent settlement there. President Harrison, on January 20, recommended to the Senate and the House of Representatives that provision be made by law for the placing of these Apaches on lands in the Indian Territory. The next step in the slow-moving drama was the passing of a resolution by the Senate, January 28, directing the

Secretary of War to submit to it all the evidence in his possession bearing on the imprisonment of the Apaches, particularly with reference to the manner in which Chatto and his associates were induced by the Government to visit Washington with assurance of safe conduct and were later seized and confined as prisoners.

Accordingly, the whole mass of military correspondence and official reports that had to do with the fortunes of these Chiricahuas between July, 1886, and January, 1890, was placed before the Senate. Let it not be thought, however, that Congress took speedy action to alleviate the condition of these people. The Secretary of War promptly requested authority to make the transfer, but it was not until August 6, 1894, four years after Lieutenant Howard's report had been submitted, that Congress authorized their removal. Finally in early October, 1894, they were located on the military reservation at Fort Sill under control of the garrison. Some seventy families were represented and they numbered in all at this time two hundred and ninety-six. There were only fifty able-bodied men and they were permitted to enroll as soldiers and were subject to regular military discipline. Each family was allotted a fenced plot of ground for cultivation. A thousand acres of virgin prairie was broken for them; six hundred head of cattle were bought for them by the Government; a sawmill was erected to supply them with building material; and the children were sent to near-by Indian Schools. A good many of the Chiricahuas became fairly good farmers and cattlemen, and grew more and more attached to the little farms apportioned to them. By December, 1909, they owned stock, implements, and other property valued at one hundred and sixty-two thousand dollars.

The Fort Sill Military Reservation was within the bounds of the territory that had been allotted to the Kiowa and Comanche Indians. By a treaty made in February, 1897, the Kiowas and Comanches ceded to the Apache pilgrims enough additional land in their reservation to provide each Apache, man, woman, and child, a farm of one hundred and sixty acres. But let not the unwary reader leap to the conclusion that this land actually came into the possession of those for whom it was provided. Twelve years passed, and in 1909 they were still deprived of individual ownership of this land. Meantime, additional tracts had been set aside for them, specifically; so that now the territory they occupied amounted to approximately eighty thousand acres. Yet it was necessary for the Board of Indian Commissioners in 1909, and again the next year, to point out emphatically to the Government that the land upon which these Apaches were settled had been provided for them by special agreement, and that in all honor it ought now to be allotted to them in severalty. Very able Army officers who had been in command on the reservation and had observed the steady progress made by these prisoners were urging that they now be given individual ownership of their farms. One of these officers, Captain (later General) Hugh L. Scott, who had jurisdiction over them for many years, said that while they were in his charge "they built more than 70 houses, hauling the material 33 miles from the railroad. They dug their own wells with a well machine, around 200 feet in depth. . . . They raised in one year at Fort Sill 300,000 pounds of Kaffir Corn, put up and sold to the Government 1,000 tons of hay, 500 tons of it being baled by their own labor, besides building fences, taking care of 2,500 head of cattle, various gardens, etc." He concludes: "They know how to work if opportunity and encouragement are given them."

In 1909, in their annual report to the Secretary of the Interior, the Board of Indian Commissioners had this to say: "As a whole, older and younger together, these Apaches have made remarkable progress in the arts of industry and in habits of self-support. We believe that the time has come to recognize this fact, and to change their status from that of prisoners of war to that of free men." Yet in the light of all the facts stated above, it was not until 1913 that these Indians were given their land in severalty. At that time each Apache prisoner was personally interviewed and given his choice whether he would remain at Fort Sill or be removed to the Mescalero Reservation in New Mexico. During the year 1913, one hundred and eighty-seven members of the band stated that they desired to return to Mescalero. The remainder, most of whom had grown up in captivity under the supervision of competent and humane Army officers, and, in consequence had known nothing of the tribal life of their turbulent ancestors, were allotted suitable tracts of land at Fort Sill. So by March, 1914, twenty-eight years after their entrance into captivity, the last prisoner was released from the jurisdiction of the War Department. It was understood that those who decided to return to the old tribal life on the Mescalero Reservation should have individual allotments of land there instead of holding their property in common with other members of the tribe.

"Old" Nana, one of the fiercest and ablest of the renegade chiefs, survived to reach Oklahoma, and there died at a great age—unreconstructed. Loco lived to reach Fort Sill and died there. He was a capable and famous chief. In general he was not ill-disposed toward the white man. Milder than most of the other renegade chiefs, he was more sinned against than sinning. After coming in with Crook in 1883, he enlisted as a scout and remained loyal to the Government. He was a member, with Chatto, of the delegation that Miles persuaded to visit Washington, and was sent to Florida with the rest. At Fort Sill he enlisted as a soldier and remained a quiet, well-behaved Indian. He died saying that he felt as if he had no country. Two sons survived him, Dexter, who came to Mescalero and died there, and Johnny Loco, who lives in Oklahoma.

Chihuahua was among the seventy-seven renegades who surrendered to Crook in March, 1886. With the rest he was brought to Fort Bowie and sent to Fort Marion, Florida, April 7. During the remainder of his life he was sober and well behaved. He tried his best to be a good Christian, attending Church, and positively refusing to drink or gamble. In Florida he was rather laughed at by his associates for walking thus so seriously in ways of righteousness. He reached Oklahoma, enlisted as a United States soldier, and died at Fort Sill, still a prisoner of war. Two remarkable children of Chihuahua, Ramona and Eugene, now in their late sixties, reside at White Tail on the Mescalero Reservation. They have an enlarged, framed photograph of their father which they show with pride. Both of them talk good English. I visited Ramona in her tidy, well-furnished little home at White Tail. She is a fine, intelligent Christian woman, a member of the Dutch Reformed Church, the best example of what education and religion can do for an Apache that I met on the reservations. Ramona's husband is Asa, son of Juh, successor of Cochise as war chief of the Chiricahuas. Eugene, Ramona's brother, is an industrious and successful farmer. He has a grandson named Chihuahua for his great-grandfather.

Chatto was among those who came back to the ancestral hunting grounds. In his youth he had been a violent renegade —a leader of extraordinary skill and daring. He admired Crook exceedingly and tried hard to follow his advice and establish himself in the ways of the white man; but his treatment by the Government after July, 1886, was grievous and depressing. All the remaining years of his life were embittered by the thought of it. O. M. Boggess, formerly superintendent of the Mescalero Reservation, writes: "I knew him very well, indeed. He was an excellent citizen, had a satisfactory home, and was favorably known to both the reservation Indians and to the white residents of Otero County." The Reverend Richard Harper, also, who was missionary at Mescalero, and saw much of Chatto, speaks highly of him. He describes him as a man of striking bearing and dignity of character, and states that he was held in general respect by his tribesmen. He lived to be a very old man. He died on the reservation in March, 1934, as the result of an automobile accident. With others, he had been visiting up in a canyon, and the entire party had been drinking. On the way down the Canyon the automobile left the road and turned turtle in the creek. Chatto had two ribs broken, pneumonia followed, and he died within three days. In the agency safe at Mescalero are the medal given him by the Government in 1886, and his copy of Britton Davis' *The Truth about Geronimo.*

Geronimo died at Fort Sill, February 17, 1909. Throughout his life he displayed marked gifts as an advertiser. White exploiters, too, made the most of him during the period of his captivity at Fort Sill. He was given ample opportunity to display his vanity and bravado at the St. Louis World's Fair, and at the Buffalo and Omaha Expositions. He was permitted to appear as a sensational figure in the procession in honor of the inauguration of Theodore Roosevelt. Indeed, wherever supreme whoopee was made, there Geronimo was to be found in the midst. This was all very pleasing to him, as he was able to turn a good many extra pennies by the sale of bows and arrows and photographs of himself. As for mawkish white sentimentalists, male and female, nothing gave them more exquisite enjoyment than to shake hands with one so notorious for deeds of infamy and bloodshed. Geronimo was never a chief. He belonged to the band of which Juh, and later

Nachez, was chief. At the height of his career he held the allegiance of only a small number of his own band. He was feared as a medicine man. Apaches believed that no bullet could kill him. He was a man of immense courage, energy, and effrontery; was resourceful, daring, and impudent; but for the rest he was a cruel, perfidious rascal, hated and distrusted by Apaches and white men alike.

In 1903 Geronimo joined the Dutch Reformed Church, but his attendance at services was irregular. Surely, whatever may have been his profession, he was a poor practitioner. Honor and integrity, whether in accordance with Apache or Christian standards, were alien qualities to him. On the Jicarilla Reservation, I talked with Miss Hendrina Hospers, field matron of the Dutch Reformed Church. She spent many years at Fort Sill and Mescalero. She knew Geronimo well. On the day that he met with the accident that resulted in his death, she met him on the road as he was on his way to Lawton to sell a bow and arrow. She wanted to buy them herself, but did not have any cash with her, so Geronimo drove on to town. With the money he received for the bow and arrow he got drunk; and on his way back home fell out of the buggy. A cold rain was falling, and he lay there in the road all night. When discovered, he was taken to the military hospital where he died a few days later. His widow and his son Robert were among those who returned to the Mescalero Reservation. During the World War Mrs. Geronimo bought a Liberty Bond and wore a Red Cross button. Robert Geronimo is a leading Indian at Mescalero, President of the Cattlegrower's Association, and the most successful stockman on the reservation.

Nachez was among those who returned to the Mescalero Reservation and settled at White Tail. General Hugh L. Scott records that in captivity he retained a high degree of self-respect and did with docility whatever was required of him. At Fort Sill he held a place of leadership among his tribesmen and was praised and respected by the white people. Cochise was his father; and, though he did not inherit the prowess and force of personality of that mighty warrior, Scott affirms that he was a sterling and capable man. On the Mescalero Reservation he was one of the Indian police; and up to his death was recognized as the leading man of his tribe. During all his years at Mescalero he lived a sober and righteous life. He was an honored member and regular attendant of the Dutch Reformed Church, speaking and praying in public, and doing everything he could, by precept and example, to plant the Christian religion deep in the hearts of his people. He did not harbor resentment because of his treatment by the Government. In conversations with Mr. Harper he sometimes commented on the great hardships and dangers that the Apaches endured on the warpath, and expressed approval of the present manner of life at Mescalero. Both Mr. Wilson, Agency farmer, and Mr. Harper knew him intimately for years, and both of them genuinely admired him, and spoke with enthusiasm of his superiority and earnestness of character. He died in the hospital at Mescalero of influenza in 1921. Four children: a daughter Amelia and a son, Christian Naiché,[2] on the Mescalero Reservation, a married daughter in Oklahoma, and Barney, a fireguard on the San Carlos Reservation. His son Christian is a member of the Tribal Council, and associate judge. He leaves several grandchildren, also, the great-grandchildren of Cochise.

Of the historic figures who were sent to Florida as prisoners in 1886, and who later returned to New Mexico, there remain five to be accounted for: Noche, Kayitah, Martine, Ka-ya-

---

[2] From the time of his surrender, Nachez is usually referred to as Naiche, and his name is spelled Naiche in the Mescalero Agency records.

ten-na, and Toklanni. Noche was one of Crook's trusted scouts. After Miles took command, he consulted Noche as to the best means of capturing Nachez and Geronimo. Noche's advice was to send two Chiricahua emissaries into the camp of the renegades to propose terms of surrender. It was he who named Kayitah as the best man to send, and advised that it be left to him to choose a companion. Both Kayitah and Martine were related to Geronimo by marriage, and Noche believed that no other two men could have entered the camp alive. Noche died of tuberculosis at Mescalero, April 14, 1914. Mr. Harper esteemed him highly, and was with him at the time of his death. Uncas, the blind interpreter at Mescalero, is a son of Noche, and a grandson, the son of Uncas, is a Boy Scout.

Kayitah died of old age at Mescalero, February 15, 1934. He was interested in farming and appreciated his home at White Tail. He was a man of milder temper than Martine, and was pleasant to deal with. He was never a troublemaker; nor did he have much to say by way of complaint because he was sent with the hostiles into captivity, though he always affirmed that Miles made them big promises in case they succeeded in bringing in Geronimo. Martine, now almost eighty years old, is still living at Mescalero, and I talked with him there. Very feeble in both body and mind, he is cared for at the Agency hospital. He was in one of the stores in the village the day I saw him. His son George, who talks good English, introduced me and helped me in my conversation with him. Ka-ya-ten-na, who disputed the authority of Britton Davis at Turkey Creek, was, in consequence, sent to Alcatraz Island for eighteen months, and later, wholly reformed, became one of Crook's most useful scouts, died in the hospital at Mescalero of pneumonia in 1918. Mr. Harper states that he was of medium size, not at all militant in appearance; was, indeed, so mild and respectful on the reservation that it seemed difficult to realize that what history records about him could be true. Bourke, at the close of Chapter XXIX of his book, *On the Border with Crook,* names Toklanni as one who was sent a prisoner to Florida and dealt with in the same manner as were the renegades, though he was not a Chiricahua at all but had only recently married a wife of that band, and though he had never been on the warpath, except as a soldier of the United States. Toklanni is still alive at Mescalero, hale and hearty. He is nearly six feet tall, and is alert and soldierly. He has a genial, winning smile, possesses a sense of humor, and everyone who knows him is his friend. He presented himself before me neatly dressed, displaying on the breast of his blue coat a bright badge of the Veterans of Indian Wars.

So much for the prodigals and prisoners! But now what about the good Apaches who stayed at home and worked for their Uncle Sam? This is a long story, too, and most difficult to set down in brief. In order to sum up and interpret the net result of these fifty years of peace, I have patiently scanned the reports of Indian agents, Army officers, officers of the Bureau of Indian Affairs, and special commissions covering the whole half-century from 1886 to 1936. Moved by a deep desire to be accurate and just, and to bring the record down to the moment, I have also visited the Apache reservations several times during the past four years to observe for myself the present condition of the Apaches. After such studies one vividly realizes how slow and painful has been the struggle of the Apaches toward civilization and enlightenment.

The forces against which these people have had to contend were twofold: that which operated from within—their own deep-seated habits of savagery, and that which constantly beset them from without—the greed, hatred, stupidity, and injustice of the white man. These forces have acted and reacted upon

TOKLANNI, WARM SPRING APACHE

Photograph by Superintendent
E. R. McCray

ANTONIO ROMERO, JICARILLA APACHE

EVELYN MAY SIMMS, JICARILLA APACHE, LEGALLY ADOPTED
DAUGHTER OF THE REV. AND MRS. J. DENTON SIMMS

Courtesy of Rev. R. H. Harper

each other with concomitant and almost equal strength; and certain it is that neither the force working within nor the force working from without has tended greatly toward righteousness. Let it be remembered that fifty years ago these Indians were still nomadic, murderous savages by instinct and habit. They still adhered to their primitive fetishes, superstitions, and customs, and still nursed in their breasts the untamed passions of their ancestors. They dressed in primitive fashion and were primitive in all their ways of living. They loved liberty and felt that it was their right to roam. They lusted for what belonged to others and actively cherished the doctrine

> *That they should take who have the power,*
> *And they should keep who can.*

They were polygamists. They were superstitious; were largely under the sway of the medicine men, and the medicine men were often bad men. They were deeply addicted to the vices of gambling and drinking.

Now from the point of view of the American all this had to be changed; and the moment we gained physical control over the Apaches attempts were made to enforce these changes. Sad to say, during the two or three decades they had been more or less in contact with the American, they had found little in him to arouse their admiration, and certainly nothing that provided them with "the expulsive power of a new affection." Yet, from this time on, Army officers, Indian agents, and Christian missionaries were to be their monitors and judges; and the degree to which they gave up their former ways and took on the ways of the American was to be the mark and test of their progress toward civilization. Army officers and the Indian agents tried to get them to dress as white people did, to settle in one place, to live in houses, to raise crops and breed cattle, and to do other useful work, to give up gambling and tizwin drunks, to live with one wife, to send their children to school, to come to the doctor when they were ill and, when necessary, go to the hospital for treatment, to maintain law and order and democratic government through native justices and policemen of their own choosing; and, when the missionaries came, they tried to induce them to attend church and become Christians. We shall nearly all agree, I think, that these were good American ways, well calculated to forward the civilization of these Apaches. I have listed these various objectives as standards by which to record the degree of progress made by these people during this half-century. These are the points that I find stressed as I read the annual reports of the Indian agents to the Bureau of Indian Affairs, and of the Commissioners of Indian Affairs to the Secretary of the Interior. These reports point out, year by year, improvement or lack of improvement in all these things.

In spite of the devil, of themselves, and of their white enemies and detractors, these Apaches manifestly have improved during the past five decades. But before attempting a general summary of their progress, I must give a little attention to the obstacles they have had to overcome from without. In the first place, the Government itself was at fault. Indifference, vacillation, procrastination, and, at times, downright injustice marked its dealings with these people. During the earlier decades, agents were paid little and were shifted often. The Indians received an insufficient supply of food and clothing, and what they did get was of poor quality; there was failure to provide good seed for planting at the proper time; the buildings at the agencies were little more than adobe shacks, too small to house properly either agents, pupils, or sick people. There was frequent change of policy. High officers of the Government recommended from time to time that permission be given to citizens and corporations to work the mines, or cut the big timber, or control the ranges on the various reservations. From the moment that hostilities ceased there was petty, insistent, groundless opposition to the program of peaceful progress that humane and Christian citizens were earnestly trying to promote. For example: Governor Zulick, of Arizona, in his annual report to the Secretary of the Interior, September, 1886, urges that the Apache Reservation be cut down in order that white men may occupy it. The next year this same governor, though he makes no charge that depredations have been committed, arraigns the Apaches in Arizona as bitterly as he and other citizens had denounced the Chiricahua renegades in their most violent days, and once more demands that they be removed from the Territory. Governor Wolfley, his successor, in his annual report of 1889, recommends that the San Carlos Reservation be cut down, and that the coal lands be taken from the Apaches. In his report of September, 1888, Governor Edmund G. Ross of New Mexico demands that the Jicarilla Reservation be cut down for white occupation, though he admits that the Jicarilla Indians are doing well, and are causing no disturbance. Likewise, Governor N. O. Murphy of Arizona, in his report of 1890, urges that the Apaches be removed and that their reservations be opened for settlement. In 1914 there was an active movement on foot by El Paso businessmen to turn the Mescalero Reservation into a National Park; and, as late as 1918, Mr. Malcolm McDowell, Secretary of the Board of Indian Commissioners, reported that leading men of El Paso were again attempting to introduce a bill in Congress looking to the turning of the Mescalero Reservation into a National Park.

If, to all that the Government did or failed to do for these groping savages, we add the barking of political hyenas, the clamorous greed of citizens who desired to exploit the Indians, the crafty and persistent attempts of vile traders and viler whisky dealers to invade the reservations, or, failing of that, to hang upon the outskirts just beyond reach of the federal arm, we are able to get some idea of why the Apaches have moved forward somewhat slowly toward the shining heights of civilization. Yet progress has been made; and today, rank and file, the Apaches are very different beings from what they were half a century ago.

For one thing they have endured. They are not a decadent or diminishing race. On the contrary, we find, by comparing the annual reports of the Department of the Interior for 1886 and 1936, that there are in the United States today, 1,306 more Apaches than there were half a century ago. In 1886 there were 6,142 in all—5,644 in Arizona and New Mexico and 498 in Florida; in 1936 there were 7,448 in all—7,124 in Arizona and New Mexico and 324 in Oklahoma.

One other important thing is to be said before we take a final glimpse of these tribesmen on their reservations today. Repeatedly, as the decades have come and gone, we have had good reports from agents, Army officers, and civilians concerning the Apaches as workers. Crook was the first to show the Apaches that work is dignified and that it has its sure and solid rewards. From the time that he set them to raising crops, and cutting hay, and chopping wood with the assurance that they should receive full pay for such labor, the Apaches have shown themselves to be good workers. As time went on there was ever-increasing demand for their labor, not only in supplying hay and wood for the Army posts, but as toilers in the mines, as diggers of ditches, as builders of fences, and, preeminently, as road builders. More than a generation ago in Globe and other mining towns Apaches were in demand as laborers, and their behavior was so good when working for their own profit on the reservation that it was not difficult to get permission to work wherever they could find jobs.

In 1905, under the direction of American engineers, the Apaches became famous for the construction of one of the best roads built in Arizona up to that time—the eighty-mile stretch along the original Apache Trail between Phoenix and the Roosevelt Dam site. Those who observed these Indians at their work declared that they seemed to have an inborn knack for road building—employing dry masonry, yet choosing their material with such care and laying it with such skill that the result was a solid and enduring roadbed. Some of the work they did at that time has lasted longer than the concrete and steel work that was done at the same time. The Apaches helped to build several of the best roads that were constructed in Arizona a generation ago. They carried on whether or not under the eye of the foreman; took pride in their work; and could be depended upon for steady labor in hot weather as well as in cold.

In 1904 Mr. Louis C. Hill was supervising engineer in charge of Roosevelt Dam construction work. He was among the first to employ Apaches in large numbers for day labor. In an extended letter to me under date of April 12, 1937, he gave an account of his experience with these Indians as workers at that time. I quote: "They used to work all day on the road like the white men, but when the day was finished and the foremen yelled 'All off,' the Indians started for home up the canyon and ran to the top of the hill and on over to their camp at a good fast dog trot. They ran from about where the foot of the grade is now clear up to the old town of Roosevelt near Cottonwood Creek. My opinion is that if they had been properly treated by giving them time and thought and interest, so that they would feel they were getting somewhere, there would never have been any trouble. They were good workers, and I never knew an Apache to beg." They are good workers today, as I can testify from my extensive travel through all four reservations in Arizona during this month of June, 1937.

There are no finer tracts of land in the world than those on which the Apaches now securely dwell. They comprise more than three million acres of mountainous country at an average altitude of about five thousand feet. The sun continually shines over these vast expanses; the stars forever burn in bright splendor. The temperature is rarely either very hot or very cold. Surely nowhere on earth are there grander mountains, finer cattle ranges, more fertile fields, trout streams swifter, cooler, more retired. Of late the Government seems to have done its best to match Nature in material benefits. On every reservation there are modern schoolhouses and hospitals as well equipped and satisfactorily conducted as are the schools and hospitals in the typical American town. Up-to-date sanitary dormitories house the Indian boys and girls during the school year. The agency grounds resemble college campuses in rural towns, adorned as they are with flowers, trees, and smooth-clipped lawns. Superintendents have homes comparable in comfort and convenience with those of superintendents of schools in large towns, while other employees live either in modern attractive cottages near the agency offices, or in well-conducted agency clubhouses. Good roads are maintained throughout the reservations. Telephone lines reach the remote homes of head stockmen, rangers' stations, and fireguards in their mountain lookouts. Pure water is piped into every home and public building at the agency; houses and other buildings are electrically lighted; radios are common; and moving pictures are presented at suitable times in school auditoriums.

All these things Nature and Uncle Sam are now doing for the Apache Indians. What additional benefit or pleasure could be desired by the physical man? Surely, no outward comfort is lacking. If anything good is lacking, it must come from within. So we turn now to consider whether the Apache has the desire and ability to utilize this civilized life that has been built around him.

More and more, on all the reservations, the Apaches are adapting themselves to the modern manner of dress. The men nearly all have barbershop haircuts, though now and then one sees an old man from far back on the reservation whose uncut hair extends to his shoulders; and on the Jicarilla Reservation men and women alike plait their hair in two long braids that fall over the shoulders in front. On all the reservations the men wear Levy's with soft shirts of various colors and qualities, and all have large black or gray hats that they wear cowboy-fashion. Both men and women buy comfortable store shoes of fairly good grade, with low heels. The women continue to array themselves in voluminous calico skirts that fall to their heels, with loose blouse of the same brilliant material. It requires fifteen yards for a dress pattern. They make their own garments, and apparently dress in this style from a genuine sense of modesty. The younger girls, at the schools and around the agencies, wear shorter skirts, but when they return to their remote wickiups out on the reservation, they revert to the earlier fashions, shamed into so doing by the ridicule of their elders and the potent power of custom. The women wear no hats, and allow their hair to fall loosely around their shoulders as of old. As of old, too, a woman carries her papoose in a light, cradle-shaped basket, supported by a broad strap over her head.

Housing conditions vary greatly on the different reservations. On the White River and San Carlos Reservations the Indians nearly all continue to live in primitive wickiups. Here and there very small frame houses are occupied, or partially occupied, for short periods; but usually they give evidence of abandonment and neglect. Sometimes they are turned into storage sheds for corn, saddles and saddle blankets, and farm tools. They are almost wholly unfurnished, and, if occupied in cold weather, windows and doors are kept tight shut, and refuse is allowed to accumulate, so that, on the whole, they are more unsanitary than wickiups; for it is a prime virtue of a wickiup that it may be burned down when dirt and garbage become unendurable, or when a death occurs.

The Jicarillas are a pastoral people. In winter they drive their flocks to the warm open grazing grounds at the southern end of the reservation, and live in tents, or extemporized shelters. In the mountainous areas at the northern end of their territory they occupy log or adobe shacks and huts, or, still more commonly, now, square canvas tents. Almost none of them live in tepees or wickiups.

The most marked improvement in housing I found on the Mescalero Reservation. Here there is scarcely a wickiup to be seen. For the Chiricahuas who returned to Mescalero in 1913 and 1914, the Government built small frame houses at White Tail, eighteen miles from the Agency. During their long captivity the Chiricahuas had learned to dwell in houses, so, at once, they set a good example to their kinsmen on the reservation, and, as a result, not a few abandoned their wickiups for houses. At present, Mr. E. R. McCray, the superintendent of this Agency, is promoting the most ambitious housing program that has ever been attempted on an Apache reservation. His plan includes the erection of one hundred and fifty new, up-to-date little four-room frame houses, with adjoining barn, chicken house, and privy. These cottages are fitted out with neat, substantial modern furniture—a wood stove for the living room, a good range and sink for the kitchen, and, for other rooms, iron bedsteads and suitable chairs, tables, and dressers. All this furniture is of as good quality as is to be found in the home of the ordinary white man. Some of these houses have already been erected to replace those built for the Chiricahuas twenty-five years ago. Already, a little community of old people (humorously referred to as Townsend's Village) no longer able to work, and regularly rationed by the agency, are living in these new, attractive cottages. When the program shall have been completed every Indian on the reservation will have a sanitary, well-furnished house to live in if he will occupy it; and the encouraging fact is they are actually living in them.

At present, on all the reservations, the Apaches are industrious and prosperous. In consequence of the somewhat too lavish expenditure of federal money at this time, no one is without a job who is able and willing to work. A good many of the older Apaches still draw pensions as former Army scouts; many intelligent younger people are employed in various indoor positions at the agencies; and still others are engaged in manual labor on various projects. Most of these Indians own cattle or sheep, and a great many have horses. Some years ago the Government gave to every adult Indian who was willing to care for them, each with his own private brand, an allotment of cattle or sheep. This stock is herded on the reservations under the supervision of experienced white stockmen, the Indians themselves serving as cowboys and shepherds. Once a year, or oftener, there is a general round-up; the cattle are taken to the nearest shipping station, are there sold and weighed, and each holder of a brand is paid for the stock he markets. A small percentage of the money received goes into the Tribal Fund for general and administrative expenses incurred. The rest goes into the pockets of the individual owners.

On all the reservations the superintendents are doing their best to induce each adult Indian to take over a small allotment of farm land to hold and cultivate for himself. These little farms are selected and worked with the advice and aid of the white farm manager of the agency. Many of the Indians, in addition to running their cattle, are now successfully working their small plots of land. As in many other respects the greatest progress in farming has been made by the Chiricahuas on the Mescalero Reservation. They had practiced farming to a considerable extent during their long sojourn in Oklahoma, and in other particulars had taken on the ways of civilization. Most of them speak English as well as does the ordinary immigrant farmer from Europe, and they dress very much like other farmers throughout the United States. Nearly all of them are good and fairly industrious agriculturists. Their small fields, of from five to twenty acres, and adjoining modern cottages are situated in lovely canyons or valleys at an elevation of seven or eight thousand feet, with views of lofty mountains in every direction. They have horses, cows, and chickens, farm wagons, and a good many now have Fords or Chevrolets.

Economically the Jicarilla Indians present an interesting situation. This is a small tribe, numbering only about seven hundred and fifty. Until recently they have seemed to be the weakest and most backward of the Apache groups. About two decades ago they were dying off rapidly from tuberculosis. Then the Government took active steps to check the inroads of this disease. They were dying from insufficient food and lack of shelter. Through the timely and vigorous efforts of local white men, Mr. Emett Wirt and Mr. Denton Simms, the Commissioner of Indian Affairs was brought sharply to book and the Jicarilla tribe was saved from destruction. A hospital was established particularly for the treatment of tuberculosis. The death rate was quickly checked, and then, steadily, year by year, the Jicarillas began to increase in numbers. Large flocks of sheep were bought for them, to be paid for later out of the Tribal Revolving Fund, and as a result of all this wise action they are now financially more secure than are the members of any of the other tribes. The average income from the sale of wool is large; nearly every family is self-supporting; and some men among them, the more intelligent and industrious, are growing well-to-do.

Until recently it has been very difficult to persuade the Apaches to go to white doctors when they are sick, or to enter the hospitals for treatment. Of late, though, they have been freeing themselves, more and more, from their old superstitions, and there has been gradual weakening of the hold of the medicine men upon them. Every reservation now has a good hospital, with trained doctors and nurses in charge, and more than ever before sick people are entering these hospitals for treatment. It is rather common now for Apache women to come to the hospital to have their babies, and men and women alike are now willing to go there for surgical attention and for the treatment of serious illness; so the beds are usually nearly all occupied. Doctors and nurses are careful when possible to remove patients who are at the point of death to tents or rooms outside; for it is hard for the Apache to conquer his horror of a building that has been contaminated by death.

On all the reservations now there are good schools, and children between six and eighteen who are mentally and physically able to go to school are in attendance. Some of the best of these schools are conducted by religious denominations, but of course the bulk of the school population attend Government schools. Buildings, playgrounds, inside equipment, and teaching efficiency are about on a par with the average small-town school for white children throughout the United States. Not many pupils show a desire for higher education, but a few become ambitious to learn more and to fit themselves for definite positions in life. What hope there is of steady and solid advancement for the Apaches is to be found in these very few young people who catch visions of higher things. Here and there a teacher or a missionary has pointed out to me a girl or a boy in whom he centers his pride and his hope.

In matters moral and religious there is at present little to encourage the missionary and the humanitarian. Neither young people nor old show marked progress in goodness and sobriety, in loftiness of aim, or stern self-control. On the whole the white man, as he presents himself today, is not a very lovely being to imitate, yet, always, the Indians are exhorted to follow in the steps of the white man. Unhappily it is easier to follow the vices of the white man than his virtues. It is the general impression of agency officials, missionaries, and other serious-minded white people who have long resided on the reservations that drinking and gambling are on the increase at present among both old and young; and they think there is considerable moral laxity between sexes. Drink has always been the chief curse of the Apache; and men and women alike have always had a passion for gambling. At present the Indians continue to have their secret tulapai parties, in spite of the vigilance of the officials. In addition they now buy liquor from saloons adjacent to the reservations, and from bootleggers. Now, also, they are able to buy at the stores ingredients from which to concoct powerful intoxicants. The white people at the agencies believe that this increased tendency to drinking, especially among the young, is traceable to the repeal of prohibition and the resulting marked increase in drinking and drunkenness among citizens everywhere. It seems impossible to eradicate the gambling habit among the Apaches; but, fortunately, the effects of gambling are not so deadly and degrading as is addiction to the drink habit. As to all these vices, including sexual promiscuity, it is my belief that the Apaches are no worse than the white men in average American communities. On the reservations marriage must now be entered into in accordance with the federal law. Divorces, however, may be granted by the Tribal Council. Separation has become rather easy; so there are a good many divorced men and women on the reservation.

The Christian religion is making almost no headway among the Apaches. Never has the Apache nature seemed to respond to Christian doctrine and conduct. For a generation or more missionaries of very high quality intellectually and morally have labored devotedly among them and have been greatly respected by them. The Indians attend their services and their mission schools to some extent; but their course of life, except in rare cases, has remained almost unaffected by the Christian creed and code of action. Some of the Chiricahuas on the Mescalero Reservation do appear to have become genuine Christians; and the same is true, I believe, of a few young people on the Jicarilla Reservation. Nearly all the returned Chiricahuas incline toward the Protestant faith, as they had early been brought under the influence of the Dutch Reformed Church at Fort Sill. Many of them are now consistent members of this church. I think, for example, of Ramona, Chihuahua's daughter, and of Uncas, son of Noche. These two fine elderly people seem to me to exhibit the true marks of Christianity—sober, mild, industrious, and kindly as they are. Both have suffered deeply, and both seem to have learned from their suffering lessons of godliness and submission. I am not sure but that two or three very young Jicarillas whom I saw give evidence of those refinements of character and conduct that we like to call Christian.

I have asked myself often, and I asked missionaries, teachers, traders, and Government officials on the reservations, "What is the best that we may hope for the Apaches—twenty-five, fifty, one hundred years from now?" It is hard to believe that much can be expected beyond what I have recorded in the paragraphs written above. If still further progress is made, it must come as the result of some inward light and propulsion. No force from without, however wise and humane, can avail to draw the Apache upward to racial attainment, enlightenment, greatness of character. The ideal, the motive power, must emanate from within if the Apache is ever to mount upward to a place of nobility and distinction among the races of men. No people can achieve independence and win a worthy place for itself among civilized nations unless it can generate its own lofty racial ideals and an accompanying passion to make these unique ideals prevail. At this time it does not seem likely that there reside in the Apache nature the passion and the power to attain racial eminence and independence.

BIBLIOGRAPHY

Annual Reports of the Bureau of Indian Affairs, 1886–1936.

Annual Reports of the Secretary of War, 1895, 1896, 1897.

DAVIS, O. K. "Our Prisoners of War." In *North American Review*, March, 1912.

HODGE, F. W. *Handbook of American Indians*. Washington, 1907.

Literary Digest, October 25, 1924.

Outlook Magazine, May 25, 1912.

Reports of the Governors of the Territories of Arizona and New Mexico, 1887–1912.

Senate Executive Document No. 83, 51st Congress, 1st Session.

WELSH, HERBERT. *The Apache Prisoners in Fort Marion*. Philadelphia, 1887.

INDEX